THE SONG OF THE SINGING ASSEMBLY

A Theology of Christian Hymnody

THE SONG OF THE SINGING ASSEMBLY

A Theology of Christian Hymnody

JUDITH M. KUBICKI

Foreword by VIRGIL FUNK

GIA Publications, Inc.
Chicago

7404 S. Mason Ave.
Chicago, Illinois 60638
www.giamusic.com

G-9419

ISBN: 978-1-62277-234-6

Library of Congress Cataloging in Publication Control Number : 2017028924

Cover and layout design by Martha Chlipala.
Printed in the United States of America.

"A Mighty Fortress Is Our God" by Martin Luther, tr. *Lutheran Book of Worship* © 1978, *Lutheran Book of Worship*, admin. Augsburg Fortress. All rights reserved. Used by permission.

"A Mighty Fortress Is Our God" by Martin Luther, adapt. and rev. Omer Westendorf © 1964, World Library Publications, www.wlp.jspaluch.com. All rights reserved. Used by permission.

"A Place at the Table" by Shirley Erena Murray © 1998, Hope Publishing Company, Carol Stream, IL 60188. All rights reserved. Used by permission.

"Come Join the Dance of Trinity" by Richard Leach © 2001, Selah Publishing Co., Inc. All rights reserved. Used by permission.

"Draw Us in the Spirit's Tether" by Percy Dearmer (1867–1936) from *Enlarged Songs of Praise* 1931. Copyright © 1931, Oxford University Press. Reproduced by permission of Oxford University Press. All rights reserved.

"God, beyond All Names" by Bernadette Farrell © 1991, 1994, OCP. All rights reserved. Used by permission.

"Let Kings and Prophets Yield Their Name" by Carl P. Daw, Jr. © 1990, Hope Publishing Company, Carol Stream, IL 60188. All rights reserved. Used by permission.

"Sing a New Church" by Delores Dufner, OSB © 1991, Delores Dufner, OSB. Published by OCP. All rights reserved. Used by permission.

"Touch the Earth Lightly" by Shirley Erena Murray © 1992, Hope Publishing Company, Carol Stream, IL 60188. All rights reserved. Used by permission.

"Two Doxologies" from *Lord, Open My Lips* by Cyprian Consiglio © 2003, OCP. All rights reserved. Used by permission.

"When the Lord in Glory Comes" by Timothy Dudley-Smith © 1967, Hope Publishing Company, Carol Stream, IL 60188. All rights reserved. Used by permission.

Painting of "The Last Supper" by Bohdan Piasecki reproduced on page 187 © We Are Church Ireland (www.wearechurchireland.ie).

This book is dedicated with admiration, affection, and appreciation to three teachers:

Mary Collins, O.S.B.
Joseph A. Komonchak
Fred Moleck

In various and sundry ways
they planted the seeds that have blossomed into this book!

Table of Contents

FOREWORD

VIRGIL FUNK

The Song of the Singing Assembly is a theology of Christian hymnody. Judith Kubicki is first and above all a teacher, indeed a professor at Fordham University in New York, and an academic scholar. Judith Kubicki makes a significant contribution to the study of hymns, not only in the explanation of their texts as theology, but also in an academic analysis of how and why hymns are important to Christian worship. So who will benefit from reading *The Song of the Singing Assembly*?

Pastoral musicians and everyone interested in hymnody will find the analysis of over fifty hymns interesting. Those who work professionally in church music—publishers, directors of music ministry, organists, and choir directors—will find the commentary on the hymns a form of meditation, bringing texts to life that may have grown stale by repetition. And since the hymns selected are so widely used ecumenically, *The Song of the Singing Assembly* might even serve as a mini-retreat in six chapters for church musicians of all denominations.

> The sampling of hymn texts is meant to whet the appetite for taking a closer look at the theology expressed through the metaphors and images found in Christian hymn texts.

The thoughtful student will be surprised to discover how the hymns selected for analysis provide a foundation course in theology, including eschatology, soteriology, Christology, ecclesiology and even feminism. And, because hymn texts are non-doctrinal, they provide a wonderful presentation of the end-times, salvation, the image of Christ, and the Trinity, in language that is understandable and easily grasped. For me, Kubicki's treatment of the current language issues connected with feminism in chapter six is worth the price of the book. Many religions have made their hymnbook into their catechism; Judith Kubicki has arranged the classic hymns in such a way that they are a fundamental course in theology.

For the pastor or parish who have become discouraged in making the effort at congregational singing, *The Song of the Singing Assembly* will serve as a reminder about the importance of hymn singing, not just for the liturgy, but the for life of the parish. For as Kubicki reminds us:

> There is perhaps no other physical activity that so engages the body, the mind, the spirit, and the emotions of an individual and an assembly than wholehearted singing. The activity of hymn singing allows an assembly to recognize itself as believers and as members of a faith community.

But *The Song of the Singing Assembly* makes an even more important contribution to the field of hymnology. Prior to the Second Vatican Council, vernacular singing at low Mass was introduced, first in Germany, in the form of *Gemeinschaftsmesse* in 1943, and then into the English-speaking world in the form of the four-hymn mass. While drawn mainly from the Protestant experience these hymns had a ritual function: to accompany the ritual processions of the liturgy at the entrance, the presentation of gifts, communion, and dismissal. When the vernacular was introduced in 1969, there were few hymns written by Catholic composers for the liturgy. The strict musical theorists claimed that hymns should not to be used at Mass; rather processional psalms should be used following the structure of the liturgy as expressed in the Latin *Liber Usualis* first published in 1898. Nevertheless, the American bishops wisely gave permission for the use of English hymns in the liturgy in 1972. But the conservative theorists have continued to hold on to their position that hymns should not be used in the Latin Liturgy, with the statement that we should sing the liturgy and not at the liturgy (referring to hymns).

Judith Kubicki's analysis of the theology of the hymn contributes to that discussion by not only demonstrating how some hymns draw their sources from the Psalms, but also by her very persuasive discussion of the symbolic and metaphorical nature of hymn texts as speech communication and provides a strong foundation for the evolution of the liturgy by use. In other words, by demonstrating the worthiness of hymns as vehicles of theology, she establishes the legitimacy of hymn singing as part of the on-going evolution of the liturgy in our times.

> A hymn can serve as a mediator of reality. The symbolizing activity of singing hymns involves active participation of subjects in mediating connections and in discovering their identity and place in their particular social world. ... Singing texts that articulate the Christian attitudes of joy, praise, thanksgiving, forgiveness, contrition, etc., has the potential to form the singers in those Christian attitudes. All the symbols of the liturgy, language and music included, have the potential to shape us in those "right attitudes" that are peculiar to the heart of Christian worship.

Kubicki is not only a teacher, but she is also an academic scholar. Her own work examining the music of Taizé is vitally important to the continued development of repertoire in the English language. Repertoire development must be developed with a critical ear.

> The Taizé corpus teaches us that we do not necessarily become one by singing about unity. Rather, the very act of singing together, attentiveness to the other, a willingness to walk in another shoes (or sing in another's native tongue) can be far more effective vehicles for promoting unity, reconciliation, and respect.
>
> The reality is that trying to capture mystery in images can never be fully achieved. What we, as Church, can only hope to do in the face of this mystery is to continue to sing. In this

way, we offer our humble, but confident assent to mystery with a resounding "Amen!" This we continue to do, even when it is not always easy.

The Song of the Singing Assembly is an important book, a must read by those committed to liturgy and music, because it makes a major contribution to the development of the link between hymns, hymn singing, and theology.

Rev. Virgil C. Funk
President emeritus, National Association of Pastoral Musicians

ACKNOWLEDGMENTS

It is with deep joy and profound gratitude that I acknowledge the many individuals and groups who have helped to bring this book project to a successful conclusion. My thanks to Fordham University for awarding me the Faculty Fellowships that provided the time for research and writing and to the E. Rhodes and Leona B. Carpenter Foundation and the Gallucci Creative Foundation for their financial support. I am also grateful to James Wilson and Celinett Rodriguez in the Fordham Office of Research and Sponsored Programs for their advice and encouragement.

Special thanks to colleagues in the North American Academy of Liturgy (NAAL), especially the Liturgical Theology Seminar, the Liturgical Music Seminar, and the Liturgical Language Seminar for their ongoing input as my writing progressed. I owe special thanks to Gail Ramshaw for her thoughtful suggestions regarding specific chapters. I am grateful to members of *Societas Liturgica* for their suggestions and critique of my writing in its earlier stages. Special thanks goes to Virgil Funk for writing the generous foreword to this book. He has challenged and encouraged my thinking and writing over many years. Also special thanks to the National Association of Pastoral Musicians (NPM) for their invitation to speak on topics covered in this book at their DDMD Winter Colloquium in 2014. Their enthusiasm and feedback were invaluable.

I am also grateful for the support and encouragement of my colleagues in the Theology Department, including three chairs, Leo Lefebure, Terrence Tilley, and J. Patrick Hornbeck, for the support and interest extended through faculty colloquia, and the Julio Burunat Foundation Lecture Series. It was Leo who first suggested that I design the course "Great Christian Hymns." I am especially grateful to my colleague, Harry Nasuti, for his careful reading and helpful suggestions on the biblical material. Over the years, I enjoyed the smart and dependable service of graduate teaching assistants, especially Gregory Tucker, Taylor Bartlette, and Edward Dunar. I am also grateful to my undergraduate students in my Great Christian Hymns classes over the years. Their interest, enthusiasm, and questions encouraged me to pursue this research and write this book.

I would like to acknowledge Liturgical Press for their permission to use an article published in *Worship* in September 2010 in a reworked version as chapter four. I owe a debt of gratitude to the late R. Kevin Seasoltz, O.S.B, former editor of *Worship* for his encouragement and support of my work as writer of the Liturgical Music Column. My thanks also go out to GIA Publications for taking on this project and to Michael Silhavy who was an important conversation partner during the writing of this book. Finally thanks to Kirin Nielsen, associate editor at GIA, for the final shepherding of the book into the light of day.

My family, my religious community, and the many liturgical assemblies of which I have been a part have been an ongoing source of strength, encouragement, and inspiration. I am grateful for their understanding, patience, love, and friendship. The Church Musicians' Guild of Buffalo (CMG), today a local chapter of NPM, has also been an important formative influence in my early years as a church musician. There are so many friends that I dare not mention just some.

The three teachers mentioned in the dedication influenced my thinking and my research when I was a student for two degrees at The Catholic University of America. Mary Collins, O.S.B., directed my dissertation on the topic of liturgical music as ritual symbol. Joseph Komonchak's ecclesiology course presented the first opportunity to explore images of church in classic Christian hymns. Fred Moleck taught a Church Music History course when I was working on my Masters in Liturgical Music. Later, through the NPM and NAAL and the *GIA Quarterly*, Fred continued to be a source encouragement and support for my writing. In addition to these three teachers, there have been countless other pastors, music directors, organists, and teachers reaching back to my childhood. All of them have inspired me to be passionate about the song of the singing assembly, to promote it, support it, and to understand it better. Seeds planted over a lifetime have finally blossomed forth in this book! *Deo Gratias*!

Judith M. Kubicki, CSSF
Fordham University
Bronx, New York

INTRODUCTION

In the middle of the twentieth century, the great hymnologist Erik Routley (1917– 1982) wrote these words: "The only reason I have for attempting the present book is a conviction that there is work to be done by those who can bring to the study of church music a sense of theology."[1] Throughout his career, Routley's research and writing provided both knowledge and inspiration to the study and practice of Christian hymn singing. My hope is that this present book will in some small way contribute to the work that Routley envisioned as both necessary and important, not only for academic purposes, but also for the flourishing of the life of the church.

The topic of Christian hymnody is enormous. Any attempt to account for Christian hymnody in all historical periods and in all languages and in all Christian churches would require an encyclopedia of countless volumes. The potential breadth of the subject therefore necessitates drawing parameters regarding the goals and specific subject matter of this monograph. This is not a history of Christian hymnody although historical influences will be taken into account as one of the contexts of both composing and singing Christian hymns. Neither is this a musicological analysis of hymnody although music and its influence as context for the text is a significant consideration. The book will examine hymns in English, yet does not (and could not) consider the hymnody of every English-speaking country. Some hymns originally written in other languages such as Hebrew, Greek, Latin, and German, among others, will be considered in English if they are being sung in English translation.

---

1   Erik Routley, *Church Music and Theology* (Philadelphia: Fortress Press, 1959), 11.

My particular perspective is that of a Roman Catholic living in the United States. Aware of the fact that since the Second Vatican Council there has been significant ecumenical sharing of repertoire and resources, I am hopeful that my work here will be found useful well beyond my own RC context.

This project focuses on developing a theology of Christian hymnody, or perhaps more accurately, a method for discovering such a theology. Its approach is twofold: 1) discovering a theology expressed within the hymn texts and 2) discovering a theology expressed by the action of communal hymn singing in a worship context. The idea for this project has developed slowly over years of study, teaching, writing, and pastoral practice in the areas of liturgical music, English language and literature, and liturgical and sacramental theology. More recently, it has been teaching an undergraduate theology course entitled "Great Christian Hymns" at Fordham University for more than a dozen years that has enabled my thinking to take shape and become expressed in these pages.

Throughout the book, I will often make reference to "church." My primary understanding of this term comes from the writings of the New Testament where church or ekklesia refers to the people gathered for worship. Another way of defining the term is to say that the church is the gathering of the People of God, the Christian faithful, in order to worship the Triune God. This is accomplished first of all through liturgical celebrations such as the Eucharist (Mass) or the Lord's Supper, the sacraments, and the Liturgy of the Hours. Secondarily, it is also accomplished through extra-liturgical or para-liturgical celebrations of an assembly or a local community of faith understood to be church.

Bringing together insights from the world of music, language and symbol and putting them into conversation with theology can be an exciting and enlightening, yet dangerous project. There is always the possibility of using texts to prove or support one's particular perspective. There is likewise the possibility of being blind to the influence of one's own life perspective (*Sitz im Leben*—"situated in life") on one's thinking. Yet the task is an important one to take up for several reasons. In offering a method for interpreting hymns theologically, this book will offer an explanation for how syntax, imagery, and symbol interact with other elements of the liturgy to express faith, provide theological meaning, and help shape a group of singers into an assembly that is able to perceive itself as a particular instance of church, that is, the Body of Christ.

OUTLINE OF CHAPTERS

The book consists of six chapters. The first lays the groundwork for understanding how hymn texts do theology by exploring select definitions of "hymn" and of "theology." This is followed by an exploration of Maxwell Johnson's insights into Prosper of Aquitaine's famous dictum, "Lex orandi, lex credendi" and Brian Wren's understanding of hymns as "condensed" theology. Four specific contexts for hymn texts—music, space or architecture, history, and ritual—are introduced as having significant impact on the theological meaning of a hymn, both as it is expressed and the way it is received. The chapter then proposes the first aspect of a method for analyzing the theology of hymn texts by examining concrete images. These are understood to be those that appeal to one of our five senses: seeing, hearing, tasting, touching, or smelling. The first chapter closes by offering an analysis of three hymns for Epiphany by examining each text's concrete images.

Chapter two examines two aspects of liturgical hymn texts: their biblical and symbolic characteristics. Beginning with the premise that language is about relationships, this chapter locates language as one among many aspects of ritual. Since the psalms are in many ways the building blocks of Christian hymnody, the first part of the chapter examines them as both Scripture and liturgy. In this first section, the practice of interpreting the psalms Christologically is explored through a comparative analysis of Psalms 72, 23, and 98 and their metrical versions, including the Christmas carol "Joy to the World." A discussion of Canticles in the Hebrew Scriptures and in the New Testament concludes this first section. Symbolic language is the topic of the second section. Here the philosophy of semiotician Michael Polanyi and the theology of Louis-Marie Chauvet form the basis for positing hymn singing as symbolizing activity. An analysis of the Easter hymn, "Jesus Christ Is Ris'n Today" provides a concrete example of how a hymn functions in this way.

Chapter three includes several textual analyses that explore metaphor as a way to find the theological pulse of a hymn text. The nature of metaphoric language, particularly as religious language is examined by incorporating the thinking of such scholars as Philip Wheelwright, Gail Ramshaw, Mark Searle, and Sallie McFague, among others. The chapter goes on to explore four points: (1) different approaches to Christian eschatology in hymn texts; (2) understandings of redemption through Jesus Christ in a variety of hymn genres; (3) shifts in metaphoric language in hymn texts created since the Second Vatican Council; and (4) theological implications of some of these shifts

Chapter four begins with a focus on three classic hymns on the topic of church. Its purpose is to discover how singing them can both express and shape our understanding of who we are as a church. The ecclesial and symbolic nature of the liturgy, and specifically of hymn singing, is discussed. Since hymn singing is an act of ecclesial meaning, the chapter also traces changes to these three hymn texts that have appeared in hymnals over the years. A post-Vatican II hymn on church is offered by way of comparison with some of the traditional hymns studied earlier in the chapter. The final section explores the ecclesiology of Taizé and how their music structures their worship while also embodying a clear and compelling theology of church. The chapter concludes with some observations that draw on a theology of the assembly and the rich diversity of hymns on the topic of church.

Chapter five examines the performative and transformative power of classic hymn texts. It begins by considering the meaning of "classic," particularly as presented by twentieth-century scholars Hans-Georg Gadamer and David Tracy. Building on the thinking of J. L. Austin, the chapter develops the argument that hymn singing is a performative speech act. This is followed by a consideration of the phenomenological understanding of disclosure. Building on the philosophical thinking of Robert Sokolowski, the chapter explores how hymn singing can function as an event of disclosure. These somewhat abstract ideas are made more concrete by considering hymns that exhibit characteristics of performativity and disclosure. The final section of the chapter considers the transformative power of hymn singing. The specific focus of this section is hymn singing as formative for Christian living, particularly living lives that promote the Gospel, living a just life, and becoming the One Body of Christ.

Chapter six explores the question of how hymn singing enables us to name God. The chapter brings the rich tradition of naming God—including biblical, early Christian, and medieval sources—into conversation with contemporary theologians, philosophers, and hymn text writers. A brief excursion into the world of the visual arts is made to make an important point about the power of metaphor in shaping the religious imagination. The chapter also examines contemporary examples of hymn texts and the Trinitarian formula that grapple with expressing the mystery of God in more inclusive ways. These reflections naturally lead to the question of how we name ourselves. The Bible, Christian tradition, and cultural usage are used to explore possible solutions to this contemporary dilemma. This involves the willingness to edit classic texts, a practice with a long and distinguished history.

THE INTEGRAL NATURE OF HYMN SINGING IN LITURGICAL CELEBRATIONS

One goal of this project is to present a clear and convincing argument for the integral role of hymn singing in the liturgy. While all the elements of liturgical ritual interact with each other to generate theological meaning, the role of the assembly's song in accomplishing this task is irreplaceable. That is, no other ritual element can accomplish what the singing assembly accomplishes. When an assembly sings the liturgy with gusto and conviction, its participation is enhanced and promoted on all levels and in all aspects of community life. Some worshiping assemblies, particularly in the Roman Catholic tradition but not only there, have given up on attempts to promote the song of the assembly. Discouraged and worn out by failed attempts, these communities have settled for mediocre participation or none at all. It is especially in these situations that renewed commitment, resources, and effort are especially needed. My hope is that this book will resonate with those who read it so that the song of the singing assembly—infused with the breath and the fire of the Holy Spirit—can in some small way be renewed for the life of the entire Church!

CHAPTER 1

HOW DO HYMNS DO THEOLOGY?

DEFINING OUR TERMS

HYMN

When we ask how hymns do theology, we are asking a big question. There is the matter of the hymn text and the music that accompanies it. There is also the matter of constantly changing contexts such as the ritual or worship event within which the hymn is sung, place or architectural space, historical period, and cultural and social aspects that all impact transmission of meaning. This first chapter will lay some groundwork by considering the meaning of familiar terms. So, for example, before proceeding with the task of discovering how hymns, particularly hymn texts, do theology, it might be helpful to consider what we understand by the simple term "hymn." While we might like to assume that the term "hymn texts" does not need much explanation, still there are varying definitions or understandings of the term "hymn." Some are broader and some narrower. This is true especially as the hymn has continued to evolve, within the Judaic-Christian tradition, and particularly since the Second Vatican Council (1962–1965).

Augustine of Hippo (354–430 CE) offered a quite simple definition when he described a hymn as the praise of God by singing. Augustine explained it this way: "A hymn is a song embodying the praise of God. If there is merely praise but not praise of God, it is not a hymn. If there be praise, and praise of God, but not a song, it is not a hymn. For it to be a hymn, it is needful," insists Augustine, "for it to have three things—praise, praise of God, and these sung."[2] It may come as a surprise to some that Augustine spoke of worshiping God through hymn singing in the early days of the Church. Some associate hymn singing with the beginning of the Protestant Reformation. But hymns are an ancient form of worship that dates back even further than Augustine to our ancestors in the Judaic tradition. The Hebrew Scriptures are filled with many instances when a particular passage is actually a hymn, probably sung during communal worship. Exodus 15:1–21 records the "Song of Victory" sung when the Israelites witnessed the destruction of Pharaoh's army in the sea. As it is being sung, Aaron's sister, Miriam, leads the women in a victory dance. This canticle of thanksgiving eventually becomes the first of the canticles that the Christian liturgy borrowed from the Hebrew Scriptures. It is used even now as the psalm response for the Exodus reading at the Easter Vigil in the Roman Rite, among others.

It was not only ancient Israel that engaged in hymn singing, however. Ancient Greece did as well. In *Worship Music: A Concise Dictionary*, the entry for the word "hymn" explains that the word comes from the Greek *hymnos* and meant a song praising gods or heroes. The first entry in the dictionary defines hymn as a free poetic form set to music and sung liturgically; the second defines it as strophic poetry set to music and sung liturgically and extra-liturgically. The dictionary notes that hymns in the Eastern Church are in free poetic forms.[3] In his preface to *Anatomy of Hymnody*, Austin Lovelace begins with this definition: "A hymn can be defined as a poetic statement of a personal religious encounter or insight, universal in its truth, and suitable for corporate expression when sung in stanzas to a hymn tune."[4] On the other hand, *The History of American Catholic Hymnals Since Vatican II*, defines "hymn" simply as a religious poem set to music.[5]

Perhaps a more substantive and inspiring definition is the one found in the Preface to the hymnal, *Congregational Praise*, published by the Congregational Union of England and Wales in 1951:

---

2   Boniface Ramsey, ed., *The Works of Saint Augustine: A Translation for the 21st Century. Expositions of the Psalms 121–150*, translation and notes by Maria Boulding (Hyde Park, NY: New City Press, 2004), 490.

3   Robin A. Leaver, "Hymn," in *Worship Music: A Concise Dictionary*, ed. Edward Foley (Collegeville, MN: The Liturgical Press, 2000), 149–150.

4   Austin Lovelace, *Anatomy of Hymnody* (New York: Abingdon Press, 1965), 5.

5   Donald Boccardi, *The History of American Catholic Hymnals Since Vatican II* (Chicago: GIA Publications, 2001), xi.

This at least may be said, that a hymn is intended for singing, and for singing together. Its subject must therefore be worth singing about, and it should express the common faith of Christendom. Nothing is so worthy of our singing as the glory and majesty of God, His creative power and redeeming grace. The greatest hymns are never far from the sublime scenery of our redemption. The singing of a hymn is an act of corporate worship, and as our fellowship is not only with one another but also with the saints above, our reach will often exceed our grasp, but we must avoid the idiosyncrasies of personal feeling and experience.[6]

This brief definition captures many important aspects of hymn as understood within the Christian church. While the idea of singing may generally be assumed, the fact that a hymn is intended for singing *together* highlights the communal quality of this activity. Generally, a hymn is not meant for solo singing or private singing, but for singing with a group of people with whom one has bonds of faith, if not of care and love. The last sentence of the definition states very clearly that singing a hymn is an act of corporate worship. Singing is *not* an interruption of worship, but rather a heightened expression of our communal act of worshiping God.[7] At various points in history, some Christian traditions have embraced this insight more than others. Furthermore, the definition points out that the subject of the hymn must matter; it cannot be trivial.

It is the last sentence of this quotation, however, that offers another reason for hymn singing that is often overlooked. Not only is singing an act of our corporate worship of God that expresses our fellowship with each other, but it is also an expression of our fellowship with the saints who, we might recall, are engaged in the endless praise and worship of God. There is both a horizontal and a vertical dimension involved. Scripture has made this point in several places, particularly in the Book of Psalms, Isaiah, and

---

6   Congregational Union of England and Wales, *Congregational Praise* (London: Independent Press, 1951), iv. Erik Routley was a member of the committee preparing this hymnal and General Secretary to the committee.

7   This claim is not meant to suggest that song is simply decorative. In general, because liturgy is ritual, its various components are typically heightened, whether it be speech, gesture, or movement, depending on the degree of solemnity of the occasion.

Revelation where heaven is depicted as a veritable songfest (see Is 6:1–5, Rev 5:13, and Rev 14:3). When we raise our hearts and voices in song to worship God, we join with the angelic voices and all those who have gone before us who sing God's praise unceasingly. Because of this, the hymn best serves this sublime activity if is not idiosyncratic or too narrow in its vision or experience. A creative tension normally exists between the private and individualistic and the personal and communal aspects of our public prayer.

The hymnal, *Congregational Praise*, does not cite the author of the definition we have been considering since many on the committee probably had input into its construction. However, its content and spirit point to the significant influence of Erik Routley who served on the committee that published *Congregational Praise*. He also served as General Secretary for the committee. One of the most renowned hymnologists of the twentieth century, Routley observed that knowing which hymns a given group loves to sing will reveal which aspects of Christianity mean the most to them.[8] It is an explication of the principle that the content of our prayer reflects the content of our faith.

In a similar way, Brian Wren, contemporary hymn text writer, describes hymns as "poems of faith." He further develops this idea by adding that a hymn is

> a congregational song consisting of a sequence of units, called stanzas, with or without a repeated refrain. Such sequences have the capacity—not always realized—to develop a theme and reach a conclusion. A good hymn lyric has flow and direction, and keeps its quality as it unfolds. An outstanding lyric may even "mend in length," as George Herbert puts it, meaning that it improves as it goes on. It *takes us somewhere* (emphasis added) as it tells a story, paraphrases scripture, or develops a theme.[9]

---

8   Erik Routley, *Christian Hymns Observed: When in Our Music God Is Glorified* (Princeton, NJ: Prestige Publications, 1982), 3.
9   Brian Wren, *Praying Twice: The Music and Words of Congregational Song* (Louisville, KY: John Knox Press, 2000), 253.

There have been exceptions to this rule, of course. For example, many of Charles Wesley's hymns were written for evangelistic field preaching, where "line-by-line" impact seems to have mattered most, and the total weight of accumulated imagery was apparently more important than its overall pattern."[10] Today, the Internet, instantly available on multiple digital devices, is beginning to fashion new ways of thinking that are neither primarily linear nor sequential. But as a hymn text writer, Wren argues that hymns need to be more than a collection of fragmentary elements. Though other genres of liturgical song such as acclamations and litanies may have poetic qualities, hymns, in Wren's judgment (and I agree) are the most developed form of poetry in the category of congregational song—at least up to this historical point in liturgical development.[11]

THEOLOGY

Perhaps the more elusive word in the question posed at the beginning of this chapter is the word "theology." In the first edition of his classic tome, *Catholicism*, Richard McBrien makes the point that it is important to distinguish faith, theology, and belief. His distinctions can be helpful since we often speak of "expressing our faith" and "forming faith" when we talk about sung prayer or hymns.[12] But what exactly does the word "faith" mean? According to McBrien, faith is personal knowledge of God. Christian faith is personal knowledge of God in Christ. Note that his emphasis is on the *personal* rather than on the *cognitive* or the *propositional*: "Faith is not primarily belief in truths (propositions) which have been revealed to us by God through the Bible and the Church; rather, it is the way we come to knowledge of God as God. The proper object of faith, in other words, is not a doctrine or a sacred text, but God, our Creator, Judge, and Savior."[13] Later in his writings, McBrien underscores the point that Christian faith

---

10   Madeleine Forell Marshall and Janet Todd, *English Congregational Hymns in the Eighteenth Century* (Lexington, University Press of Kentucky, 1982), 87.

11   Wren, *Praying Twice*, 253–254.

12   Bishops' Committee on the Liturgy, *Music in Catholic Worship* (MCW) (Washington, DC: USCCB Publications Office, 1972, 1982), no. 1,6 and Committee on Divine Worship, *Sing to the Lord: Music in Divine Worship* (STL) (Washington, DC: United States Conference of Catholic Bishops, 2008), nos. 13, 27, 30, 69, 130; *General Instruction of the Roman Missal* (GIRM) published in *A Commentary on the General Instruction of the Roman Missal*, ed. Edward Foley, Nathan D. Mitchell, Joanne M. Pierce (Collegeville, MN: Liturgical Press, 2007), nos. 20, 39–40; *Sacrosanctum Concilium (Constitution on the Sacred Liturgy)*, gen. ed. Austin Flannery (Northport, NY: Costello Publishing Co., 1996), no. 59.

13   Richard P. McBrien, *Catholicism: Study edition* (New York: HarperCollins, 1981), 25. See also revised edition (1994), 20.

is "a gift of God by which we freely accept God's self-communication in Christ. Catholicism [as any other Christian denomination] is a [particular kind of] communal, ritual, moral, spiritual, and intellectual *expression* (emphasis added) of Christian faith."[14] Furthermore, we can distinguish "faith" from "the faith." The latter refers to the entire composite of beliefs held by Christians in general or by Catholics in particular. This is what we usually mean by the word "doctrines."[15] We speak of the doctrine of original sin, the doctrine of grace and redemption, or the doctrine of the real presence of Christ in the Eucharist.

Furthermore, according to McBrien, faith is personal knowledge of God; it is our perception of God in the midst of daily life. It does not and cannot exist in isolation. So while faith is not theology, it cannot exist independent of theology. Theology comes into play at that moment when a person of faith becomes intellectually conscious of her or his faith. In other words, theology is the critical reflection on faith.[16] This book's goal is to provide a critical reflection on the faith expressed in our Christian repertoire of hymnody and in our many acts of liturgical singing.

Perhaps a concrete example will help to illustrate the point. Let us say that I have a deep faith in God's presence in my life. I visit a member of my local parish who is dying in the hospital. After the usual small talk about the weather and the quality of the hospital meals, my dying friend confides her doubts about the afterlife and God's forgiveness. The conversation that ensues is a type of "doing theology" because through it my friend and I reflect on and interpret our experience of God in our living and in her dying through the lens of faith and informed by our Christian belief.

Thus we can say that faith is personal knowledge of God; theology is consciously and critically reflecting on that faith. The Benedictine monk, philosopher, and Archbishop of Canterbury, St. Anselm (d. 1109) defined theology as "faith seeking understanding" (*fides quaerens intellectum*). In other words, "theology is that process by which we bring our knowledge and understanding of God to the level of expression. Theology is the

---

14 Richard P. McBrien, *Catholicism: Completely Revised and Updated Study Edition* (New York: HarperCollins, 1994), 19.
15 McBrien, 1981, 25.
16 McBrien, 1994, 20.

articulation, in a more or less systematic manner, of the experience of God within human experience."[17]

In a broad (and less systematic) sense, theology can emerge in many venues: music, theater, a painting, a dance, a church, a posture. Of course, it is also perhaps even more accessibly found in the written, spoken, or sung word. However, an important caution needs to be raised. There is no guarantee that all theology is good theology. We can be mistaken in interpreting our experience or knowledge of God. We might even have a distorted or false experience of God in the first place. Recall the Gospel story where the Pharisees want to know whose sin—the blind man's or his parents'—caused the man's blindness (Jn 9:1–3). Jesus corrected their mistaken notion and told them that it was not caused by the sin of the parents or the son. We can perhaps think of our own examples, often in our childhood, where something bad happened and the reason (theological interpretation) offered was that it is a direct punishment of God. History records that within the Christian church there have been theological wanderings and sometimes missteps. Sometimes unwittingly, texts have been written that have strayed or contradicted the Christian faith. This has even been the rare case among some of the finest hymn text writers.[18]

Nevertheless, we can agree with McBrien when he asserts that faith exists always and only as it is expressed in some type of theological form. The question is which theological interpretation is best suited to the task at a particular moment. This is not an idle question. For in every age, the Christian tradition needs to be expressed and interpreted in a way that will speak to the people of a specific time and place.[19] This focus on context was part of the Second Vatican Council's effort to read the signs of the times and it continues to be one of the Church's priorities in the twenty-first century. It is the reason why we need to sing, not only the great classic hymns of the past, but also write and sing new hymns for the People of God today and in the future.

---

17   McBrien, (1981) 26.
18   See *Psalter Hymnal Handbook*, Emily R. Brink and Bert Polman, editors (Grand Rapids, MI: CRC Publications, 1998), 743. For example, Charles Wesley wrote "Love Divine, All Love Excelling" with four stanzas. The original second stanza is usually omitted because the text can be interpreted as asking God to take away our free will.
19   McBrien, 1981, 26.

But theology in its strictest sense is not the only outcome of faith. The pastoral leadership of the Church, from time to time, may formulate normative rules that are referred to as "doctrines" (teachings). Those promulgated with the highest solemnity are called dogmas (what is right).[20] In addition to theology and doctrines, worship and moral behavior are also outcomes of faith. And so one of the goals of this book is to examine the relationship between the singing of hymns in Christian assemblies and the Christian faith of those assemblies.

In this way we can say that if theology is a process (of reflection or interpretation), then belief is one of its several products. That is, a belief is a formulation of our knowledge of God through faith.[21] Doctrine is an official teaching that expresses what we believe, but it is not the only one. There are many expressions of belief: Scripture, liturgy, and of course, doctrines and dogmas, all of which may lead to living a moral life. Thus the one Christian faith has multiple forms of expression: letters, liturgical documents, theological reflections, narratives, officially approved or mandated cults (e.g., liturgies), and sacramental celebrations through which the community ritualizes in word and action and song what it believes in the depths of its heart and consciousness.[22] The liturgy we celebrate and the hymns we sing express and nurture our faith. Oftentimes, however, that expression can be mechanical and uninspired, a risk involved whenever human beings engage in repetitive behavior. And indeed, liturgy or worship is ritual behavior that involves repeated patterns of prescribed actions. These actions have included communal singing of some sort since the very beginning.

"LEX ORANDI, LEX CREDENDI": ANOTHER LOOK AT PROSPER OF AQUITAINE'S DICTUM

The familiar axiom of the fifth-century writer Prosper of Aquitaine (c. 390–c. 455), "lex orandi, lex credendi," has often been quoted as a way to explain the relationship of worship to belief. The phrase translated means that "the law of praying is the law of believing." Sometimes it is translated, "the law of praying determines the law of faith." However, the Latin quote

---

20 McBrien, 1994, 20.
21 McBrien, 1981, 27.
22 McBrien, 1981, 28.

above is a shortened form of what Prosper actually said: "ut legem credendi lex statuat supplicandi" (That the law of supplication (rule of prayer) might establish the rule of faith).[23] It is from this axiom that the basis for calling liturgy *theologia prima* derives. Many liturgical theologians[24] have argued that worship or liturgy is our first source of theology. Citing Prosper was especially in vogue as a result of the Liturgical Movement that eventually ushered in the reforms of the Second Vatican Council. But making a clear link between worship and theology is not simply a contemporary interest. Many of the early Fathers of the Church approached not only liturgical texts, but also the rituals themselves as a location of theological disclosure. In fact, this was the basis of *mystagogy*[25] in the Early Church. Thus we can say that the work of exploring the theological meaning of Christian hymn texts is part of an ancient and illustrious Christian tradition of reflecting on the liturgy in order to discover theological meaning.[26] However, as is the case with any slogan or sound bite, the original or full meaning is often lost, misrepresented, or significantly altered when it is applied to situations very different from its original usage. In other words, problems emerge when Prosper's dictum is taken out of its original historical context. So what is the original story?

Theologian Maxwell Johnson has done a great service to liturgical theologians through his investigation and synthesis of the origin of Prosper's dictum.[27] Prosper of Aquitaine was a monk in the region of Marseilles and a strong proponent of Augustine's position against the semi-Pelagian school of Lerins.[28] According to Dom Cappuyns, Prosper penned the document entitled the *Celestinian Capitula*[29] as part of his defense of Augustine's position. The

---

23   The Latin text is in *Series Latina* (1844 ff.) 51:209–210; also in H. Denzinger & A. Schönmetzer, eds. *Enchiridion Symbolorum. Definitionum et Declarationum de Rebus Fidei et Morum* (Freiburg im Bresigau: Herder, 1965), 246.

24   See for example the work of Aidan Kavanagh, David Power, Alexander Schmemann, and David Fagerberg.

25   "Mystagogy" refers to the liturgical catechesis that initiated a catechumen into the mystery or Christ. More specifically, it refers to the period of instruction, based on the rites of Initiation just experienced, that followed an adult reception of Baptism. See "Mystagogy" in John T. Ford, *Glossary of Theological Terms* (Winona, MN: St. Mary's Press, 2006).

26   Judith M. Kubicki, *The Presence of Christ in the Gathered Assembly* (New York: Continuum, 2006), 3.

27   Maxwell E. Johnson, *Praying and Believing in Early Christianity: The Interplay between Christian Worship and Doctrine* (Collegeville, MN: Liturgical Press, 2013). See chapter one.

28   Semi-Pelagianism refers to the doctrine upheld in the fifth century about human nature. While not denying the necessity of grace for salvation, semi-Pelagians maintained that humankind was capable of taking the first steps toward Christianity and that grace supervened only later. See *The Oxford Dictionary of the Christian Church*, 3rd rev. ed., ed. by F. L. Cross and E. A. Livingstone (Oxford University Press, 2005, published online 2009). www.oxfordreference.com/view/10.1093/acref/9780199659623.001.0001/acref-9780199659623

29   The *BCL Newsletter* December 1980, 237 & 239, explains in a footnote that the axiom in question comes from the so-called *capitula Coelestini* that were annexed to a letter of Pope Celestine I (422–32). However, they are probably the work of Prosper of Aquitaine (c. 440).

Capitula enjoyed *auctoritates* (authority) because it was believed to come from Pope Celestine (422–32).[30] Recall that the actual wording of the adage is "ut legem orandi legem statuat credendi." This has been translated as follows: that the law of supplication determines (or founds) the rule of faith.[31] Prosper's *Capitula* was written to prove the necessity of divine grace for faith. Chapter 8 of this work refers specifically to the rites of priestly supplication or intercessions *in such a way that the order of supplication determines the rule of faith* (emphasis in original). What Prosper does here is invite the reader to consider the rites of supplication made by the priests. He asserts that these rites are celebrated uniformly in the entire church since they have been transmitted since the time of the apostles.[32] The intercessions of Good Friday would be an example of such universal practice. Prosper cites these prayers which ask that God give grace to various categories of people—unbelievers, idolaters, Jews, heretics, schismatics, and catechumens. In other words, all humankind is in need of God's grace. Prosper cited the prayers of Good Friday because their practice supported his argument that the act of believing is God's gift of grace. This was the original point of the argument against the semi-Pelagians. However, the sources for this conviction are not simply liturgical, but include Scripture and the decisions of the Apostolic See (popes and councils). In chapters 1–6, Prosper includes excerpts from Pope Innocent I (401–417) and Pope Zosimus (417–418). Chapter 7 cites the Council of Carthage (418).[33] The liturgical piece is a part of Prosper's argument, but not even the primary one.[34] Rather, what Prosper is claiming is that the *lex supplicandi* (law of supplication (prayer)) can be said to "constitute" the lex credendi because the lex supplicandi conforms to traditional and biblical doctrinal teaching of the church. That is why Prosper appeals to the liturgy. Not because it is liturgical, but because of its apostolic roots.[35] For Prosper, Scripture and tradition are the primary sources.

---

30   Paul De Clerck, "Lex orandi": The Original Sense and Historical Avatars of an Equivocal Adage," *Studia Liturgica* 24(1994), 180.

31   De Clerck, 182.

32   De Clerck, 182. Most scholars agree that early church worship was characterized by a great deal of variety rather than the uniformity that gradually came to become standard practice. Nevertheless, while the claim that something was universally observed strengthens the argument, it does not necessarily imply that the manner of observance was the same everywhere.

33   De Clerck, 180.

34   Michael B. Aune, "Liturgy and Theology: Rethinking the Relationship," *Worship* 81(January 2007), 67. See also De Clerck, 182–183.

35   Paul V. Marshall, "Reconsidering 'Liturgical Theology': Is There a *Lex Orandi* for All?" *Studia Liturgica* 25:2(1995), 140.

It is helpful to take a look at another piece of writing by Prosper in order to get a fuller understanding of the basis for his argument. In *De vocatione omnium gentium*, Prosper refers to a passage from 1 Timothy 2:1–6 to argue against the semi-Pelagians.[36] Here is the key passage:

> First of all, then, I ask that supplications, prayers, petitions, and thanksgivings be offered for everyone, for kings, and for all in authority, that we may lead a quiet and tranquil life in all devotion and dignity. This is good and pleasing to God our savior, who wills everyone to be saved and to come to knowledge of the truth. For there is one God. There is also one mediator between God and the human race, Christ Jesus, himself human, who gave himself as ransom for all.

Neither Augustine nor Prosper limit their arguments to liturgical prayer. This point is critical for understanding the original context and usage of Prosper's adage. In fact, it is not even the primary argument in the original *Capitula*. Because of its misuse and misinterpretation, the scholar Michael Aune has suggested retiring "Prosper's axiom" from our discourse on liturgical prayer and belief.[37]

Nevertheless, there is significant value to examining the relationship between worship and belief for the ways in which that relationship enriches both. In doing so, however, we need to acknowledge that the relationship is fluid and subject to change in different cultural and/or historical contexts. Aside from arguing the truth of Prosper's dictum, we can agree that both worship and belief influence and nurture each other. And because it is ritual activity that involves language and symbolizing activity, worship expresses theological meaning.[38] As Paul Bradshaw points out, it is a two-way relationship: the Church expresses its faith in the act of worship and the act of worship nurtures and forms the faith of the church.[39]

---

36 De Clerck, 182–185.
37 Aune, 65–68.
38 See also Judith Marie Kubicki, *Liturgical Music as Ritual Symbol: A Case Study of Jacques Berthier's Taizé Music* (Leuven, Belgium: Peeters, 2006).
39 See Paul Bradshaw, "Difficulties in Doing Liturgical Theology," *Pacifica* 11(June 1998), 187.

The great Orthodox theologian, Alexander Schmemann, insists that theology must be rooted in the very experience of the faith and that experience is given and received in the Church's liturgy, that is, in her *lex orandi*.[40] In assessing Schmemann's view, Maxwell Johnson concludes that for Schmemann, the *lex orandi* is the Church's *lex credendi* and "the theological task is ultimately an interpretive and descriptive process that attempts to grasp the 'theology' as revealed in and through liturgy."[41] Such an approach is fine as long as it does not become an excuse for using the liturgy as a proof text for a particular theological perspective. Like the symbols and the symbolizing activity of which they are comprised, liturgies are by their nature multivalent. And it is this multiplicity of meaning that is especially significant when one claims that the liturgy constitutes primary theology. Aidan Kavanagh, a theologian who promoted an understanding of liturgy as primary theology, also observed: "The language of the primary theologian, however, more often consists in symbolic, metaphorical, sacramental words and actions which throw flashes of light upon chasms of rich ambiguity."[42] It is this rich ambiguity in the liturgy that enables it to mediate meaning over time and across multiple cultural contexts. Furthermore, it is this rich ambiguity that can be lost when a misunderstanding or misuse of Prosper's adage encourages a unilateral view of liturgy that views it as a proof text for supporting a singular interpretation.[43] So, while praying does shape believing, the reverse is also true.[44] For this reason, many liturgical scholars are rethinking the significance of Prosper's phrase and its appropriate application to liturgical theology.

HYMN TEXT AS CONDENSED THEOLOGY

Thus far we have been considering theology from the viewpoint of the systematic theologian, specifically Richard McBrien and various contemporary

---

40 Alexander Schmemann, "Liturgy and Theology," *The Greek Orthodox Theological Review* 17 (1972), 95.

41 Alexander Schmemann, "Liturgical Theology, Theology of Liturgy, and Liturgical Reform," *St. Vladimir's Theological Quarterly* (1969), 218. Cited in Maxwell E. Johnson, *Praying and Believing in Early Christianity: The Interplay between Christian Worship and Doctrine* (Collegeville, MN: Liturgical Press, 2013), 19.

42 Aidan Kavanagh, "Response: Primary Theology and Liturgical Act," *Worship* 57 (July 1983), 322–333. This piece was a response to an earlier piece by Geoffrey Wainwright in which Wainwright offers an overview of his new book, *Doxology: The Praise of God in Worship, Doctrine, and Life* (New York: Oxford University Press, 1980). The subtitle describes the text as a systematic theology. The "primary theologian" that Kavanagh refers to in the quote is the person in the pew whom he affectionately called "Mrs. Murphy."

43 See P. Marshall, 135; Bradshaw, 187–188; M. Johnson, 16.

44 M. Johnson, *Praying and Believing*, x. See also P. Bradshaw, "Difficulties..." 181–193.

liturgical theologians in both Western and Eastern Christianity. Now let us take a look at theology from the viewpoint of a contemporary hymn text writer, Brian Wren, whose definition of hymn we considered earlier in this chapter. In his book, *Praying Twice: The Music and Words of Congregational Song*, Wren poses the question whether hymns can do theology. He begins chapter 10 by likening the professional theologian who shows an interest in the lyrics of hymns to an American visiting Australia—or speaking with a native Australian just about anywhere. It is a perfect metaphor for the experience of conversing in the same language and totally missing the message. As a doctoral student at CUA, I lived down the hall from a doctoral student from Australia. I recall one experience when, looking me straight in the eye, she uttered a simple sentence. I did a double take. I heard every word and recognized each as English. Nevertheless, I had no idea what she had said. The language sounded simultaneously familiar, yet foreign. So it is also with a hymn text. Even though, in a hymn text, the Christian story is told and doctrines or theological viewpoints expressed, "a hymn lyric's theological work—if any—is done within the syllable count, stress patterns, and rhyming options of English stanza, and the limits and possibilities of rhetorical devices such as epigram, simile, antithesis, and metaphor."[45] These are the building blocks of hymn texts. These are not the materials with which systematic theologians normally work. Recall that earlier Richard McBrien defined theology as the articulation, in a more or less systematic manner, of the experience of God within human experience. This "systematic" theology is understood to be a form of reasoned inquiry, an ordered, reasoned account of Christian faith. The *Westminster Dictionary of Christian Theology* defines theology as "the rational account given of Christian faith," while Alister McGrath's *Christian Theology: An Introduction* defines it as "the systematic study of the fundamental ideas of the Christian faith. Karl Rahner defines theology as "the conscious and methodical explanation and explication of the divine revelation received and grasped in faith."[46]

If we hold up these definitions of theology to our hymn texts, Wren reasons, we would be forced to conclude that hymn texts cannot do theology.

---

45   Wren, *Praying Twice*, 349.
46   Wren, *Praying Twice*, 350.

First of all, their brevity and form are ill suited to systematic reasoning. Furthermore, a hymn invites us not to step back from faith and examine it, but to step into faith and worship God. That is one of the important ways that congregational singing functions as a participatory event. It is not simply about joining in the singing. We know from our own experience that worship is laden with theological insights. In worship, theology is acted out or expressed in the enacting of the entire ritual.[47] Wren suggests that as elements of worship, hymn texts might be considered "vehicles of theology." But, he admits, vehicles generally do not transform their passengers nor reshape their experience. Rather, expressing a theological concept in stanza entails moving from concept to metaphor, from elaboration to epigram, from balanced prose to the energy of rhyme and rhythm. Because of limited word length and time frame, the poet must be selective, highlighting some themes while omitting others. It is unlikely, therefore, that a hymn lyric can "carry" theological concepts without also interpreting them. Thus, at least in some limited and unique way, hymns do theology.[48]

In the process of concluding that hymns are capable of doing theology, Wren necessarily creates a wider definition of theology, one that involves music, drama, and the visual arts. In other words, he makes the theological "umbrella" bigger so that it is capable of covering more categories. By extension, we can say that theology can also be done through the verbal arts— such as hymnody—that draws more on metaphor, story, and description than on reasoned argument.[49] Following this line of reasoning, we can consider music, drama, the visual arts, and hymnody expressions of theological insight. Wren concludes his argument with this definition: "Hymns are a particular way of using words, a specific genre of verbal theology, different from narrative, history, parable, sermon, lecture, and reasoned treatise. Hymns are a particular genre of theological song."[50]

Wren coins the term "condensed" theology to describe the kind of theology that hymns do. While a hymn may express a theological point of view, it does not do so in the sustained manner of systematic theology. Instead, a hymn

---

47   Wren, *Praying Twice*, 351.
48   Wren, *Praying Twice*, 352.
49   Wren, *Praying Twice*, 364.
50   Wren, *Praying Twice*, 365.

offers condensed arguments. The hymn will not so much try to convince us of a theological insight, as it will invite us to celebrate anew an insight that we have already embraced. It does this by stating, pithily and vividly, theological insights whose claims are argued elsewhere. Using economy of phrase by means of such tools as epigram, imagery, and metaphor, a hymn text expresses theological viewpoints using only a few words.[51]

Some of these epigrams or "economy of phrase" include such familiar phrases as "Amazing grace," "Hark! The herald angels sing," "There is a balm in Gilead" "Were you there" "Lo, how a rose e're blooming," "How can I keep from singing," "There's a wideness in God's mercy," "We shall overcome someday," "It came upon the midnight clear," "At the cross her station keeping," "Now the green blade rises," "As fire is meant for burning," and "Sing a new church...."

To summarize, we can say that faith is personal knowledge of God; theology is consciously reflecting on that faith; and belief is the product of that faith, expressed as Scripture, doctrine, and/or liturgy. Hymns express theological insights in a way that allows us to express and nurture our faith. Its content or reference is the Christian tradition, that is, that set of beliefs that Christians hold in common. Some examples would be our belief that God is Triune, that God created the world; that Jesus Christ is fully human and fully divine, suffered death, and rose from the dead for the salvation of all humankind; that Mary is the Mother of God; that Christ is present in the gathered assembly, the presider of Eucharist, the Word proclaimed, the bread and wine, and in the sacraments; that God is love.

Since we sing hymns during worship, we want the texts to be excellent in their theological viewpoints or insights (how they interpret our experience of God and articulate our Christian beliefs). Because we sing these texts, we want our hymns to have musical excellence. And as human beings we want the theology expressed in hymns to touch our hearts, capture our imagination, and inspire our living. Mediocrity is not an option since we are engaged in something that is far too important.

---

51   Wren, *Praying Twice*, 369.

Looking at Context

Hymns are sung prayer performed within the larger context of worship or liturgy. Therefore, we cannot study them simply as words and music on a page. Rather, we need to study hymns as they exist and interact within multiple contexts. Four contexts, alluded to at the opening of this chapter, are particularly important for this study: (1) music, (2) space or architecture, (3) history, and (4) ritual. Musicians and congregations alike know that a hymn tune must be good if the hymn is to become beloved in a worshiping assembly. If the music is unfamiliar, too difficult, or poorly rendered, the hymn will fail no matter how good the text. Furthermore, the musical setting of a hymn text can significantly influence the reception of the text by highlighting certain words through repetition, tempo changes, melodic and harmonic treatment, and accompaniment.

Music making occurs within a particular space or environment, usually a room or building. Sometimes it may also occur outdoors. When music making occurs within a space that is clearly delineated as sacred, the space and the music interact to create or sustain an experience of the holy. Even if the space is not a sacred space (e.g., a school gym), the music making itself may create a sonic environment that clearly delineates a worship space. The space within which we worship needs to be acoustically supportive of singing and instrumental performance. In addition, the style and size of the space can speak volumes (one way or another) about God's transcendence/immanence and the worshiping assembly's experience of itself as one. The space can also have an impact on how the assembly and individual members are able to hear themselves singing. This can affect their ability to receive the hymn's message and enhance or impede their awareness of themselves as the one body of Christ.

Each hymn is created within a particular moment in the history of the church and in the life of a particular community or group of people. So it can be helpful to know some basic history, as for example, the impact of the Reformation on the growth and development of Protestant hymnody, the role of slavery in the genesis of the Black spiritual, the impact of the Second Vatican Council on hymns written in the later twentieth and early twenty-first centuries. In addition to the significance of the historical moment in which a hymn emerged is the significance of the historical moment when a hymn continues to be sung and interpreted. Knowing that John Newton wrote "Amazing Grace" to convey his conversion experience after years of slave trading helps us to appreciate the original theological import of that hymn. However, the American experience of singing "Amazing Grace" during the days immediately after the disaster of September 11, 2001 has changed the relationship Americans have with the meaning of that text in significant ways.

Lastly, hymns are meant to be sung during worship. Therefore, experiencing hymns sung within actual liturgical celebrations can provide a more accurate understanding of their meaning and message. Ultimately, anything that we say about a text needs to be considered within these several contexts in order to comprehend the larger picture. But, because we are dealing with symbols and metaphors and ritual, we will never exhaust the potential meanings that can be generated.

We return to our fundamental question: how do hymns do theology? Furthermore, how do hymn texts, within a specific musical context, do theology? Wren proposes that hymn texts are capable of doing condensed theology (as opposed to systematic theology) by means of such literary devices as metaphor, epigram, story, rhyme scheme and meter, among other things. When a particular instance of hymn singing is sung at the appropriate ritual moment with a particular worshiping assembly, the result can be theologically meaningful and spiritually inspiring.

To illustrate what we have been talking about more specifically, let us take a look at the theology expressed in three hymns or carols for the feast of Epiphany. The hymn texts are printed without music, but the tunes commonly sung are included. This procedure will be observed throughout the book since interlining[52] makes it difficult, if not nearly impossible, to appreciate fully the presentation of ideas or story. Indeed, this practice may well be a contributing factor to a congregation's inability to fully appreciate and/or understand the theological message of even familiar and beloved hymn texts. The custom of printing the words of a hymn alongside the music, as is done in many British

---

52   "Interlining" is a technical term that simply means that the text is placed within the music as we usually see it in our hymnals, especially those published in the United States.

or Australian hymnals, among others, may be a practice worth considering in the United States.

Recall that our earlier discussion pointed out that theology explores and describes rich, multilayered, and multidimensional realities about our life in God. The history of the Church is a great example of the fact that over the centuries, different aspects of the same mystery have been understood and celebrated in a variety of ways. This does not necessarily mean that one century got it right and another got it wrong. Nevertheless, when the various aspects of a particular mystery are kept in healthy balance or creative tension, such balance may more readily enable the mystery to shine forth clearly. The point of the analysis that follows is not to say that the theology of one hymn is better than another. This may or may not be the case, based on a variety of criteria. Rather, it may simply be that at a particular time, a certain aspect of theology speaks more directly to the assembly's lived experience. In other words, the people of one period of time may be in need of focusing on or hearing about a certain aspect of a mystery of the faith simply because of the challenges they face in their daily experience.

Looking for Concrete Images

Our first step is to take a look at the concrete images in each of the texts. By this term we mean those words or brief phrases that appeal to one or more of the five senses: sight, taste, touch, smell, and sound. Concrete images serve as the connections between the original event or experience and the experience of the singers, either in the act of singing or in recalling a previous similar experience. In hymn texts, they also serve as connections with the various aspects of ritual that appeal to the five senses. Good ritual celebration, like good hymn texts, will engage as many of our five senses as possible. In addition to the primary experiences of hearing and seeing, there is also the sense of smell as in the use of incense, holy oil, and flowers—to name the obvious. Additional scents can be introduced through the texts of the readings and of the hymns and songs. The sense of touch can be awakened through the tactile quality of various objects in the ritual setting, contact with each other at the sign of peace, the signing with oil and the washing with water during Initiation rites and other sacramental celebrations. Taste is an important dimension of receiving the Body and Blood of Christ in Communion as well as an important metaphor for the experience of God in our lives. The analysis that follows examines two traditional hymns and one contemporary hymn that celebrate the feast of Epiphany.

EPIPHANY HYMNS

The first hymn text is the nineteenth-century carol, "We Three Kings"[53] based on Matthew 2:1–11. John H. Hopkins, Jr. wrote both the text and also composed the tune, KINGS OF ORIENT. The meter is 88 44 6 with refrain (italicized). This hymn is typically sung during the Christmas season, and particularly on the feast of the Epiphany, which for Churches in Western Christianity may be celebrated on January 6 or the Sunday nearest that date.

> We three kings of Orient are;
> Bearing gifts, we traverse afar
> Field and fountain,
> Moor and mountain,
> Following yonder star.
>
> *Refrain:*
> *O star of wonder, star of night,*
> *Star with royal beauty bright,*
> *Westward leading,*
> *Still proceeding,*
> *Guide us to the (thy) perfect Light.*
>
> Born a King on Bethlehem's plain.
> Gold I bring to crown him again;
> King forever,
> Ceasing never,
> Over us all to reign. *Refrain*

---

53   "We Three Kings," *Worship* (2011), #452.

Frankincense to offer have I;
Incense owns a Deity nigh;
Prayer and praising,
Gladly raising,
Worshiping God on high. *Refrain*

Myrrh is mine: its bitter perfume
Breathes a life of gathering gloom;
Sorrowing, sighing,
Bleeding, dying,
Sealed in the stone-cold tomb. *Refrain*

Glorious now behold him arise,
King and God and Sacrifice;
"Alleluia,
Alleluia,"
Sounds through the earth and skies. *Refrain*

The first stanza has many sensory images. They include three kings, Orient, gifts, field, fountain, moor, mountain, and star. The last image, star, is central to the story and is picked up in a significant way by the refrain. The refrain mentions star three times. It is contrasted with night and then spoken of in connection with the "perfect Light." This perfect Light is described in the second stanza as born a King. Other images include Bethlehem's plain, gold, and again king. Although crown is used as a verb, it conjures up images of the crown worn by a king. This newborn king is described as reigning over everyone and forever. What kind of king wields that kind of power? Slowly, the idea emerges that this king is different from all others. The refrain repeats with its images of star and perfect Light once again. Frankincense is the primary image of stanza three. It is a sign of the Deity or the nearness of the divine. The final line describes the traveling kings worshiping the King born in Bethlehem as God. The refrain with its images of light follows once again. The tone shifts in stanza four with the introduction of the gift of myrrh. Images include bitter perfume, gloom, bleeding, and stone-cold tomb. All of these allude to the future suffering and death of Christ and the use of myrrh for his burial. The refrain follows. The final stanza clearly focuses on the resurrection of Christ. We behold him "arise." The Risen One is described as King, God, and (paradoxically) Sacrifice. Both heaven and earth join in singing "Alleluia!"

Let us consider some initial points about the use of these images and the story and theology that the text expresses. The point of view is personal as each of the three kings speaks (sings) a stanza about his gift and its meaning. In the unfolding of the story, the identity of Christ, who by the way is never described as a baby, unfolds. Christ is king who reigns over all humankind. Christ is God and we worship him as God. Christ is human and he will suffer and die, but he will also rise from the dead as King, God, and Sacrifice for our redemption. The entire Paschal Mystery is celebrated in the story of the three visitors.

Furthermore, the refrain with its images of light vs. darkness and Christ as light, reinforces notions of Christ's royalty and kingship. The word "royal" in the phrase, "Star with royal beauty bright," clearly refers to Christ, not to the three kings. But perhaps one of the most significant lines in the entire carol is the line "still proceeding." The refrain is in the present tense, not the past tense. It is still proceeding. It is leading us still today. It is still guiding us to the perfect Light. What does the star represent? Is it the presence of Christ in the world? Is it the Holy Spirit? The practice of using the image of light for Christ has a long tradition with clear biblical roots that will be discussed later in the book. Most carolers enjoy singing the refrain with its often-exaggerated rendition of the syllable "O." Perhaps it is because of the music's similarity with folk music or, indeed, with drinking songs, that congregations cannot resist joining in, at least on the refrain. There is a certain earthiness about the music. This quality makes it an appropriate accompaniment to a text that celebrates the manifestation of the God-become-human to the three visiting kings who represent all humanity throughout the ages.

The second hymn is also a nineteenth-century carol. The text of "As with Gladness Men of Old" is by William C. Dix. The tune entitled DIX is by Conrad Kocher and adapted by William H. Monk. The meter is 777777. Like "We Three Kings," the scriptural reference is Matthew 2:1–11, but only for the first three stanzas. Scripture references for stanzas 4 and 5 are Revelation

21:23 and 22:5. The hymn is usually sung on the feast of Epiphany and throughout the Christmas/Epiphany season. Because of some interesting differences in the rendition of the text in three hymnals, an alternate version is offered in parenthesis.[54]

As with gladness men of old
Did the guiding star behold,
As with joy they hailed its light,
Leading onward, beaming bright,
So, most gracious Lord, may we
Evermore be led to thee. (your splendor see)

As with joyful steps they sped
To that lowly manger bed,
There to bend the knee before
Him, whom heav'n and earth adore;
So may we with willing feet (hurried pace)
Ever seek the mercy seat. (Run to seek your throne of grace)

As they offered gifts most rare
At that manger (c)rude and bare;
So may we with holy joy (this holy day),
Pure and free from sin's alloy, (Drawn to you without delay)
All our costliest treasures bring,
Christ! To thee (you), our heav'nly King.

Holy Jesus, ev'ry day
Keep us in the narrow way;
And, when earthly things are past,
Bring our ransomed souls at last
Where they need no star to guide,
Where no clouds thy (you) glory hide.

---

54   *Worship* (2011) #450, *Gather* (2011) #465, *RitualSong* (2016) #551, *People's Mass Book* (2003) #226, and *One in Faith* (2015) #405 published the adapted text given in parenthesis. *Journeysongs* (2012) #334 published the original text without revision or adaptation.

In the heav'nly country (city) bright
Need they no (none shall need) created light;
Thou (You), its light, its joy, its crown,
Thou (You) its sun which goes not down;
There for ever may we sing
Alleluias to our King.

Concrete images in stanza one of "As with Gladness" include men, star, and light. The message of the stanza is simple: the "men of old" behold or notice the star with joy. The second stanza describes joyful, quick steps. That kind of enthusiastic movement we can see. The men have responded to what they have seen and decided to take action—to travel. There is also "lowly manger bed," bending the knee, heaven and earth, feet, seat or throne. The images in stanza three set up a contrast between rare gifts and the poverty of the manger described as crude and bare. (I suspect there was some straw.) Costliest treasures and heavenly king are two other images in this stanza. The images in the fourth stanza are less tangible and therefore more abstract. The phrase "earthly things" is a somewhat vague reference. The two strongest images are star and clouds. In both cases, however, neither the star nor the clouds will be present when earthly things are past. The stanza has a decidedly eschatological[55] thrust to it. This continues in stanza five, where in the heavenly city there will be no need of created light. This would include no need of the star that the "men of old" followed. Christ is hailed as heaven's light, joy, crown, sun that never sets, and finally again, King.

What can we say, then, about this text? Notice, first of all, that the structure of the first three stanzas is such that the first four lines of each stanza look back at the story in the past. That is actually what is meant by "of old." The song is not specifically commenting on the age of the travelers. Then, for each of the first three stanzas, the last two lines bring the focus into the present. As "men of old" were led by a star, so may we be led to Christ. As the travelers sped to visit and worship Christ, so may we hurry to Christ's throne of grace. As the men of old offered rare gifts, so we hope to offer to Christ our costliest

---

55 Eschatology has often been described as the theology of the last things: death, judgment, heaven, and hell. However, the focus of this theology is really more on the final realization of God's reign, begun by the death and resurrection of Christ and realized in its fullness in the second coming of Christ.

treasures. The costliest of these, of course, is the gift of our very self. The last two stanzas look to the future when we, having been ransomed by Christ, no longer need a star to guide us. Nor will clouds hide Christ's glory. Rather, with the light of Christ shining, we can spend eternity singing glory to Christ our King who is our light, our sun that never leaves us in the dark.

Notice that the star is introduced early in the text. The image of light weaves in and out of the five stanzas. Christ is described as King twice, but the visitors are never referred to as kings (although they offer gifts most rare) and their number and gifts are not specified as was the case in the previous hymn. Nevertheless, this hymn does mention the manger—lowly, crude, and bare—but it seems more as a foil for the rare or costly gifts the visitors bring. The main focus seems to be on what we can learn from the story. This is evident in the last two lines of the first three stanzas and also the fourth and fifth stanza in their entirety. There is a clear movement from past to present and then to the future eschaton, as we ponder the meaning this event has in our own lives. What costly treasures do we have to offer our King? Is the path of the "men of old" similar to the "narrow way" we ask Christ to keep us on? The hymn tune, DIX, usually associated with this text, is also often yoked with "For the Beauty of the Earth" and some new, less familiar texts as well. Kocher, who wrote the original version of the hymn tune, was fond of the music of Mozart and Haydn. Also, as a Lutheran, he would have been familiar with the traditional Bar form (AAB) of chorale melodies. These influences can be heard in the classic AAB form of the tune. In this way the music perfectly mirrors the development of the text. The first four lines recall the original event and the last two focus on the present. Each time the shift is made, the melody changes from A to B.

Our last hymn in this section is fairly new. Francis Patrick O'Brien composed the text to "Epiphany Carol" in 2002.[56] Published with the tune BEACH SPRING, the carol's meter is 8787D.

> Ev'ry nation sees the glory
> Of a star that pierced the night.
> As we tell the wondrous story

---

56 *RitualSong* (2016) #549.

We are bathed in radiant light.
Star sent forth from highest heaven,
Dancing light of God's design,
Shine upon the gift that's given:
Word made flesh now born in time.

Ev'ry tongue shall sing the praises
Of his birth in deepest night.
He is healing for the ages;
He is Christ, our God's delight.
He proclaims within his being
All our hopes, our great desires.
He shall die to rise, redeeming
All who follow with their lives.

Once again may we discover
Word made flesh sent from above.
In our neighbor, sister, brother,
In the lonely and unloved.
May we touch him, may we hold him,
May we cradle him with care
As we learn to love each other,
Bringing hope from out despair.

Gather, God, the world together
In the brightness of your day.
Fill our hearts with joy forever;
Help us walk the holy way.
May your justice rule the nations;
May all people live as one.
Now we see our true salvation
In the glory of your Son.

The title neither mentions nor alludes to kings or wise men or men of old. Its subject is the experience of epiphany or the revelation of God's glory. While the original story is clearly in the background, present experience is in the foreground. Let us look at the images.

Verse one includes every nation, star, night, light, heaven, gift, and flesh. Star and light are each mentioned twice. The descriptions of light are particularly vibrant, spoken of in lush terms: "bathed in radiant light," "dancing light of God's design." The second stanza includes tongue, night, Christ. Many lines mention abstractions such as healing, hopes, desires that cannot be said to appeal to one of the five senses directly. This might suggest the more elusive and ethereal nature of an epiphany experience. A more concrete focus returns in the third stanza with the inclusion of the noun "flesh" as the primary concrete image. The verbs—touch, hold, and cradle—suggest that this "Word of God" has truly taken on human flesh and that we can still experience this "Word" in the flesh of one another. The last stanza speaks of "brightness of your day," hearts filled with joy, nations ruled by justice, and the glory of your Son. The distance between present and future disappears as we witness an epiphany of the glory of God's Son in our own day.

The text does not mention gifts or magi. Instead, the gift introduced in stanza one is Christ, the word made flesh. Stanza two elaborates on this gift as God's offer of healing, hope, and redemption *for us*. There is also no mention of the manger of Bethlehem. Rather, stanza three directs our attention to the lonely and unloved in our midst. This is where we may discover the Word made flesh alive among us, once again. The last stanza brings together the themes expressed throughout the text. We pray that the brightness of God's day, like the star over Bethlehem, bring us joy and help us walk the path, the holy way. The three kings or magi, left unmentioned in the text, were led on their holy way. We also have a holy path to follow. This path includes having the nations ruled by Christ's justice, having all people live as one. At the end of this path, we will see our salvation revealed in the glory of Christ, as did the men who traveled westward to find the newborn king. This final revelation is the epiphany, the revelation of Christ. Furthermore, we are reminded that this epiphany is for every nation—as the first line of the carol makes abundantly clear. Like the prophet Simeon who spoke of Christ as light for the gentiles and the glory of Israel, the text echoes his canticle recorded in Luke 2:29–32. This hymn lays the miracle of the epiphany at our very feet. Christ continues to reveal himself to us today. We are bathed in radiant light. Do we have the eyes to see the "dancing light" of God's design? No need for nostalgia. We have our own epiphany in the "now."

BEACH SPRING is a lyrical melody that resembles a ballad. Originally published as part of *The Sacred Harp* (1844), the tune has a recognizable American character to it that can assist in situating the singers' focus on their present experience. The lyrical expansiveness of the middle section tugs at the imagination and coaxes the heart to respond to the challenge of the Christian mission.

Focusing on the concrete images in these three hymns for Epiphany highlights their power to carry a story and to engage the imagination. But interpretation requires a specific type of discipline and care. All three texts made clear connections with Scripture, either Matthew 2, Revelations, or Luke 2. It is not the case that "anything goes." The poets of these texts derive their songs from the Christian tradition expressed in the Scriptures and in the liturgical feasts celebrated each year. These sources are the basis for creativity and interpretation. However, the Church's experience, both communally and individually, are in dialogue with the tradition. Such interchange enables us to discover fresh insights for familiar texts and pray our lives into being through the singing.

This chapter has explored the meaning of such familiar terms as "hymn," "theology," and "faith." With the assistance of Maxwell Johnson's research, it has also taken a fresh look at Prosper of Aquitaine's famous dictum, "*Lex orandi, lex credendi*," or more accurately, "*ut legem credendi lex statuit supplicandi.*" It becomes clear that the influence is not only in one direction. not one way. Rather, worship and faith mutually enrich each other. Brian Wren's useful distinction between systematic and condensed theology enables us to affirm that hymn texts, along with multiple contextual support (music, history, space, and rite), do indeed do theology. Finally we examined and compared three hymns on the topic of epiphany to discover how concrete images, meter and repetition serve to express theological meaning. Building on the assertion that hymn texts are capable of expressing theological meaning, the next chapter will explore two specific aspects of the language of hymns: the biblical and the symbolic.

CHAPTER 2

THE LANGUAGE OF LITURGICAL HYMN TEXTS:
BIBLICAL AND SYMBOLIC

INTRODUCTION

L anguage is about relationships. The language of Christian hymn
singing, as part of the wider and richer interplay of liturgical
symbols, orchestrates a complex web of relationships that enable
connections between God and God's people, among each of the members
of the worshiping assembly, and even our relationship with ourselves. These
relationships are in constant motion and are multi-leveled and complex. This
is the case because hymn singing within the context of Christian ritual is an
integral part of the symbolizing activity that we call liturgy or worship.

Language is one of many aspects of ritual that—together with gesture,
space, sacred objects, vesture, music, sound and silence—comprise the
liturgy. At its best, liturgical language is biblical, symbolic, metaphoric,
poetic, doxological, communal and ecclesial, repetitive, embodied, and
revelatory. In this chapter, we will focus only on the biblical and symbolic
nature of liturgical language. Insofar as this language directly relates to the
official prayers of the Mass, sacramental rites, and scripture proclamation,
it is subject to a rigorous process of review before new texts are composed
or revisions are made and approved.[57] Composing or revising the language
of hymnody, however, while perhaps appearing to be held to less rigorous

---

57 I am speaking particularly about my own Roman Catholic tradition. Not all churches observe the levels of
    scrutiny and oversight that are currently in place within the Catholic Church, particularly where the English
    language is concerned.

standards, can often receive strong responses from the congregations that sing them. These responses, whether positive or negative, support the common wisdom that words really do matter.

BIBLICAL LANGUAGE: PSALMODY

From the earliest days of Christian worship, the texts of sung prayer have been deeply rooted in sacred Scripture, both the Old and the New Testaments. The Book of Psalms is the heart of biblical prayer. Not only has Christian prayer appropriated the psalms in whole or part for its own worship song, but in many ways it has also observed its structure, focus, and stance before the Holy One. Therefore, in order to better understand and appreciate Christian hymnody, it is helpful to pause and consider the legacy of the Psalter that has been handed on to us from our Jewish brothers and sisters.

Let us begin by clarifying some terminology. We have already made reference to the "psalms," the "Book of Psalms," the "Psalter," and "Psalmody." The term "psalm" refers to one of the 150 individual songs or poems included in the Book of Psalms in the Hebrew Bible. For our purposes, the Book of Psalms, the Psalter, and Psalmody, all refer to the collection of psalms as they are found in the Hebrew Scriptures. Hans-Joachim Kraus defines the Psalter as "a collection of the songs, prayers, and wisdom teachings of the Old Testament people of God, which for the most part were sung or spoken in the sanctuary in Jerusalem."[58] The psalms were an important component in ancient Jewish worship in the Temple, domestic feasts, and in the ancient synagogue. Today they continue to play a significant role in synagogue worship.[59] "Psalmody," on the other hand, usually means the singing of psalms, or that part within the Liturgy of the Hours when they are sung.[60] Finally, the term "Psalter" refers to the 150 psalms in the Hebrew Bible, usually in translation. A book that contains a collection of biblical psalms for worship is referred to as a Psalter, even if it does not contain all 150.[61] If we look at the Greek root of these

---

58   Hans-Joachim Kraus, *Theology of the Psalms*, trans. Keith Crim (Minneapolis: Augsburg Publishing House, 1986, 1992), 12.
59   Michael J. Gilligan, "Psalm," in *Worship Music: A Concise Dictionary*, ed. Edward Foley (Collegeville, MN: Liturgical Press, 2000).
60   John K. Leonard, "Psalmody," in *Worship Music: A Concise Dictionary*, ed. Edward Foley (Collegeville, MN: Liturgical Press, 2000).
61   Frank C. Quinn, "Psalter," in *Worship Music: A Concise Dictionary*, ed. Edward Foley (Collegeville, MN: Liturgical Press, 2000).

words, we discover that "*psalmos*" meant "a song sung to a harp." Psalmody had multiple meanings: (1) the art of singing the psalms; (2) the arranging and/or composing of psalms for singing; or (3) a collection of psalms for singing or reciting.[62] The important aspect in the etymology of the words is that singing was the presumed method of prayer. This was often performed in ancient times to the accompaniment of a harp.

The psalms serve as the veritable building blocks of so much of Christian hymnody. Since many of the earliest disciples of Christ were practicing Jews familiar with Temple worship and the observances of Judaism, the Book of Psalms would have been a natural choice for prayer. Jesus himself often referred to the Scriptures when he preached and regularly prayed—that is— sang the psalms. By about 200 CE the psalms held a regular place in the Eucharist. They were also an essential element of the Divine Office (Liturgy of the Hours) from the very beginning. The practice of interpreting the psalms Christologically was also evident in the practice of affixing a Trinitarian doxology at the conclusion of each psalm since the fourth century.[63]

Psalms have a double identity in that they are both scripture and liturgy. As scripture, that is, as part of the inspired Word of God, they serve a canonical function in relation to other liturgical material. This is especially evident in that the psalms have served as models for writing other hymns and prayers. Old Testament scholars believe that the psalms originated as songs composed for public and private occasions of worship. Within Christianity, the forms and intentions of the psalms, as well as their motifs and vocabulary, have shaped the liturgical creativity of the church, sometimes consciously and sometimes more subliminally.[64]

The Psalter confesses the faith of a worshiping community, whether the original Israelite community for which it was composed or communities that have adopted these prayers for their worship today. It is when texts emerge from worshiping communities that the theologies contained therein are truly vibrant. The Hebrew Scriptures tell the story about the living God encountered in worship. Such a context assures strong connections to real

---

62   John T. Ford, Psalmody, *Glossary of Theological Terms* (Winona, MN: St. Mary's Press, 2006).
63   Gilligan, "Psalm."
64   James Luther Mays, *The Lord Reigns: A Theological Handbook to the Psalms* (Louisville, KY: Westminster John Knox Press, 1994), 4–6.

life and to the dynamism of a community.[65] In other words, we can say that, while the Psalter is not a work of systematic theology, it is nonetheless a concentration and selection of theological material in the Hebrew Scriptures made in the context of ancient Israel's worship.[66] When we speak about the psalms, Hans-Joachim Kraus observes, it is clear that in their correspondence to their subject matter, praise and prayer are the basic forms of theology.[67] Borrowing from Karl Barth, Kraus defines theology as "a task that not only begins with prayer and is accompanied by it, but one that is to be carried out appropriately and characteristically in the act of prayer."[68]

What kind of God emerges in the Psalter? It is a God who is "in relationship" with humankind. This God is both loving and faithful. This is particularly expressed through two words repeated throughout the psalms: *hesed* and *ĕmet*. *Hesed* is a relational term that characterizes God's relationship with humankind as one of steadfast love and mercy. *Ĕmet*, on the other hand, has its root in the sense of truth, or trustworthiness. In other words, God's relationship with humankind is one of fidelity that inspires trust. The psalms have therefore been described as songs of a community of individuals related both to God and to each other. They are also intrapersonal instructions exploring the delicate web of human, divine, and natural relationships.[69]

Biblical scholar Harry Nasuti makes the point even more strongly. He observes "that of at least equal importance for a theology of the Psalms is an understanding of the way these texts *make available* (emphasis added) a relationship between God and the believing individuals and communities that have used them."[70] Throughout the history of Judaism and Christianity, the psalms have continued to be used in the relational contexts of liturgy and personal prayer. Because of this, the psalms have been not only a source of theology, but also of theological anthropology. This is the case since the

---

65   W. H. Bellinger, Jr., "The Psalms as a Place to Begin Old Testament Theology," in *Psalms and Practice: Worship, Virtue and Authority*, Stephen Breck Reid, ed. (Collegeville, MN: Liturgical Press, 2001), 37.

66   Bellinger, "The Psalms," 33.

67   Kraus, *Theology*, 12–13.

68   Cited in Kraus, *Theology*, 13. See Karl Barth, *Einführung in die evangelische Theologie* (Zurich: EVZ Verlag, 1962), 180–181.

69   Rolf A. Jacobson, "'The Faithfulness of the Lord Endures Forever': The Theological Witness of the Psalter," in *Soundings in the Theology of Psalms: Perspectives and Methods in Contemporary Scholarship*, ed. Rolf A. Jacobson (Minneapolis: Fortress Press, 2011), 114.

70   Harry P. Nasuti, "God at Work in the Word: A Theology of Divine-Human Encounter in the Psalms," in *Soundings in the Theology of Psalms: Perspectives and Methods in Contemporary Scholarship*, ed. Rolf A. Jacobson (Minneapolis: Fortress Press, 2011), 29.

human side of the relationship is present in its own voice.[71] And since the psalm texts continue to be used in contemporary worship as first-person speech, they are not only part of ancient Israel's theological witness, but also part of an ongoing—and still revelatory—conversation that believers continue to have with God today.[72]

In speaking of the impact of praying the psalms, James Luther Mays explains that "the words of the psalms are the vocabulary of a particular 'language world.' By means of the psalms, we must enter and live in that 'language world' if praise and prayer with their words are to be authentic."[73] When speaking of a "language world," Mays does not simply mean issues of grammar, syntax, and vocabulary, but a sphere of meaning and the particular understanding and rendering of "world" and "existence" expressed in them.[74] Furthermore, by "language," Mays does not mean the language of a particular national group such as English, Spanish, or French, but speech that is part of a distinctive way of viewing, experiencing, and acting in the world.[75] The psalms provide us with a language whereby God, the world, and human life are grasped in terms of the reign of God.[76] In such a world, there is a clear relationship between creator and creature. The Creator showers creation with steadfast love and providential care. The response of creatures is to acknowledge their utter dependence on the Creator and express praise, thanksgiving, and awe for all their blessings.

Biblical scholar Walter Brueggemann appeals to some of the major accents found in philosopher Paul Ricoeur's programmatic work. He does this in order to explore how the psalms function. Ricoeur identifies two hermeneutical moments of suspicion and new symbolization. Brueggemann adopts Ricoeur's schema in order to support his own explanation that the dynamic of life as movement is not regular or patterned. Rather Brueggemann insists, life is characterized by disorientation and reorientation.[77] In the midst

---

71 Nasuti, "God at Work," 29–30.
72 Nasuti, "God at Work," 30–31.
73 Mays, 6.
74 Mays, 6.
75 Mays, 6.
76 Mays, 7.
77 Harry P. Nasuti, *Defining the Sacred Songs: Genre, Tradition and the Post-Critical Interpretation of the Psalms.* Journal for the Study of the Old Testament Supplement Series 218, (Sheffield, UK: Sheffield Academic Press, 1999), 58. In n. 2, Nasuti reminds his reader that Brueggemann himself cautions against using this schema as a "straightjacket." Rather, it functions more as a "paradigm" or "heuristic" tool.

of this situation, the human person struggles to maintain some measure of equilibrium in his or her life.[78] Brueggemann proposes "that the sequence of *orientation-disorientation-reorientation* is a helpful way to understand the use and function of the Psalms."[79] Certainly the Book of Psalms has been accurately described as that prayer book that gives expression to the entire gamut of human emotion. In other words, the psalms express the heights of ecstatic joy or the depths of despair or grief. Brueggemann himself asserts that the enduring authority of the psalms is found in their ability to touch the extremities of human life, extremities that he characterizes as disorientation and reorientation.[80] Psalms of disorientation remember better times and express the desire to return to the equilibrium of the past. These psalms often express anger and resentment and, as psalms of lament, enable the individual and/or the community to enter into the disorientation. The psalms of reorientation welcome a newness that gives rise to wonder, amazement, and thanksgiving. The new situation is recognized as gift or grace.[81]

Why should Christians pay attention to this interpretation of the psalms? How does it speak to contemporary faith and spirituality? The answer lies in the centrality of the death and resurrection of Jesus Christ to the Christian faith. Brueggemann's schema for understanding the ways in which the Psalms mirror and express human experience can be further understood in terms of the Paschal Mystery. This important term is taken from the Greek *pascha*, meaning "Passover," and *mysterion*, meaning "a secret rite" or "secret doctrine." Paschal Mystery refers to Christ's redemption of all people through his life of sacrifice, especially his Crucifixion, death, and Resurrection.[82] Because Christians are baptized into Christ's Paschal Mystery, their lives participate in his dying and rising. An apt way of describing this can be in terms of disorientation and reorientation. Our lives are filled with the joys, disappointments, struggles and successes of human existence. The psalms can be a school for a Christian's living out

---

78   Walter Brueggemann, "The Psalms and the Life of Faith: A Suggested Typology of Function," in *Soundings in the Theology of Psalms: Perspectives and Methods in Contemporary Scholarship*, ed. Rolf A. Jacobson (Minneapolis: Fortress Press 2011), 4.
79   Brueggemann, "The Psalms and the Life of Faith," 5.
80   Brueggemann, "The Psalms…," 11
81   Brueggemann, "The Psalms…," 9–10.
82   John T. Ford, "Paschal Mystery," in *Glossary of Theological Terms*. Essentials of Catholic Theology series (Winona, Minnesota: St. Mary's Press, 2006).

the Paschal Mystery even as they were and continue to be a path to God for the Jewish people.

The language of the psalms enables human beings to describe their experience and express their emotional response. And while the psalms bring human experience to expression so that it might be embraced as the real situation in which persons live, that is still not the whole story. In dramatic and dynamic ways, many of the psalms also evoke and form new realities that did not exist until, or apart from, the actual singing of the psalm. In this way the psalms are *anticipatory*. They enable worshipers to embrace the new reality as old worlds are relinquished.[83] Because the individual or community praying these psalms of anticipation and relinquishment are praying these texts as first person speech, the opportunity to engage them in a personal way opens them to transformative grace.[84]

Singing the psalm texts has an aesthetic effect that is similar to what is experienced when singing a congregational hymn. In addition to metaphor, the presence of such poetic devices as sound and structure (including but not limited to parallelism) rhythm, pitch, and tonality[85] involves the singer in ways that are not fully translatable into cognitive terms. The power of this aesthetic dimension suggests that limiting humanity's relationship with God to the cognitive dimension is woefully inadequate.[86] The God who is encountered through praying the psalms reaches out to be in relationship with humankind in a personal way. The person praying is not praying as an isolated individual, but as one rooted first of all in the history of Israel and then carried on by the faithful communities of Judaism and Christianity throughout the ages. This encounter with God in the psalms is at the same time a present reality. For this reason, the God encountered is a "living God" who interacts with those praying the psalms in their real life situations. Finally, the psalms highlight the eschatological urgency with which they describe God's actions among God's people. This eschatological orientation results from the psalms' persistent

---

83 Brueggemann, "The Psalms," 20–24.
84 Nasuti, "God at Work," 39. The significance of this dynamic will become more evident when we discuss the transformative power of congregational singing in chapter five.
85 Of course, every discussion of poetic elements of the psalms must always be aware that Christians are not singing them in their original language. Translation changes the impact of poetic devices as well as their nature and presence in the text. Nevertheless, translators generally approach their task with the intention to preserve the poetic dimensions of the original language in the receptor language. Approaching translation by observing "dynamic equivalence" assigns a priority to achieving poetic expression in the receptor language.
86 Nasuti, "God at Work," 45–47.

expectation of God's future activity. Nevertheless, the attitude of expectation is always rooted in a divine-human encounter in the present made possible through the psalms themselves. As an important site of this present encounter, the psalms continue to serve as one of the most effective ways that both God and humankind work to ensure that their relationship continues.[87]

In studying the worship practice of the early and medieval church, we discover that psalmody provided a rich source of prayer, for both Daily Prayer (Divine Office or Liturgy of the Hours) and the Eucharist. Settings varied from plainchant to polyphony. The proper antiphons sung in the entrance and communion rites have been and are today, often a stanza of a psalm. In the current Roman Rite, the congregation sings the refrain of the Responsorial Psalm after the first scripture reading. This ritual element offers the assembly the opportunity to proclaim with pithy phrase and heightened voice the main focus or theme of the Scripture readings for the day.

In the sixteenth century, the Protestant Reformation retrieved the practice of singing in the vernacular (the language of the people) rather than in Latin or Greek.[88] Often hymns were sung a cappella and in unison. Because of the theology of the influential Swiss Reformer John Calvin, many Protestant churches limited their repertoire to singing only Scripture texts. In practice this usually meant the psalms and a few biblical canticles. One of the great achievements of the Reformation was the publication of the *Genevan Psalter*, a collection that went through several revisions before its final edition in 1562. It includes all 150 Psalms with 125 different tunes and 110 different meters. It also includes some of the canticles.[89]

Reformed churches also adopted a new musical form developing at that time—homophony. However, the structure of the psalm texts—as they are presented in the Bible—did not easily fit into the regular metrical schemes of homophonic music. Hebrew psalms have a unique poetic structure very different from the meter and rhyme scheme of Western hymnody today. Contemporary translations of the psalms present texts in free poetic form rather than in stanzas. That is, the length of individual lines and number of lines

---

87   Nasuti, "God at Work," 47–48.
88   The ancient Church worshiped in Greek until approximately 380 CE when it changed to Latin because it was the vernacular at that time.
89   See Paul Westermeyer, *Te Deum: The Church and Music* (Minneapolis: Fortress Press, 1998), 154. See also Erik Routley, *The Music of Christian Hymns* (Chicago: GIA Publications, 1981), 33, 36.

in a stanza vary widely even within a single psalm. This structure resembles free verse more than the structure of a metered stanza. In any case, such free-flowing poetry is more easily sung by the various patterns of chant and psalm tones than metric hymn tunes. In the psalms, it is the ideas that rhyme rather than the words.[90] The following quote explains the notion simply and clearly:

> Meter, insofar as it exists in Hebrew poetry, is actually the rhythmical counterpart of parallelism of thought. Rhythm is not due to syllabic quantities but to the less definable instinct of balancing parts whose exact accentual values are not measurable and probably never were . . . In Hebrew poetry regularity of stress is subordinated to regularity of balanced ideas. Thus the tendency to fill out lines with incomplete parallelisms by means of compensation . . . is due to the desire to oppose word-masses of about the same weight while varying and emphasizing the thought.[91]

The three ways that the ideas in the psalms rhyme is synonymously, synthetically, and antithetically. In other words, the two-part rhyme may consist of the first part that says something coupled with a second part that either says the same thing in other words (synonymously), offers more information to support or build on the first line (synthetically), or offers a contrasting, but not contradictory thought (antithetically).[92] While these neat distinctions may seem helpful, James Kugel cautions that trying to force everything into one of these three categories obscures the potential subtleties of the text. In fact, the possible relations between the *stichoi* (verse halves) are endless.[93]

Because the reformers favored psalms for congregational song and because psalms texts did not naturally fit set patterns of rhyme and meter, text writers set about reworking them. As a result, psalm texts were rearranged to fit the metrical schemes of familiar hymn tunes. Naturally, the metrical scheme of

---

90   See Westermeyer, *Te Deum: The Church and Music* (Minneapolis: Fortress Press, 1998)20. Here Westermeyer references Kenneth Hart as making this claim.

91   Robert C. Tannehill, "The Magnificat as Poem," 269. Tannehill quotes from N. K. Gottwald, *Interpreter's Dictionary of the Bible* (Nashville, Tennessee: Abingdon Press, 1962), 834.

92   Westermeyer, *Te Deum*, 19. Robert Lowth is generally credited with the discovery of biblical parallelism.

93   James L. Kugel, *The Idea of Biblical Poetry: Parallelism and its History* (New Haven: Yale University Press, 1981), 12–15.

the psalm would depend on the tune the text writer chose to set the metered text. So, for example, Harry W. Baker arranged Psalm 23 as "The King of Love My Shepherd Is." He chose the tune ST. COLUMBA whose meter is 8787. On the other hand, Isaac Watts set Psalm 23 as "My Shepherd Will Supply My Need." He chose the tune RESIGNATION whose meter is 8686D or CMD. The two different arrangements of the text of Psalm 23 cannot be sung interchangeably with these two texts because the meter is different. The result was a blurring of the distinctions between hymnody and psalmody—a hybrid so to speak—that we call the metrical psalm. In addition to reworking the texts for purposes of rhythm and rhyme, these originally Jewish prayers were often given a Christological interpretation. The metrical psalms of Isaac Watts are a good example of this practice. Perhaps one of his most radical reworkings is his hymn (metrical psalm) "Jesus Shall Reign," based on Psalm 72. The first eleven verses of the psalm are quoted below:[94]

> [1] Give the king your justice, O God,
>
> and your righteousness to a king's son.
>
> [2] May he judge your people with righteousness,
>
> and your poor with justice.
>
> [3] May the mountains yield prosperity for the people,
>
> and the hills, in righteousness.
>
> [4] May he defend the cause of the poor of the people,
>
> give deliverance to the needy,
>
> and crush the oppressor.
>
> [5] May he live while the sun endures,
>
> and as long as the moon, throughout all generations.
>
> [6] May he be like rain that falls on the mown grass,
>
> like showers that water the earth.
>
> [7] In his days may righteousness flourish
>
> and peace abound, until the moon is no more.

---

94   *The New Oxford Annotated Bible. New Revised Standard Version with the Apocrypha.* NRSV Third edition. Michael D. Coogan, editor (New York: Oxford University Press, 2001). All biblical quotes are taken from the NRSV unless otherwise indicated.

[8] May he have dominion from sea to sea,

and from the River to the ends of the earth.

[9] May his foes bow down before him,

and his enemies lick the dust.

[10] May the kings of Tarshish and of the isles

render him tribute,

may the kings of Sheba and Seba

bring gifts.

[11] May all kings fall down before him,

all nations give him service.

The original psalm text is a prayer for the king (David and his dynasty). Watts incorporates many of the ideas and images from the psalm into his hymn, "Jesus Shall Reign." However, the focus of the hymn shifts significantly from the focus of the original psalm. Psalm 72, a royal psalm, is a prayer of blessing *for* the monarch. Watts' hymn prays to (rather than for, of course) Christ as King. Since Jesus was of the house of David, it was, for Watts, perhaps a natural development to move from this psalm for the king to the notion of Christ as King. As a result, the Psalm that asked God for blessings for the king is now a prayer celebrating the blessings of Christ's reign. A key focus of the psalms is the reign of God. Since Christians believe Jesus is divine, Watts' move makes perfect theological sense. At least it makes sense to Christians. Recent scholars have taken note of the distinctive power of the metaphor of God as king.[95] Note also that verse 10 of Psalm 72 mentions distant kings coming bearing gifts and offering homage. Christians see in that verse a reference to the story of the Magi. Assigning Psalm 72 as the Responsorial Psalm for the feast of the Epiphany is itself a Christological interpretation of the psalm. Watts' hymn, "Jesus Shall Reign," is usually sung to the tune DUKE STREET whose meter is 8888, commonly referred to as long meter (LM).[96] follows:

---

95   See Harry Nasuti, "God at Work," 36 and n. 31. See also James L. Mays, "The Center of the Psalms: 'The LORD Reigns' as Root Metaphor, in *The Lord Reigns: A Theological Handbook to the Psalms* (Louisville, KY: Westminster John Knox Press, 1994), 12–22; William Brown, *Seeing the Psalms*, 188. Brown comments that God as king is "one of the most prominent metaphors in the Psalter."

96   "Jesus Shall Reign," *Worship* (2011), #569.

Jesus shall reign where'er the sun
Does his successive journeys run;
His kingdom stretch from shore to shore,
Till moons shall wax and wane no more.

To him shall endless prayer be made,
And praises throng to crown his head;
His Name like sweet perfume shall rise
With ev'ry morning sacrifice.

People and realms of ev'ry tongue
Dwell on his love with sweetest song;
And infant voices shall proclaim
Their early blessings on his Name.

Blessings abound where'er he reigns;
The pris'ner leaps to lose his chains;
The weary find eternal rest,
And all who suffer want are blest.

Let ev'ry creature rise and bring
Blessing and honor to our King;
Angels descend with songs again,
And earth repeat the loud Amen.

This Christological interpretation of Psalm 72 also includes a reference to Psalm 8:1–2 that refers to infant voices praising God's name. The verses follow:

O Lord, our Sovereign,
    how majestic is your name in all the earth!
You have set your glory above the heavens.

    Out of the mouths of babes and infants
you have founded a bulwark because of your foes,
    to silence the enemy and the avenger.

The last two lines of stanza three quoted above refer to infant voices praising God's name in a similar way to the first two verses of Psalm 8.

Watts also did a metrical setting of Psalm 23. In this instance, however, he keeps very closely to the original psalm text. For the pious Jew praying Psalm 23, the Shepherd would signify God. For the pious Christian, it signifies Jesus Christ, who referred to himself as the Good Shepherd during his public ministry. The biblical text is rendered as follows in the NRSV:

[1] The Lord is my shepherd, I shall not want.

[2] He makes me lie down in green pastures;

he leads me beside still waters;

[3] he restores my soul.

He leads me in right paths

for his name's sake.

[4] Even though I walk through the darkest valley,

I fear no evil;

for you are with me;

your rod and your staff—

they comfort me.

[5] You prepare a table before me

in the presence of my enemies;

you anoint my head with oil;

my cup overflows.

[6] Surely goodness and mercy shall follow me

all the days of my life,

and I shall dwell in the house of the Lord

my whole life long.

A Christian can pray this text wholeheartedly, even without the Christological interpretation. Both Judaism and Christianity believe in the one God and Jesus himself prayed the psalms. So even though there are no Christological allusions in the psalm, it is a favorite of Jews and Christians alike. Watts' metrical setting of Psalm 23 is entitled "My Shepherd Will Supply My Need." His text does not mention Christ by name. There really is no need to do so since within the

Christian community, the image of shepherd has been traditionally associated with Christ. Watts' text, "My Shepherd You Supply My Need," follows[97]:

> My Shepherd you supply my need;
> Most holy is your name;
> In pastures green you make me feed,
> Beside the living stream.
> You bring my wand'ring spirit back,
> When I forsake your ways;
> And lead me for your mercy's sake,
> In paths of truth and grace.
>
> When I walk through the shades of death,
> Your presence is my stay;
> One word of your supporting breath
> Drives all my fears away.
> Your hand, in sight of all my foes,
> Does still my table spread;
> My cup with blessings overflows,
> Your oil anoints my head.
>
> The sure provisions of my God
> Attend me all my days;
> O may your house be my abode,
> And all my work be praise!
> There would I find a settled rest,
> While others go and come;
> No more a stranger or a guest,
> But like a child at home.

On the other hand, Henry W. Baker's metrical hymn setting of Psalm 23, "The King of Love My Shepherd Is,"[98] includes the words "cross" (fourth stanza line 4) and "chalice" (fifth stanza line 4). Both are strong and familiar

---

97   "My Shepherd You Supply My Need," *Worship* (2011), #708.
98   "The Kind of Love My Shepherd Is," *Worship* (2011), #712.

Christian symbols. In addition, there are other words that express more subtle Christian expressions. For example, in stanza two, line two, the word "ransomed" suggests redemption won by Christ. In the fourth line of the same stanza, "food celestial" is an allusion to the Eucharist. Together, these re-workings provide a subtle but unmistakably Christological interpretation. Bakers' text is offered below:

The King of love my Shepherd is,
whose goodness fails me never;
I nothing lack if I am His,
and He is mine forever.

Where streams of living water flow
my ransomed soul He's leading,
and where the verdant pastures grow
with food celestial feeding.

Confused and foolish oft I strayed,
but yet in love He sought me,
and on His shoulder gently laid,
and home, rejoicing, brought me.

In death's dark vale I fear no ill
with you, dear Lord, beside me;
your rod and staff my comfort still,
your cross before to guide me.

You spread a table in my sight,
your saving grace bestowing;
and oh, what transport of delight
from your pure chalice flowing!

And so through all the length of days
your goodness fails me never,
Good Shepherd, may I sing your praise
within your house forever.

One last example will illustrate yet another way in which Christian text writers have incorporated the psalms into Christian hymnody. Many might be surprised to learn that the beloved Christmas Carol, "Joy to the World," was created from Psalm 98, Psalm 96:10–12, and a reference to Genesis 3:17–18. Watts' primary inspiration for this carol was Psalm 98. Parts of the carol can also be found in Psalm 96. These excerpts, for the most part, are similar to stanzas or sentiments also found in Psalm 98.[99] The Genesis reference alludes to how the coming of Christ undoes the sin of Adam and Eve and the curse on the earth.

Psalm 98 is the Responsorial Psalm for Christmas Day Mass in the Roman Liturgy. The psalm celebrates God's rule, inviting all of creation to acknowledge God's kingship. Phrases such as "all the ends of the earth have seen the victory of our God" (v. 3b) and "Make a joyful noise to the Lord, all the earth" (v. 4) highlight the universal quality of God's rule and creation's praise. Indeed, it is this fourth stanza that opens Watts' carol—Joy to the world! Recall the earlier observation regarding the centrality of the "king" metaphor in the Book of Psalms. Here is a prominent example of its appropriation by Christian hymn text writers.

Psalm 98

[1] O sing to the Lord a new song,
for he has done marvelous things.
His right hand and his holy arm
have gotten him victory.
[2] The Lord has made known his victory;
he has revealed his vindication in the sight of the nations.
[3] He has remembered his steadfast love and faithfulness
to the house of Israel.
All the ends of the earth have seen
the victory of our God.

[4] Make a joyful noise to the Lord, all the earth;
break forth into joyous song and sing praises.

---

99   See Emily R. Brink and Bert Polman, *Psalter Hymnal Handbook* (Grand Rapids, MI: CRC Publications, 1999), 487.

⁵ Sing praises to the Lord with the lyre,

with the lyre and the sound of melody.

⁶ With trumpets and the sound of the horn

make a joyful noise before the King, the Lord.

⁷ Let the sea roar, and all that fills it;

the world and those who live in it.

⁸ Let the floods clap their hands;

let the hills sing together for joy

⁹ at the presence of the Lord, for he is coming

to judge the earth.

He will judge the world with righteousness,

and the peoples with equity.

In the case of this carol, Watts does not attempt to follow the psalm as closely as he did in "My Shepherd You Supply My Need." Instead, he reworks and rearranges the material, providing a decidedly Christological interpretation. Note also that the characteristic Hebrew reference to God as a God of steadfast love (*hesed*) and faithfulness (v. 3) also highlights that God is true to God's promises. In the Hebrew prayer this steadfast love was expressed in God's presence to God's people and his protection of Israel from its enemies. In the Christian interpretation of the psalm, that faithfulness is celebrated in the birth of the Messiah, Jesus Christ. Verses 7–9 of Psalm 98 call upon all of creation—the sea and sea creatures, floods, and the hills—to sing for joy because the Lord is coming. For Israel, this declaration would have been an act of faith in God's presence and protection. Watts weaves these ideas into his exuberant phrases describing "fields and floods, rocks, hills, and plains" repeating "the sounding joy"!

The connection between announcing the coming of the Messiah in the carol with the story of the Fall of Adam and Eve in Genesis 3 is a logical step theologically. For Watts, the Lord's coming is a fulfillment of God's promise to send the Messiah for the salvation of all humankind. The Christmas carol heralds the coming of the Christ who brings blessings for all, that is, "as far as the curse if found." In other words, Christ's birth will undo the curse that all of humankind and all of creation have been under as a result of the disobedience of our First Parents. This is indeed cause for worldwide rejoicing! Much psalm scholarship interprets the phrase "the Lord reigns" or "the Lord has become king" with the notion of victory that is expressed in the first stanza of the psalm. This imminent, present quality is picked up by the carol as well. Verse 9 of the psalm points to the future implications in its description of the way the world will be judge and ruled from now on. The carol nicely catches this eschatological element as well.[100] The tune of "Joy to the World"[101] is ANTIOCH and is based on music by George F. Handel. The meter is CM with repeat.

> Joy to the world! The Lord is come:
> Let earth receive her King;
> Let ev'ry heart prepare him room
> And heaven and nature sing, (2x)
> And heaven, and heaven and nature sing.
>
> Joy to the world! The Savior reigns:
> Let us, our songs employ;
> While fields and floods, rocks, hills, and plains;
> Repeat the sounding joy, (2x)
> Repeat, repeat the sounding joy.
>
> No more let sin and sorrows grow,
> Nor thorns infest the ground;
> He comes to make his blessings flow
> Far as the curse is found, (2x)
> Far as, far as the curse is found.
>
> He rules the world with truth and grace,
> And makes the nations prove
> The glories of his righteousness,
> And wonders of his love, (2x)
> And wonders, wonders of his love.

---

100 Many thanks to my colleague, Harry P. Nasuti, for sharing these insights with me and critiquing this chapter before publication.
101 "Joy to the World," *Worship* (2011), #424.

Therefore, regarding the presence and use of psalmody in Christian worship, we can say that psalmody is prayed and sung in the liturgy both as biblical texts and as metrical hymns. Furthermore, psalmody's ability to enable worshipers to enter into personal relationship with God both individually and communally has been appropriated by hymnody. This is particularly true when the tradition has remained faithful to praying and singing the psalms.

Biblical Language: Canticles in the Hebrew Scripture

The previous section has argued that the Book of Psalms has been, and continues to be, a major resource for Christian worship throughout its history. However, in addition to this important collection of Jewish hymns, there are also numerous songs or hymns—often referred to as canticles—that are also sung in Christian worship.[102] A familiar example is the Canticle in Exodus 15. Some scholars actually speak of two canticles: The Canticle of Moses and the Canticle of Miriam. The first begins at verse 1:

The Song of Moses

1 Then Moses and the Israelites sang this song to the Lord:
"I will sing to the Lord, for he has triumphed gloriously;
horse and rider he has thrown into the sea.
2 The Lord is my strength and my might,
and he has become my salvation;
this is my God, and I will praise him,
my father's God, and I will exalt him.
3 The Lord is a warrior;
the Lord is his name.
4 "Pharaoh's chariots and his army he cast into the sea;
his picked officers were sunk in the Red Sea.
5 The floods covered them;
they went down into the depths like a stone.
6 Your right hand, O Lord, glorious in power—
your right hand, O Lord, shattered the enemy.

---

102 This discussion will observe the common practice of calling any song in the Bible that is not located in the Book of Psalms by the term "canticle." This includes both testaments.

⁷ In the greatness of your majesty you overthrew your adversaries;

you sent out your fury, it consumed them like stubble.

⁸ At the blast of your nostrils the waters piled up,

the floods stood up in a heap;

the deeps congealed in the heart of the sea.

⁹ The enemy said, 'I will pursue, I will overtake,

I will divide the spoil, my desire shall have its fill of them.

I will draw my sword, my hand shall destroy them.'

¹⁰ You blew with your wind, the sea covered them;

they sank like lead in the mighty waters.

¹¹ "Who is like you, O Lord, among the gods?

Who is like you, majestic in holiness,

awesome in splendor, doing wonders?

¹² You stretched out your right hand,

the earth swallowed them.

¹³ "In your steadfast love you led the people whom you redeemed;

you guided them by your strength to your holy abode.

¹⁴ The peoples heard, they trembled;

pangs seized the inhabitants of Philistia.

¹⁵ Then the chiefs of Edom were dismayed;

trembling seized the leaders of Moab;

all the inhabitants of Canaan melted away.

¹⁶ Terror and dread fell upon them;

by the might of your arm, they became still as a stone

until your people, O Lord, passed by,

until the people whom you acquired passed by.

¹⁷ You brought them in and planted them on the mountain of your own possession,

the place, O Lord, that you made your abode,

the sanctuary, O Lord, that your hands have established.

¹⁸ The Lord will reign forever and ever."

¹⁹ When the horses of Pharaoh with his chariots and his

chariot drivers went into the sea, the Lord brought back the waters of the sea upon them; but the Israelites walked through the sea on dry ground.

Miriam is introduced at verse 20. She leads the women in dance repeating the same text attributed to Moses in verse 1 of this canticle. The women's dance and Miriam's song are narrated in Exodus 15:20–21.

The Song of Miriam

[20] Then the prophet Miriam, Aaron's sister, took a tambourine in her hand; and all the women went out after her with tambourines and with dancing.
[21] And Miriam sang to them:
"Sing to the Lord, for he has triumphed gloriously;
horse and rider he has thrown into the sea."

Old Testament scholar Michael D. Coogan points out that Exodus 15:1–18, called "the Song of the Sea" or "The Song of Miriam," is one of the oldest parts of the Bible. As the story is told and retold, it becomes magnified. Its purpose is to praise God for Israel's rescue from Egypt.[103] The role of Miriam and the other Israelite women is significant. In Exodus 15:20–21, Miriam, whose name is mentioned for the first time and who is identified as prophet and Aaron's sister, leads the Israelite women in a victory song and dance. Women often led such celebrations, and indeed often actually composed the victory hymns.[104]

Again, notice that in the Exodus texts quoted above, the Song of Miriam in verse 21 is identical to the text attributed to Moses and the Israelites in verse 1. Coogan suggests a possible explanation: "Later tradition transfers that credit to Moses, both because of the tendency to attribute so many traditions to him and also perhaps as a patriarchal suppression of the significant role that women had in the formation of the literature of ancient Israel. Nevertheless,

---

103 Michael D. Coogan, *The Old Testament: A Historical and Literary Introduction to the Hebrew Scriptures*, 2nd ed. (New York: Oxford University Press, 2011), 93, 100.
104 Coogan, 103. Such hymns are attributed to the women of Israel welcoming Saul and David after their victories (1Sam 18:6–7) and to Deborah (Judges 5:1) who, like Miriam, is called a prophet (Judges 4:4).

the presentation of women in the Exodus narrative suggests that women had status in ancient Israelite society on several important levels."[105]

In any case, it is important to emphasize that Miriam's dance and song are specifically cultic actions since they are described as worship and praise of God. In this way, Miriam occupies a role similar to that of Judith: she is leading the women in praise of God on occasion of God's victory. Dancing is widely attested as part of life in numerous societies in the ancient world. It functioned as a natural expression of joy, but also within religious and cultic life. Like many other instances of ritual dance, Miriam's victory dance was part of a larger cultural environment of song and dance. Indeed, it is best understood as a dramatic re-presentation as well as celebration, of God's victory over the Egyptians at the sea.[106] According to Rita Burns, "Dance was a recurring feature in celebrations of victory among the Hebrews. Moreover, . . . since the victory celebrations were cultic in nature, the dance therein must be regarded as religious ritual. Ritual, properly understood and executed, is never empty. It is symbol. It expresses meaning and keeps it alive."[107] Burns specifically uses the term "re-presentation" since the likely purpose of the dance was "to make effective in the present the creation and sustenance of life which past victories accomplished."[108] Quoting Martin Noth, Burns further explains that re-presentation is founded on this—that God and his actions are always present, while we in our inevitable temporality cannot grasp this present-ness except by re-presenting the action of God over and over again in worship.[109]

The frequency of references to music and dance in the Bible provides evidence of the pervasiveness of these arts in the life of ancient Israel. The most frequently mentioned biblical form of music is, of course, the song. This was used to celebrate major life events and feasts of the liturgical year.[110] Exodus 15 celebrates God as warrior-king, where God finally defeats Pharaoh at the sea. The language shows the influence of the ancient myth of

---

105 Coogan, 103.
106 Rita J. Burns, *Has the Lord Indeed Spoken Only through Moses? A Study of the Biblical Portrait of Miriam*, SBL Dissertation Series 84 (Atlanta: Scholars Press, 1987), 18–19, 25.
107 Burns, 29.
108 Burns, 30.
109 Burns, 30. See also Martin Noth, "The Re-Presentation of the Old Testament in Proclamation," in *Essays on Old Testament Hermeneutics*, ed. Claus Westermann (Richmond, Virginia: John Knox, 1963), 85.
110 Coogan, 457–458.

the storm god's battle against Sea, that chaotic power hostile to God's rule. In this case, however, the sea is no longer the enemy, but the weapon by which the Egyptians are defeated.[111]

It is important to note the prominence of this segment of the Exodus story and the canticle from Exodus 15 in the service of readings in the Easter Vigil. Its inclusion reminds Christians of their own rootedness in the Judaic story of God's deliverance and presence among God's people. The expression of joy, praise, and trust in God's activity, presence, and steadfast love is explicit and wholehearted.

BIBLICAL LANGUAGE: THE NEW TESTAMENT CANTICLES

Thus far we have focused our attention on worship song as it is recorded in the Hebrew Scriptures. This included a look at a sampling from the Book of Psalms and the Canticle of Moses/Miriam recorded in the Book of Exodus. Now we turn our attention to the canticles that are found in the New Testament. The Infancy Narratives in the Gospel of Luke include three major canticles traditionally sung by the Church. They are the Canticle of Mary or Magnificat (Lk 1:46–55), the Canticle of Zechariah or Benedictus (Lk 1:68–79), and the Canticle of Simeon or Nunc Dimittis (Lk 2:29–33).[112] All three have an integral role in the Church's Daily Prayer and, on occasion, its Eucharistic celebrations. In addition to these three, we have the *"Gloria in Excelsis Deo"* (Lk 2:14) sung by the angels to the shepherds on Christmas night. This very brief text has been expanded into different versions of the classic doxology or "Gloria." The text appears in countless hymns and acclamations with almost infinite variations. There are other canticles found throughout the New Testament Letters (Epistles) and the Book of Revelation. The Prologue of the Gospel of John (1:1–18) is also considered a canticle.

Of the three Lucan canticles, Mary's Canticle is by far most often sung within the context of Christian worship, well beyond its daily role in Evening Prayer (Vespers or Evensong). Both hymn text writers and composers over the centuries have been drawn to create new expressions of this biblical text. For this reason, a more detailed analysis of Mary's Canticle will serve here

---

111 *New Oxford Annotated Bible*, notes, 103–104.
112 The Latin titles for these canticles come from the first word or words of each canticle in Latin.

as an example of Luke's use of the canticle in the Infancy Narrative. The Canticles of Zachary and Simeon will receive somewhat briefer treatment.

Biblical scholar Richard J. Dillon comments that both readers and scholars of Luke have sometimes looked at the Infancy Narrative canticles as mere interruptions of the more important narrative element of Luke's writing. However, Dillon argues that the canticles can be compared to arias in opera, citing an explanation of Robert Tannehill regarding the canticles:

> The artistic conventions of opera allow the composer to stop the action at any point so that, through a poetic and musical development exceeding the possibilities of ordinary life, a deeper awareness of what is happening may be achieved. A similar deep participation in the meaning of an event is made possible by the placement of this poem [the Magnificat] in Luke's narrative.[113]

In other words, Luke's insertion of a canticle into the narrative allows for reflection on the theological meaning of the event being narrated. In the first part of the canticle, Mary praises God for the favor bestowed upon her; in the second half, she sings of God's favor extended to all of Israel. In addition, Mary's lyrical outburst serves to declare the future outcome and the eschatological significance of the events being narrated. By using this type of exalted poetic discourse, the narrative yields to prophecy.[114] In other words, God's regard for a humble woman becomes the sign of God's eschatological act for the world.[115]

There are various scholarly theories about the roots of the Canticle of Mary. Some suggest that Luke revised a text whose origin was with a Jewish Christian community. Dillon favors the interpretation that argues that the author of the canticle is attempting to present Mary as the singer of a classical

---

113 Robert C. Tannehill, "The Magnificat as Poem," *Journal of Biblical Literature* 93 (1974), 265. See also Richard J. Dillon, *The Hymns of Saint Luke: Lyricism and Narrative Strategy in Luke 1–2*, The Catholic biblical quarterly Monograph Series 50 (Washington, DC: The Catholic Biblical Association of America, 2013), 2–3. Dillon cites Tannehill extensively in his book. In my own teaching of an undergraduate course in Christian hymnody, I have often referred, somewhat humorously, to Luke's technique of inserting song in the middle of important action as the precursor of the American musical. We are all basically making the same point.
114 Dillon, 3.
115 Dillon, 21.

psalm. This would involve a lyrical outburst well within the traditional lyricism of her people.[116] Echoes of Old Testament poetry run throughout the canticles. For the Magnificat, this includes Psalm 34(35):9 and Hannah's Song on the birth of Samuel in 1 Samuel 2:1–10. Such fragments suggest the author's method of composing the hymn involved a kind of collage or patchwork ("cento") of Old Testament lyric. Hannah's song, probably a later insertion into the narrative of Samuel's birth, is a national song of thanksgiving that appropriately expresses Hannah's sentiments.[117] Luke, or later redactors of Luke, places Hannah's song on Mary's lips, including a description of God as a God of reversals who is especially solicitous to the poor and the downtrodden. To continue the metaphor of opera, the insertion of the Magnificat into the action allows for the significance of what is happening to be savored.[118] In keeping with the theme of thanksgiving that characterizes Evening Prayer (Vespers) Mary's Canticle is prayed daily during this Hour.

The Canticle of Zechariah (Benedictus) resembles Mary's Canticle in many ways. Like the Magnificat, it is divided into two strophes and its primary function is to praise God for fulfilling God's promise of deliverance. The first proclaims the event of salvation at hand and the second declares the salutary effect of this event on Israel.[119] Yet the hymn is Christological since the "main reason for blessing the God of Israel is for what he has done for his people in Jesus the Messiah."[120] Zachary recalls God's promise of salvation and faithfulness to the Chosen People. Then he identifies his son, John—later to be referred to as "the Baptist"—as the messianic prophet who will prepare the way of the Lord. Christ, the one who will guide his people in the way of peace, is described as "the dawn from on high" or "dayspring," depending on the translation. This is a very early instance when light or the sun is used as a metaphor for Jesus Christ. Because dawn is a metaphor for Christ, the Benedictus is traditionally sung at Morning Prayer (Lauds or Morning Praise). Luke will pick up on this motif of light in his description of the birth of Jesus and also in the Canticle of Simeon.

---

116 Dillon, 23.
117 *New Oxford Annotated Bible* (NOAB). See note for 2:1–10.
118 Tannehill, 265.
119 Dillon, 56.
120 R. Brown, *The Birth of the Messiah*, 383.

The Canticle of Simeon (Nunc Dimittis) completes the canticles included in the Lucan Infancy narrative. The aged Simeon expresses his acceptance of death now that he has seen the child who will be "a light for revelation to the Gentiles and for the glory to your people Israel." That last phrase is significant because it proclaims Christ savior not only of the Israelites, but also of the Gentiles. In this way Simeon's Canticle serves as an important development in understanding for whom the Christ has come. In this canticle, understanding salvation is broader or more inclusive. Once again, the image of light is prominent, but this time the "nunc dimittis" (now you dismiss) theme of dismissal or death appropriately fits the themes of Night Prayer (Compline).

Biblical scholar Raymond Brown expresses the development of Luke's thought in these infancy canticles when he says:

> Now the light has shone, and the revelation that comes to Simeon in the Temple court enables him to bless the parents of the child (2:34). The Law, the prophetic Spirit, and the Temple cult have all come together to set the scene for the greatness of Jesus. The one who is called "holy" (1:35) has come to the holy place of Israel, and he begins to embody much of what was associated with the Temple. It was predicted that in the last days the Gentiles would come streaming to the mountain of the house of the Lord to be taught His ways (Isa 2:2–3); (Micah 4:1). Now in that house Jesus is proclaimed as a salvation made ready in the sight of all peoples: "A light to be a revelation to the Gentiles" (Luke 2:31–32). It was the proudest boast of the Temple theologians that the glory of God dwelt in the sanctuary (1Kgs 8:10–11); (Ezek 44:4); and now as Simeon stands before that sanctuary, he proclaims Jesus to be a glory for God's people Israel."[121]

Canticles also appear in the Gospel of John, several of Paul's letters, and the Book of Revelation. The Prologue (Jn 1:1–18) is a canticle that opens

---

121   R. Brown, 453.

John's Gospel, described in the *New Oxford Annotated Bible* as "Using language derived from the depiction of Wisdom (Pr 8:27–30; WS 9:9; Sir 24:9), Jesus is described as God's sole mediator of creation (see Col 1:16–17; Heb 1:2.)"[122] It is here that a reference to Christ as "Word," based on the Greek notion of logos, is first introduced. The exalted nature of this text, rich in imagery and poetic expression, soars in ways that can only be captured in song. This is also the case with texts designated as canticles in the Book of Revelation. These include 4:11; 5:9–10, 12–13; 11:17–18; 12:10–12; 15:3–4; and 19:1–8. The letters or epistles in the second Testament contain numerous verses that are considered canticles. These include, among others, Ephesians 1:3–23; Philippians 2:5–11; and 1 Peter 2:21–24. Biblical scholars believe that they were included in the letters because they were first sung in the worship of the early Christian communities. For example, scholars describe Paul's letter to the Ephesians as particularly poetic since they believe its language is drawn from early Christian hymns and the Hebrew Scriptures. The letter celebrates Paul's vision of the church and begins with a prayer of thanksgiving (Eph 1:3–23), excerpts of which are often set to music.[123] Later in Ephesians (5:14) Paul inserts the beloved "Sleeper, awake!" text that has been set to music throughout the Church's history. Scholars surmise that it is probably a fragment of an ancient baptismal hymn.[124] The Philippians text (2:5–11) is one of the most frequently set to music for Christian worship. Its poetic structure and proclamatory language easily lends itself to musical rendition. And 1 Peter 2:21–24 contains a poetic parallelism reminiscent of the structure of the psalms. Its message reflects the suffering servant song of Isaiah 53:5–12.[125]

Countless musical settings of the canticles and psalms have been composed throughout the Church's history, some to plainchant and others to polyphony, homophony, folk tunes, and contemporary music. Some have more closely followed translations found in the Sacred Scripture while others have been more creative and free renditions. In any case, two points are important here. The first is that the Bible, both the Hebrew Scriptures

---

122   NOAB. See note for 1:1–18.
123   See NOAB, notes, 320.
124   See NOAB, notes, 326.
125   See NOAB, notes, 397.

and the New Testament, is filled with hymns that we have referred to as psalms and canticles. The second is that much of our Christian hymnody has roots in those hymns. That this rich heritage of biblical hymns can be found in Christian worship today flows naturally from the fact that many of the biblical hymns originated within Jewish or early Christian worship. The texts emerged from within worship and eventually became incorporated into the Scriptures. In turn, the Scriptures were subsequently used in later worship as a source for the creation of new sung texts.

To describe Christian hymn texts as scriptural includes a broad spectrum of meanings. It includes the fact that hymns borrow images, phrases, or even large sections of text from the Scriptures. Many hymns also include a rich array of allusions to the persons, events, and stories in the Scriptures even when they are only indirect references. Finally, hymns incorporate the literary techniques of biblical song including parallelism, inverted word order, and root metaphors.

Symbolic Language

Up to this point we have focused on the hymn texts themselves and their potential for expressing theological meaning through language. Now we will spend some time considering the act of singing these hymns and the potential this activity has for mediating theological meaning.

Liturgy or worship—because it is a form of ritual activity—is an ensemble of signs or symbols.[126] Liturgical singing, like other elements of the liturgy, is symbolizing activity. Within this activity, both text and music contribute to the symbolizing power of hymn singing. Symbols, in the words of Michael Polanyi, "carry us away," since it is in surrendering ourselves that we are drawn into the meaning of the symbol.[127] For Polanyi, a subject's active participation in the coming to meaning of the symbol is essential. What we are talking about here is not the experience of an audience, but the experience

---

126 The position of this author is that there is a clear distinction between sign and symbol, even though these words are often used interchangeably when speaking about worship. Paul Tillich makes a useful distinction between sign and symbol in *Dynamics of Faith* (New York: Harper and Row, 1957), 41–43. In this section the focus is on symbol rather than sign. Tillich defines it as that which points to something beyond itself and participates in the reality to which it points.

127 Kubicki, *Liturgical Music*, 99. Here I borrow from the work of Michael Polanyi. See Michael Polanyi and Harry Prosch, *Meaning* (Chicago: University of Chicago Press, 1975), 72.

of an active worshiping assembly engaged in the worship of God through singing. There is perhaps no other physical activity that so engages the body, the mind, the spirit, and the emotions of an individual and an assembly than wholehearted singing. According to Polanyi, while signs function on the level of cognition, symbols function on the level of recognition. In other words, the symbolizing activity of hymn singing enables participants not so much to give assent to intellectual arguments regarding Christian doctrine. Rather, the activity of hymn singing allows an assembly to recognize itself as believers and as members of a faith community. By means of singing, the message of the text is integrated with their own experience of the Christian life within a particular social and cultural milieu. This milieu involves relationships with other persons (subjects).[128] How does this happen?

The insights of Louis-Marie Chauvet can help us understand how this works. Chauvet incorporates Polanyi's semiotic thinking into his own theological writings. This French sacramental theologian reminds us that the etymological roots of the word "symbol" is the Greek word "symballein." The word literally means "to throw together." In ancient Greece, partners in a contract would enter into an agreement by cutting an object in two. Each partner took a part. Although separately the two parts had no meaning, when brought together, they symbolized or confirmed the agreement between the two partners. In other words, the ancient practice of "symbolon" functioned as an expression of a social contract based on mutual recognition in the rejoining of the two pieces. In this way the symbol mediated the identity of the partners in the agreement.[129]

There are contemporary expressions of this ancient practice. Jewelers sell pairs of necklaces that include two chains, each chain holding a piece of silver which, when put together forms a perfect circle. The jagged edges that mark the break of the circle can only be completed by the other piece of silver. So the two pieces function as a symbol, that is, an ancient "symballein." My sister and her husband own such necklaces. They wear them as a symbol of their marriage vows or covenant of love. In other words, they recognize themselves, in those silver pieces, as in a married relationship and as married to each other.

---

128 Kubicki, *Liturgical Music*, 99–100.
129 Louis-Marie Chauvet, *Symbol and Sacrament: A Sacramental Reinterpretation of Christian Existence*, trans. Patrick Madigan and Madeleine Beaumont (Collegeville, MN: Liturgical Press, 1995), 112.

Chauvet explains that our contemporary understanding of "the semantic field of the word 'symbol' has been extended to every element (object, word, gesture, person . . .) that, exchanged within a group, somewhat like a password, permits the group as a whole or individuals therein to recognize one another and identify themselves."[130] The key here is to view symbol as negotiator of identity and relationships. Based on Chauvet's interpretive framework, we can say that hymns, particularly in their actual performance, are symbolic.

Chauvet highlights the radical nature of symbol as an integral part of human existence when he says:

> Reality is never present to us except in a mediated way, which is to say, constructed out of the symbolic network of the culture which fashions us. This symbolic order designates the system of connections between the different elements and levels of a culture (economic, social, political, ideological—ethics, philosophy, religion . . .), a system forming a coherent whole that allows the social group and individuals to orient themselves in space, find their place in time, and in general situate themselves in the world in a significant way—in short, to find their identity in a world that makes "sense," even if, as C. Levi-Strauss says, there always remains an inexpungible residue of signifiers to which we can never give adequate meanings.[131]

Chauvet's claim that all reality is mediated can be applied to our analysis of hymn singing. In other words, it is possible to say that a hymn can serve as a mediator of reality. Language as symbol mediates reality by negotiating connections. These connections, within the context of Christian worship, allow members of the assembly—as a social group and as individual believers—to make sense of their world and to find their identity by discovering relationships. In this case, their world would be their Christian faith and its relationship to the larger world and even to the cosmos. The

130 Chauvet, 112.
131 Chauvet, 84–85.

symbolizing activity of singing hymns involves active participation of subjects in mediating connections and in discovering their identity and place in their particular social world.[132] The singing of hymns is one of those worship symbols that enables this to happen.

A pertinent example will help illustrate the point. Imagine a situation where a group of Christians, none of whom knows each other (hard to imagine, and fictional), gathers for worship in a magnificent cathedral on Easter Sunday morning. The opening hymn is "Jesus Christ Is Risen Today." Everyone rises, opens their hymnals and begins singing along with full organ accompaniment, choir, and brass. This traditional hymn is well beloved and has been sung in many Christian churches for centuries. The text of stanza one is taken from a fourteenth-century Latin hymn called "Surrexit Christus hodie." Stanzas two and three are adaptations from the 1708 *Lyra Davidica and The Compleat Psalmodist*, c. 1750. Charles Wesley, an eighteenth-century hymn text writer, penned the fourth stanza. For many Christian, the tune is *the* sound of Easter morning.

"Jesus Christ Is Risen Today"[133] is usually sung to the tune EASTER HYMN, meter 77 77 with alleluias. More than 400 hymnals include this hymn. In recent times, some hymnal revisions have altered the last two lines in various ways with the practice of changing Holy Ghost to Holy Spirit.

> Jesus Christ is ris'n today, Alleluia!
> Our triumphant holy day, Alleluia!
> Who did once upon the cross, Alleluia!
> Suffer to redeem our loss. Alleluia!
>
> Hymns of praise then let us sing, Alleluia!
> Unto Christ, our heav'nly King, Alleluia!
> Who endured the cross and grave, Alleluia!
> Sinners to redeem and save. Alleluia!
>
> But the pains which he endured, Alleluia!
> Our salvation have procured; Alleluia!

---

132 See Kubicki, *Liturgical Music*, 101.
133 "Jesus Christ Is Risen Today," *Worship* (2011), #516.

Now above the sky he's King, Alleluia!
Where the angels ever sing. Alleluia!

Sing we to our God above, Alleluia!
Praise eternal, as his love; Alleluia!
Praise him, now his might confess, Alleluia!
Father, Son, and Spirit blest. Alleluia!

The first stanza proclaims Christ's death on the cross for our redemption and his rising from the dead. This creedal statement, which forms the core of the Christian faith, is the shared belief of all those worshipers who fill the cathedral. The hymn serves both to identify each individual as a person who believes these words and to make connections among the assembly—everyone is a fellow believer. This group believes what the hymn proclaims and celebrates. The hymn also connects each individual and the assembly with God who is being acclaimed for the wonderful work of redemption. We feel connected in this setting because we share a common belief. We likewise feel connected because together we are confessing in song this fundamental belief of Christians, using the energy and breath of our bodies to make a joyful and robust sound! Finally, there is a connection in memory with all of our experiences of past Easters. It is likely that "Jesus Christ Is Risen Today" was sung on many former Easter Sundays. That history of performance is part of its power and its appeal. By connecting each individual in that cathedral with their past experiences of Easter Sunday worship, the hymn builds on a Christian identity that is growing and developing over time.

Furthermore, not only is the assembly making connections with those gathered in that space on Easter morning. Connections are also being made with all those who have sung this traditional text in the past and in the present in other places, albeit perhaps in different languages and different edited versions. The text connects us by naming our common faith. And because most people in that cathedral that Easter morning have probably sung that text numerous times in the past, it also serves to further negotiate the identity of each person who, over the years, has performed this hymn as an act of faith in the Easter mysteries. The meaning of the text is found in the history of its performance both synchronically and diachronically. In other words, connections are made over time and over space.

But recall that the text is joined to a familiar and beloved tune that many may consider the "sound" of Easter. The tune, appropriately called EASTER HYMN, is integrally related to the text in this instance. Together, text and tune enable the assembly to praise and thank Jesus Christ for his steadfast love and mercy in suffering, dying, and rising for the redemption of all humankind. In many ways, this hymn mirrors the structure of praise of the psalms of praise in the Hebrew Scriptures. Like the psalms, this hymn gives joyful praise for God's marvelous deeds, acclaiming God's faithfulness to God's promises.

One of the theological implications of such repetitive symbolizing activity is that, over time, this negotiating of identity and relationships enables transformation. Don Saliers observes that congregational hymn singing assists, not only in articulating but also in forming the deep emotions characteristic of the Christian life. For, it is in the process of repeatedly articulating these "right attitudes" that transformation can take place. In other words, singing texts that articulate the Christian attitudes of joy, praise, thanksgiving, forgiveness, contrition, etc., has the potential to form the singers in those Christian attitudes. All the symbols of the liturgy, language and music included, have the potential to shape us in those "right attitudes" that are peculiar to the heart of Christian worship.[134] That topic of transformation will be more fully developed in chapter five.

---

134 Don Saliers, "The Integrity of Sung Prayer," *Worship* 55 (July 1981), 293–295. Saliers develops his ideas by using Susanne K. Langer's description of ritual in *Philosophy in a New Key: A Study in the Symbolism of Reason, Rite and Art*, 3rd edition (Cambridge, MA: Harvard University Press, 1967). See also Kubicki, *Liturgical Music*, 124–125.

CHAPTER 3

LANGUAGE AND TEXTUAL ANALYSIS:
FINDING THE THEOLOGICAL PULSE OF A HYMN TEXT

INTRODUCTION

O
ver the last several years, much ink has been spilled regarding the translations of liturgical texts, the rules to be observed, and the subsequent necessity of revising musical settings of the Ordinary of the Mass. This is particularly true for the English-speaking world that worships in the Roman tradition. Translations of these texts certainly have an impact—sometimes significant and sometimes less so—pastorally, liturgically, and musically on these worship communities. Yet, there are many other texts that are publically prayed/sung that allow for significant flexibility and local application. Hymn texts, specifically those that are not settings of the Ordinary or Proper of the Mass, fall into this category. Other texts include the Prayers of the Faithful, recited or sung. All of these texts—whether intercessory, confessional, penitential, or doxological—have continued to evolve in ways that both express and shape contemporary Christian understandings of God, the people of God, our daily life, and our place in the cosmos. When we sing these texts within a ritual setting—that is, within the symbolizing activity of the liturgy—their power to communicate those Christian understandings is enhanced in important ways by interaction with other symbols and images.

Metaphorical Language

While hymn singing by its very nature is symbolic activity, hymn texts employ metaphorical language. Indeed, it is the nature of language, and most especially religious language, to be metaphorical. Language is metaphorical when two unlike entities are compared or brought together because of some perceived similarity. But metaphor is not simply a condensed comparison.[135] Philip Wheelwright provides an insightful description when he says that a metaphor is "a medium of fuller, riper knowing; not merely a prettification of the already given."[136] A similar way of thinking is expressed by contemporary hymn text writer, Brian Wren, when he explains:

> A strong metaphor does indeed save many lines of prose, but the reasons for choosing metaphor rather than prose have as much to do with impact as economy. Impact on the imagination is especially important in religious language, since "belief in God depends to a small extent on rational argument, and to a larger extent on our ability to frame images to capture, commemorate, and convey our experience of transcendence."[137]

In other words, Wren suggests, metaphor is well suited to speaking about mystery and transcendence, that is, God and the things of God. Metaphor does this by juxtaposing similar and dissimilar elements in order to create a tension that is both useful and necessary to creating an impact that serves to expand the imagination.

This is not what we learned in elementary or middle school. In English class our teachers explained that a simile was a comparison using "like" or "as" and that a metaphor was a comparison without using either of those two words. But before we criticize elementary school teachers, we need to recall that this understanding of metaphor goes back to the philosopher, Aristotle. Nevertheless, a distinction needs to be made. Aristotle's definition

---

135 Brian Wren, *What Language Shall I Borrow? God-Talk in Worship: A Male Response to Feminist Theology* (New York: Crossroad, 1989), 87.

136 Philip Wheelwright, *The Burning Fountain: A Study in the Language of Symbolism* (Bloomington: Indiana University Press, 1954), 97.

137 Wren, *What Language Shall I Borrow?*, 87. See also George Bradford Caird, *The Language and Imagery of the Bible* (London: Westminster Press, 1980), 176.

of metaphor was based on syntactical rather than semantic considerations. That is, Aristotle's concern was the grammatical role of a word and its relationship to the rest of a sentence. Semantic considerations focus on meaning and how that meaning is conveyed. Aristotle did regard metaphor as an abbreviated simile. While this explanation may have been sufficient for grammar school English classes, Gail Ramshaw observes, it is much too narrow and superficial for understanding the power of metaphor in ritual language.[138] Instead, Ramshaw offers these insights:

> Metaphor, far from being merely a decorative figure of speech, is the fundamental unit of creative thought. In metaphor the mind expands in a fresh way, imagining the new and renovating the old. Metaphor does not label: it connects in a revolutionary way. Metaphor is not merely an image, a look-alike, the reflection in the mirror. Rather, metaphor forms a comparison where none previously existed. Metaphor alters perception by superimposing disparate images. A metaphor has been called "an affair between a predicate with a past and an object that yields while protesting." The two images are logically incompatible.[139]

In this way, metaphor has an integral role in liturgical language since, as religious language, it is concerned with expressing or exploring our relationship with mystery. The ambiguity of metaphor is not a comfortable place for many of us to dwell since the twenty-first century world of scientific and digital discourse is ever striving toward greater literal precision.[140] Nevertheless, the elements of mystery (e.g., God, forgiveness, love, death, the hereafter, etc.) that liturgical language addresses require an expansiveness and confounding of meaning that is beyond the scope of the literal and the precise.

The bottom line is that metaphor plays an integral role in the liturgy. However, using the same metaphors repeatedly and exclusively can create

---

138 Gail Ramshaw, *Reviving Sacred Speech: The Meaning of Liturgical Language* (Akron, OH: OSL Publications, 2000), 8.
139 Gail Ramshaw, *Reviving Sacred Speech*, 8. See also Nelson Goodman, *Languages of Art* (Indianapolis: Bobbs-Merrill, 1968), 69.
140 Ramshaw, *Reviving Sacred Speech*, 12.

problems. When this is done, we tend to forget that they are metaphors and begin to take them literally. The resulting tendency to literalism can also lead to fundamentalism. This has often happened with religious language, particularly with our metaphors for God. Recall that a metaphor is by its nature ambiguous. Because of this, it is a particularly apt tool for speaking about mystery. But this is the very reason many contemporary Christians, not at all comfortable with ambiguity, tend toward literalism and fundamentalism. Many neither appreciate nor respect metaphor because it does not deliver the clarity they desire. John Shea has referred to this approach to religious metaphor as flat-minded literalism.[141] However, when it comes to Divine Mystery, clarity is an elusive goal, to say the least.

Another way to explain the problem is to say that when metaphors are overused so that we begin to take them literally, they lose their power or become "dead" metaphors. As Sallie McFague points out, ordinary language is full of "dead" metaphors. Obvious examples include "the arm of the chair" or "the mouth of the river." Metaphor is seeing one thing as something else. When a metaphor no long provides the possibility of spotting a thread of similarity between two dissimilar objects because the thread becomes invisible, you have a dead metaphor. Regretfully, the dead or overused metaphor continues to be used frequently, despite the fact it has reached the end of its power.[142]

In an article entitled "Liturgy as Metaphor," Mark Searle speaks about the semantic necessity of metaphor. In other words, he argues that we need metaphor to express meaning. For that reason, Searle believes that metaphor is too important to be left to the grammarians. Instead, metaphor should instead become the preoccupation of philosophers. Searle credits the philosopher Philip Wheelwright with assisting the rehabilitation of metaphor through his important distinction between "steno-language" and "tensive language."[143] His distinction can be helpful in our exploration of the meaning of metaphor and a theology of Christian hymns.

---

141   John Shea, "The Second Naiveté: Approach to a Pastoral Problem" in *Concilium* 81 (1973), 110.
142   Sallie McFague, *Metaphorical Theology: Models of God in Religious Language* (Philadelphia: Fortress Press, 1982), 15.
143   Philip Wheelwright, *Metaphor and Reality* (Bloomington: Indiana University Press, 1962), 33ff; as quoted in Mark Searle, "Liturgy as Metaphor" in *Worship* 55 (March 1981), 104–105.

According to Wheelwright, these two terms are not so much clear categories as they are a direction in which language may move. He explains "steno-language" as those words and symbols that have a more or less clearly defined reference that is shared by all who speak the same language. Words such as "house" or "tree" are examples because they are capable of definition and would point to their reference with the minimum amount of ambiguity.[144]

"Tensive language," however, is "open, undefined, ambivalent and consequently rich in associations. It refers not so much to a single and definite item of reality as to a pattern of related kinds of experience."[145] In this way, "tensive language" brings together realms of experience rather than distinguishing or separating them. In doing so, "tensive language" gives expression to the ambiguities and continuities of human experience. This is the opposite of the flat-minded literalism mentioned above.[146] Tensive language is language that is alive, according to Wheelwright. This is true whether the language is music, art, gestures, or words.[147] Wheelwright uses the Our Father as an example of a text that is tensive:

> It may become commonplace and perfunctory through careless usage, which would mean that its original linguistic vitality had been lost so its survival is merely a result of social habit; but when the gesture or the phrase reflects the religious aura that first surrounded it and gave it significance for an authentic worshiper, it has the power to elicit awe.[148]

In human experience, there is likely a tension between the wonder and humility that constitutes awe. When these are experienced in the liturgy, where ritual and rubrics come into play, the actual tension or "tensiveness" that is present will vary according to the sensitivity and disposition of each member of the assembly.[149]

---

144 Wheelwright, *Metaphor and Reality*, 33; as referenced in Searle, "Liturgy as Metaphor," 105. 142 Mark Searle, "Liturgy as Metaphor," *Worship* 55:2 (1981): 105.
145 Mark Searle, "Liturgy as Metaphor," *Worship* 55:2 (1981): 105.
146 Searle, "Liturgy as Metaphor," 105.
147 Wheelwright, 45–46.
148 Wheelwright, 47.
149 Wheelwright, 47.

Sallie McFague borrows from Colin Turbayne's three stages of metaphor[150] to highlight a similar point:

> Initially, when newly coined, it [metaphor] seems inap-
> propriate or unconventional; the response is often rejection.
> At a second stage, when it is a living metaphor, it has dual
> meaning—the literal and metaphorical—and is insightful.
> Finally, the metaphor becomes commonplace, either dead
> and/or literal-ized. At this stage, says Turbayne, we are no
> longer like the Wizard of Oz who knew green glasses made
> Oz green, but, like all the other inhabitants of Oz, we believe
> that Oz *is* green.[151]

We cannot take the power of metaphor for granted. Often we may ignore the fact that what was once a powerful way to express an insight has become commonplace, literal, and therefore dead. That is one of the reasons why poets and creators of hymn texts constantly need to search for new ways to open the assembly's imagination to Divine Mystery.

If, then, metaphorical language is foundational to religious discourse and to ritual activity, good hymn texts will be replete with metaphors. Indeed, the fundamental elements of metaphorical speech acts and sacramental embodiment intersect in the act of singing a hymn at liturgy.[152] These elements intersect in the bodies of the persons singing. This is the case since the assembly is performing a speech act in the act of singing. God's grace, active and present in this ritual action, is also embodied in the singers. In other words, both elements—performativity and sacramentality—come together in the assembly in their physicality or bodiliness. Furthermore, it is the language of this activity, both the language of the body and the language of the hymn texts, that opens up participants to multiple dimensions of faith and religious experience, inviting a response to an encounter with mystery. Such language, by its very nature, tends to be ambiguous and/or imprecise.

---

150 Colin M. Turbayne, *The Myth of Metaphor* (New Haven, CT: Yale University Press, 1962), 24–25.
151 Turbayne, *The Myth of Metaphor*, 24–25; as referenced in McFague, *Metaphorical Theology*, 41.
152 The concept of performativity and speech acts will be covered in chapter five. For now, a simple definition of a speech act is the occasion when the saying of something accomplishes the doing of something.

Exploring hymns that have strong metaphorical language will help to demonstrate, in a concrete way, how metaphor might operate in a hymn text to express theological meaning. We will do so by focusing on hymns with common theological themes. This section will explore four things: 1) different approaches to Christian eschatology in hymn texts; 2) Christian understandings of redemption through Jesus Christ in a variety of hymn genres; 3) shifts in metaphorical language in hymn texts created since the Second Vatican Council; and 4) theological implications of some of these shifts.

CHRISTIAN ESCHATOLOGY

Eschatology is often defined as the study of the last things: death, judgment, heaven, hell, and the second coming of Christ. Its focus is on the end times as the final fulfillment of the salvation won by Christ through his death and resurrection. The more biblical understanding sees eschatology as founded on the Christ-event: the announcement of the coming reign of God, the ministry, death, and resurrection of Jesus, and the outpouring of the Holy Spirit.[153] The topic of eschatology is filled with mystery and questions. It is therefore by means of metaphorical language that we are able to approach this topic and sing of it in worship.

A hymn penned in the mid-nineteenth century that describes the second coming of Christ is Henry Alford's text "Come, You Thankful People, Come."[154] The overarching metaphor is "harvest." Because of this, the hymn is often scheduled during autumn and the closing Sundays of the liturgical year. Today only four stanzas survive of the original seven. The hymn text is almost always yoked to the tune, ST. GEORGE'S WINDSOR, whose meter is 7777 D. Those four are provided below:

> Come, you thankful people, come;
> Raise the song of harvest home.
> All is safely gathered in
> Ere the winter storms begin.

---

153 Dermot A. Lane, "Eschatology" in *The New Dictionary of Theology*, ed. Joseph A. Komonchak, Mary Collins, and Dermot A. Lane (Collegeville, MN: The Liturgical Press, 1991).
154 "Come, You Thankful People, Come," *Worship* (2011), #858. See also Judith Kubicki, "Hymn Text Master Class," *GIA Quarterly* 25:3 (2014), 18–19.

God, our Maker, does provide
For our wants to be supplied.
Come to God's own temple, come.
Raise the song of harvest home.

All the world is God's own field,
Fruit unto his praise to yield;
Wheat and tares together sown,
Unto joy or sorrow grown.
First the blade, and then the ear,
Then the full corn shall appear.
Lord of harvest, grant that we
Wholesome grain and pure may be.

For the Lord our God shall come
And shall take his harvest home;
From his field shall in that day
All offenses purge away,
Giving angels charge at last
In the fire the tares to cast,
But the fruitful ears to store
In God's garner evermore.

Even so, Lord, quickly come
To your final harvest home.
Gather all your people in,
Free from sorrow, free from sin,
There, forever purified,
In your presence to abide.
Come with all your angels, come!
Raise the glorious harvest home.

Stanza one describes the harvest as complete. The produce is safely gathered in before the coming winter storms. The text acknowledges God as creator and as generous provider. Our response is to sing grateful songs of praise. But the hymn does not simply describe the harvest of fruits, vegetables and grain. Rather, it explores multiple meanings of the harvest metaphor. The first line of stanza two introduces the idea that that the world or creation is God's field. (The original text reads, "We ourselves are God's own field.") We are God's fruit or harvest, both wheat and tares as the parables in Matthew 13 explain. We pray that we, like the healthy ear of corn, will be pure and wholesome grain worthy of God's harvesting.

Interpreting the world as God's field enables the eschatological move in stanza three. That is, the focus shifts to the end times or *eschaton* when the final harvest (the gathering of humankind into the arms of God) will occur. The first line of the stanza describes the Second Coming as the harvesting of the good (fruitful ears of corn) to heaven. All offenses shall be purged away and the unworthy (tares) will be cast into the fire with the assistance of God's angels. God's storehouse or garner or home is, of course, heaven.

The final stanza expresses a keen longing that the Lord's Second Coming come quickly. With references to Revelations 22:20, the harvesting of all God's people is described as the joyful culmination of our lifelong growing into Christ. When we will be harvested for heaven, we will be free of sorrow and sin, purified and ready to abide in God's presence forever.

The metaphor of harvest works to situate the singing assembly (at least in the northern hemisphere) in the *Sitz im Leben* of their daily experience—it is a time of harvesting and enjoying the rich bounty of the earth. Perhaps in the nineteenth century a society that was more agricultural in its make-up and experience would have resonated more fully with the harvest metaphor. However, today's growing interest in farmers' markets and small organic gardens may once again support a personal appreciation for the power of this metaphor.

In this hymn, the metaphor of harvest becomes a lens for interpreting the Lectionary readings for the final weeks of the liturgical year. These readings speak of the last things and the end of the world, that is, the eschatological reality toward which we are all straining with a mix of eagerness and dread. The hymn also serves as an introduction to the season of Advent that will further develop these eschatological themes.

Timothy Dudley-Smith wrote the text for "When the Lord in Glory Comes"[155] more than one hundred years after Henry Alford wrote his. The hymn's theological focus is clearly eschatological, but very different from the harvest metaphors used in "Come, You Thankful People, Come." Dudley-Smith's text explores the mystery of God by engaging an ancient approach called *apophatic* theology. Apophatic theology, or apophasis, is also known as negative theology. Simply stated, "apophatic" (not to be confused with "apathetic") means that the text explores the nature of God by negation. In other words, the poet speaks to the imagination by stating first of all, what God is not or where God is not to be found. It begins with the assumption that God is ultimately unknowable on this side of the grave and that therefore human language is always inadequate to the task of describing God. "When the Lord in Glory Comes" has been published with Bob Moore's tune, ST. JOHN'S, having the meter 77 77 77 D.[156]

> When the Lord in glory comes
> Not the trumpets, not the drums,
> Not the anthem, not the psalm,
> Not the thunder, not the calm,
> Not the shout the heavens raise,
> Not the chorus, not the praise,
> Not the silences sublime,
> Not the sounds of space and time,
> But his voice when he appears
> Shall be music to my ears;
> But his voice when he appears
> Shall be music to my ears.
>
> When the Lord is seen again
> Not the glories of his reign,
> Not the lightnings through the storm,
> Not the radiance of his form,

---

155 "When the Lord in Glory Comes," *Worship* (2011), #863.
156 See also Judith Kubicki, "Hymn Text Master Class," *GIA Quarterly*, 26:3 (2015), 20–21.

Not his pomp and pow'r alone,
Not the splendors of his throne,
Not his robe and diadems,
Not the gold and not the gems,
But his face upon my sight
Shall be darkness into light;
But his face upon my sight
Shall be darkness into light.

When the Lord to human eyes
Shall bestride our narrow skies,
Not the child of humble birth,
Not the carpenter of earth,
Not the man by all denied,
Not the victim crucified,
But the God who died to save,
But the victor of the grave,
He it is to whom I fall,
Jesus Christ, my All in all;
He it is to whom I fall,
Jesus Christ, my All in all.

Notice how each of the three stanzas spins out a series of negative descriptions. Stanza one highlights the sense of sound. Several negative statements follow. Some mention musical sounds, e.g., trumpets, drums, anthems, or psalms. Others relate to nature: thunder or calm. Still others are heavenly sounds: shouts, choruses of praise, sublime silence. The stanza pivots on the word "time." This is followed by "but" and then the key insight of stanza one: the Lord's voice when he appears shall be music to my ears, repeated twice. We are left to imagine how that music might sound. The primary metaphor is music.

The second stanza focuses on the sense of sight. Once again, the text unfolds with negative statements regarding the Lord's appearance. The descriptions capture images of light such as glories, lightning, radiance, splendor, diadems, and gold. This stanza pivots on the word "gems" before introducing "but." This time the key insight, repeated twice, is that the Lord's "face upon my sight, shall be darkness into light." Here the primary metaphor can be described as dawn—darkness into light.

Stanza three describes the Lord's appearance to human eyes at the second coming. This time he will not come as a child (at Bethlehem), nor as a carpenter (at Nazareth), nor as the victim denied by his followers and crucified for our offenses (at Jerusalem). The negatives of this stanza are briefer and the "but" arrives sooner. Instead, this Lord is described as God, Savior, victor of the grave. The stanza pivots on the word "grave." The key insight, repeated twice, is that "He it is to whom I fall, Jesus Christ, my All in all." Adoration is our response to the Second Coming. The compelling experience will be the voice and the human face of God. These, not the cataclysm of the earth or the heavens, will enrapture us.

Theology of Redemption in Christian Hymnody

Redemption through the life, death, and resurrection of Jesus Christ is at the heart of Christian faith. Not surprisingly, expressions of that faith in Christian hymnody are richly varied in their use of images and metaphors, even though the image of the cross is central to many. So, for example, the text of Isaac Watts' classic hymn "When I Survey the Wondrous Cross"[157] contains royal imagery. The tune most often yoked with Watt's text is HAMBURG (CM), composed in 1824 by Lowell Mason. The second most often used tune is ROCKINGHAM (CM), composed by Edward Miller a little earlier than Mason's tune. The first and third stanzas of the hymn employ royal imagery directly:

> When I survey the wondrous cross
> On which the Prince of glory died,
> My richest gain I count but loss,
> And pour contempt on all my pride.
>
> Forbid it, Lord, that I should boast,
> Save in the death of Christ my God;

---

157 "When I Survey the Wondrous Cross," *Worship* (2011), #494.

All the vain things that charm me most—
I sacrifice them to his blood.

See, from his head, his hands, his feet,
Sorrow and love flow mingled down!
Did e'er such love and sorrow meet,
Or thorns compose so rich a crown?

Were the whole realm of nature mine,
That were a present far too small:
Love so amazing, so divine,
Demands my soul, my life, my all.

The second line of the first stanza speaks of Christ as "Prince of glory" and the fourth line of the third stanza speaks, paradoxically, of the crown of thorns as "rich." Both images are part of the long tradition of referring to God, and God's Son Jesus, in royal terms.[158] Using the metaphorical language of royalty to describe Christ on the cross as victim of capital punishment creates the shock of juxtaposing these two unlike ideas. We begin to think in a new way about the meaning of "king" or "royalty." This juxtaposing of opposites is set up in lines three and four of stanza one. The word pairs—gain/loss and contempt/pride—reinforce the paradoxical nature of juxtaposing cross and prince. Furthermore, the use of royal imagery signifies the unique perspective that faith provides for interpreting this specific historical event of capital punishment. Metaphor enables Watts to express the mystery, emotional turmoil, and ambiguity of Christ's crucifixion.

The use of royal metaphors for Christ is even more pervasive in another one of Watts' well-known hymns, "Jesus Shall Reign." We looked at it in chapter two as an example of a Christological interpretation of one of the royal psalms of the Hebrew Scriptures, Psalm 72.[159] The psalm is a prayer of blessing for the king of Israel. Watts takes a text that was originally a Jewish prayer for guidance and support for Israel's king (Psalm 72) and creates a hymn celebrating the kingship of Jesus Christ. What originates as a prayer

---

158 See chapter two for a discussion of the root metaphor of God's reign found in the Psalms.
159 See chapter two for the hymn text and a comparison between Psalm 72 and "Jesus Shall Reign."

of blessing that the king enjoy a long life and extensive kingdom becomes an assertion of the eternal and all-inclusive reign of Christ the King. Homage to Israel's king by kings from distant lands is a reflection on the king's prestige and power.[160]

Watts' hymn has become a staple in Christian worship, as has the metaphor of Christ as king. Of course, we have used this metaphor for Christ so often that we often unaware that we are using metaphorical language. Recall that a metaphor has the power to transform meaning. Jesus exercises his kingship, not as a despot wielding power over others (benevolently or otherwise), but as a servant of the poor and needy. The metaphor of king is transformed by its usage to describe Divine Love incarnate in Jesus Christ.

The metaphor of "king" is not the only one used to depict Christ in Christian hymnody. In Martin Luther's classic hymn, "A Mighty Fortress," the metaphor for Christ is warrior rather than king. Luther employs vivid imagery to depict our redemption won through Jesus Christ. His hymn text describes the ultimate struggle between good and evil as a battle between Christ and the devil for the souls of humankind. According to the hymn text, God sends his Son to fight for us because we are too weak to fight the devil on our own. One of the English translations published in *Evangelical Lutheran Worship* (2006) reads as follows[161]:

> A mighty fortress is our God,
> a sword and shield victorious;
> he breaks the cruel oppressor's rod
> and wins salvation glorious.
> The old satanic foe
> has sworn to work us woe!
> with craft and dreadful might
> he arms himself to fight.
> On earth he has no equal.

---

160 See note in *The New Oxford Annotated Bible* for Psalm 72:10–11.
161 "A Mighty Fortress," *Evangelical Lutheran Worship*, Evangelical Lutheran Church in America (Minneapolis: Augsburg Fortress Press, 2006), #504.

No strength of ours can match his might!
We would be lost, rejected.
But now a champion comes to fight,
whom God himself elected.
You ask who this may be?
The Lord of hosts is he!
Christ Jesus, mighty Lord,
God's only Son, adored.
He holds the field victorious.

Though hordes of devils fill the land
all threat'ning to devour us,
we tremble not, unmoved we stand;
they cannot overpow'r us.
Let this world's tyrant rage,
in battle we'll engage!
His might is doomed to fail;
God's judgment must prevail!
One little word subdues him.

God's Word forever shall abide,
no thanks to foes, who fear it;
for God himself fights by our side
with weapons of the Spirit.
Were they to take our house,
goods, honor, child, or spouse,
though life be wrenched away,
they cannot win the day.
The Kingdom's ours forever!

Notice both the military images and strong verbs associated with battle: fortress, sword, shield, rod, foe, champion, breaks, wins, fight, devour, overpower, doomed, subdues, and fights, among others. The struggle is of epic proportions. The prize for victory is huge: "the Kingdom of God is ours forever!" Even though the last stanza clearly states that God fights "with weapons of the Spirit," it is easy to forget that we are singing metaphorically. Jesus is not a "knight in shining armor" winning our battles against the devil for us, at least, not in the literal sense.

Satan is described in traditional fashion as foe who is both crafty and dreadful. The first stanza concludes by declaring him without equal on earth. This claim prepares for the amazing announcement in stanza two that God has chosen God's only Son to fight for us, to champion our cause. This gives us courage, despite the fact that humankind is surrounded by countless devils just waiting to destroy us. The third stanza ends with the line "one little word subdues him." The claim echoes other passages in Scripture. For example, in the first chapter of Genesis, each day of creation begins with the phrase: "And God said . . ." So powerful is God's word that a simple word brings about the creation of the world. God's word is true and powerful. In addition, there are numerous instances in the New Testament where Jesus speaks words of healing that are followed by miraculous cures. Immediately after this line, the fourth stanza begins with the claim that "God's Word forever shall abide . . ." In this case, the word "Word" is capitalized. This usage echoes the Prologue of the Gospel of John that begins: "In the beginning was the Word . . ." The reference is to Jesus Christ, the Word of God, who, John writes, is God and was present at creation.

Luther concludes the stanza by making a strong allusion to another Scripture story found in the Book of Job. This story highlights the power of Satan, but also the integrity of Job. The battle between good and evil is played out in the story of Job's sufferings. In the end, Job receives God's blessings again and ultimately the gift of God's Kingdom. Many Protestants swept up in the upheaval of the Reformation, interpreted the epic battle between Satan and Jesus Christ as expressive of the battle between the Roman Church and reformers. For that reason, this hymn has often been considered the battle hymn of the Reformation.

Martin Luther resonated with the *Christus Victor* or *Christus vincit* theme and often incorporated it into his hymn texts and other writings. Scripture and early and medieval church hymnody often expressed this theme. Luther, as a scripture scholar and monk would have been familiar with these texts.

Easter hymns, and in particular the Easter sequence "Victimae Paschali,"[162] celebrate this theme in a heightened way. Luther's borrowings from the Easter Sequence are clearly evident in his Easter hymn, "Christ Jesus Lay in Death's Strong Bands." The first two stanzas of "Victimae Paschali" illustrates the strong, traditional metaphors that Luther incorporates into his own work:

> Christians, to the Paschal Victim
> Offer your thankful praises!
> A Lamb the sheep redeems:
> Christ, who only is sinless,
> Reconciles sinners to the Father.
>
> Death and life have contended
> In that combat stupendous:
> The Prince of life, who died,
> reigns immortal.

Speaking of Christ as the Paschal Victim is so commonplace that most Christians accept this startling metaphor as literal language. Yet, comparing Christ to the lambs slain on the eve of the Hebrews' escape from Egypt still speaks to us today. Often, however, the allusion to the Exodus is barely acknowledged. The last two lines of stanza two highlight the paradoxical nature of what has happened. Language seems to fail attempts to be precise and clear. Luther embraces this language in his Easter hymn, "Christ Jesus Lay in Death's Strong Bands."[163] The tune, CHRIST LAG IN TODESBANDEN, is an adaptation of the chant, VICTIMAE PASCHALI, the same chant from which Luther's text is partially derived. The translation cited here originally included seven stanzas. Stanzas four and five are provided below:

> It was a strange and dreadful strife
> When life and death contended;
> The victory remained with life,
> The reign of death was ended.

---

162 "Christians, to the Paschal Victim," *Lectionary for Mass*, vol. 1, National Conference of Catholic Bishops (Collegeville, MN: Liturgical Press, 1998), 347.

163 "Christ Jesus Lay in Death's Strong Bands," translated by Richard Massie, *Christian Worship* supplement (Milwaukee, WI: Northwestern Publishing House, 2008), #720.

> Holy Scripture plainly says
> That death is swallowed up by death,
> Its sting is lost forever. Alleluia!
>
> Here the true Paschal Lamb we see,
> Whom God so freely gave us;
> He died on the accursed tree—
> So strong his love—to save us.
> See, his blood now marks our door;
> Faith points to it; death passes o'er,
> And Satan cannot harm us. Alleluia!

The last two lines of stanza two express in paradox the wonder of the *Christus Victor* theme in a manner similar to "Victimae Paschali." The third stanza employs the paschal lamb metaphor and takes it a further step by making a more fully developed comparison: "See, his blood now marks our door: ... Death passes o'er." The allusion to the Exodus is clear; the mystery of Christ's love unfolds in metaphor and allusion.

The presence of this Exodus theme is evident in hymn texts sung several centuries later and across the Atlantic in the United States of America. Gospel songs and spirituals, particularly Black spirituals, have also focused very directly on the mystery of redemption and the person of Jesus Christ. George Bennard's early twentieth-century gospel song, "The Old Rugged Cross,"[164] offers an interesting contrast to Watts' approach discussed earlier. The text reveals images and metaphors that see the cross from another perspective. Bennard also wrote the tune OLD RUGGED CROSS. The meter is 12 8 12 8 with refrain.

> On a hill far away stood an old rugged cross,
> The emblem of suff'ring and shame;
> And I love that old cross where the dearest and best
> For a world of lost sinners was slain.

---

164   "The Old Rugged Cross," *African American Heritage Hymnal* (Chicago: GIA Publications, 2001), #244.

So I'll cherish the cross, the old rugged cross,
Till my trophies at last I lay down;
I will cling to the cross, the old rugged cross,
And exchange it some day for a crown.

O that old rugged cross, so despised by the world,
Has a wondrous attraction for me;
For the dear Lamb of God left His glory above
To bear it to dark Calvary. *Refrain*

In the old rugged cross, stained with blood so divine,
A wondrous beauty I see;
For 'twas on that old cross Jesus suffered and died
To pardon and sanctify me. *Refrain*

To the old rugged cross I will ever be true,
Its shame and reproach gladly bear;
Then He'll call me some day to my home far away,
Where His glory forever I'll share. *Refrain*

The first stanza characterizes the cross as an emblem of suffering and shame. Stanza two describes the cross as "despised" and Calvary as "dark." The metaphor for Jesus is lamb, not king, nor prince, nor victor or champion in battle. Referring to Christ as "Lamb of God"[165] focuses on the suffering represented by the cross, even though it is described as beloved and beautiful. Its beauty comes from the knowledge that it represents Christ's love for us, even to death.

There is a significant common thread running between "The Old Rugged Cross" and Watts' "When I Behold the Wondrous Cross." Both hymns express a personal response that involves a commitment of one's entire life to Christ. In other words, both songs are about a relationship with Christ that is personal and total. This is expressed by such phrases as "Love so amazing, so divine, demands my soul, my life, my all," in Watts' hymn. In the Gospel song, the phrase "To the old rugged cross, I will ever be true,"

---

165 Once again we see the traditional metaphor for Christ as "Lamb of God" evident in the tradition and in a variety of genres.

expresses a similar sentiment. In addition, both hymns are sung in the first person singular.

The Black spiritual "Were You There" offers yet another perspective. While the text sometimes uses the version that asks "Were you there when they nailed him to a cross," the more familiar version uses the word "tree" instead of cross. The word would have immediately conjured up nightmare lynchings for Blacks who sang the hymn and for whom lynchings would have been a familiar occurrence, particularly during Reconstruction after the Civil War. Memories of that dark chapter in American history are vivid for many. Furthermore, in phrasing the question "Were you there? . . ." the text sets up a call that anticipates a positive response. Neither the text nor the tune is attributed to a specific person. This is one of the reasons this spiritual can be classified as a true folk song. Having emerged from the sung prayer of the African American community, this spiritual has undergone a variety of adaptations and additions. Representative stanzas are offered here:[166]

> Were you there when they crucified my Lord?
> Were you there when they crucified my Lord?
> Oh! Sometimes it causes me to tremble, tremble, tremble,
> Were you there when they crucified my Lord?
>
> Were you there when they nailed him to the tree?
> Were you there when they nailed him to the tree?
> Oh! Sometimes it causes me to tremble, tremble, tremble,
> Were you there when they nailed him to the tree?
>
> Were you there when they pierced him in the side?
> Were you there when they pierced him in the side?
> Oh! Sometimes it causes me to tremble, tremble, tremble,
> Were you there when they pierced him in the side?
>
> Were you there when the sun refused to shine?
> Were you there when the sun refused to shine?
> Oh! Sometimes it causes me to tremble, tremble, tremble,
> Were you there when the sun refused to shine?

---

166 "Were You There," *Worship* (2011), #488. See Brink and Polman, #533.

> Were you there when they laid him in the tomb?
> Were you there when they laid him in the tomb?
> Oh! Sometimes it causes me to tremble, tremble, tremble,
> Were you there when they laid him in the tomb?

This Black spiritual probably predates the Civil War although it was first published in William Barton's *Old Plantation Hymns* (1899). A white spiritual that begins "Have you heard how they crucified my Lord?" was known in Tennessee and may be an early influence.[167] However, the Black spiritual has a more personal and participatory aspect because of the framing of the question. The structure of the music suggests a call-and-response performance. It also encourages improvisation, creativity, and participation.

The Black theologian James Cone explains that for Black slaves Christ's "death was a symbol of their suffering, their trials and tribulations in a hostile and unfriendly world. When Jesus was nailed to the cross and the Romans pierced him in the side, he was not alone; blacks suffered and died with him."[168] Black slaves encountered the theological significance of Jesus' death through the experience of slavery. The Scriptures portray Jesus as someone who identifies with the poor and the helpless and takes their pain on himself. So, yes, they were there at the Crucifixion because Christ's death was for them.[169]

SHIFTS AFTER THE SECOND VATICAN COUNCIL

The years after Vatican II have witnessed a flourishing of new creativity in the emergence of new hymns and styles of worship music not seen since the Reformation (sixteenth through eighteenth centuries). This includes shifts in the use of classic metaphors and in theological emphasis. The Ecumenical Movement received new support and recognition with the promulgation of *Unitatis Redintegratio* (Decree on Ecumenism) in November 1964.[170] In

---

167 *Psalter Hymnal Handbook*, Emily R. Brink and Bert Polman, eds. (Grand Rapids: CRC Publications, 1998), #533.

168 James Cone, "Black Spirituals: A Theological Interpretation" in *Music and the Experience of God*, ed. Mary Collins et al. (Edinburgh: T&T Clark, Ltd., 1989), 45.

169 Cone, 45.

170 See Unitatis Redintegratio (Decree on Ecumenism) Austin Flannery, gen. ed., in *Vatican Council II: Constitutions, Decrees, Declarations: A Completely Revised Translation in Inclusive Language* (Northport, NY: Costello Publishing Co., 1996), 499–523.

addition to the Roman Catholic Church, many other Christian Churches set about reforming their rites and ritual books. New hymnals were published with great regularity in the latter half of the twentieth century by many denominations. In addition to new music and new texts, there was a new openness to sharing across denominational lines. Catholic hymnals began including classic Protestant tunes and texts, and some of the new composers in the Catholic hymnals began to appear in new Protestant hymnals.

Contemporary hymns, particularly those written after the Second Vatican Council, continue to use traditional metaphors in new and creative ways. So, for example, a late twentieth-century text by Carl P. Daw, Jr., explores the metaphor of Christ as King in the hymn "Let Kings and Prophets Yield Their Name."[171]

> Let kings and prophets yield their name
> To Jesus, true Anointed One,
> For whom a nation looked in hope
> Yet failed to see that God had done
> A strange and unexpected thing:
> God sent a servant, not a king.
>
> But God reveals to searching faith
> The truths that pious dogmas hide:
> When Jesus asked the twelve his name,
> Blunt Peter stepped forth and replied
> In words that seemed both right and odd:
> "You are Messiah, Son of God."
>
> Give us, O God, the grace to know
> The limits of our certainty:
> Help us, like Peter, to declare
> The still unfolding mystery
> Of One who reigns though sacrificed,
> Our Lamb and Shepherd, Jesus Christ.

---

171 "Let Kings and Prophets Yield Their Name," *Worship* (2011), #562. This hymn text is yoked with the tune, HICKORY HILL, by Ronald F. Krisman in *Worship*. However, when the text is published in a collection by Hope Publishing Co., holder of the copyright, it is set to MELITA.

This hymn is included in *Worship* 2011 in the category "Christ the King." The entire text is created on the premise that God does not do what we expect. So while Israel looked for a king, God sent a servant instead. Furthermore, by his very appearance, this Messiah lays bare the limits of human certitude: This Christ reigns by being for us both sacrificial lamb and shepherd. Metaphor assists in the "still unfolding mystery." The inclusion of this hymn in *Worship* is another example of ecumenical cooperation between publishers and composers.

Another interesting development after Vatican II was the appearance of a hymn in *People's Mass Book* published by World Library of Sacred Music in 1964 (now World Library Publications). The Second Vatican Council did not close until 1965. Yet, in 1964 the *People's Mass Book* published Omer Westendorf's adaptation of Martin Luther's "A Mighty Fortress." Westendorf used the same hymn tune and Luther's original inspiration, Psalm 46. However, Westendorf reworked the text, taking into account the political and religious landscape of the 1960s. Inspired by the Council, its enthusiastic support for ecumenism, and tensions on the political world stage, this is what Westendorf wrote:[172]

> A mighty fortress is our God,
> A bulwark never failing,
> Protecting us with staff and rod,
> His power all-prevailing.
> What if the nations rage
> And surging seas rampage;
> What though the mountains fall,
> The Lord is God of all;
> On earth is not his equal.
>
> The waters of his goodness flow
> Throughout his holy city,
> And gladden hearts of those who know

---

172 "A Mighty Fortress," *People's Mass Book* (Cincinnati: World Library of Sacred Music, 1964), #T-14. The translation Westendorf worked from was probably taken from *The Hymnal of the Protestant Episcopal Church in the United States of America* (New York: The Church Pension Fund, 1940), #551. That English version's second line reads "a bulwark never failing" as does Westendorf's. Most English Lutheran second lines read "a sword and shield victorious." See pages 76–78.

His tenderness and pity.
Though nations stand unsure,
God's kingdom shall endure;
His power shall remain,
His peace shall ever reign,
Our God, the God of Jacob.

Behold his wondrous deeds of peace,
The God of our salvation;
He knows our wars and makes them cease
In ev'ry land and nation.
The warrior's spear and lance
Are splintered by his glance;
The guns and nuclear might
Stand withered in his sight;
The Lord of hosts is with us.

The revision begins in exactly the same way as Luther's original hymn. But by the third line, it is clear that Westendorf is doing something quite new.[173] The cruel oppressor's rod (belonging to the devil) is now depicted as the protecting staff and rod of a shepherd (God). The devil is not even in the picture. Instead, the dangers that humankind faces are those of nations (war) and nature's upheaval and destruction (floods, earthquakes, etc.). Perhaps the final line of stanza one is most interesting in its change. Luther's version refers to the old satanic foe when he says "On earth he has no equal." Westendorf's line refers to God with its claim that "On earth is not his equal." Such subtleties can be deceptive if the text is not read carefully, especially because of the use of pronouns. Of course, interlining makes it even more difficult to follow the ideas as they are developed and to catch the intended meaning.

Images of water flowing throughout the city and God's tenderness and pity are clearly taken from Psalm 46. Even so, God is characterized as powerful and God's kingdom as enduring forever. It is clearly a kingdom of peace. There is no mention of Jesus Christ in the revision, even though

---

173 See pages 76–80 for the discussion of Luther's text.

Christ is a central figure in Luther's text. Westendorf does not appropriate the *Christus Victor* theme, so central to Luther's theology, in his rendering of the Jewish prayer text that is Psalm 46. Instead, the revision refers to God as the "God of Jacob," just as it appears in the psalm.

The third and final stanzas of the revision continue to borrow key images and phrases from Psalm 46. Instead of fighting our battles for us, this "God of our salvation" is a God of wondrous deeds of peace who make wars cease. Psalm 46 describes God as breaking the bow, shattering the spear, and burning the shield. Westendorf updates the description of battle gear and adds the phrase "guns and nuclear might." This reference to nuclear arms clearly locates the hymn in the last half of the twentieth century. For its time, it was a stunning move, but its point is key: with a glance, God has the power to wipe out all weapons of mass destruction. They stand withered in God's sight. Furthermore, Westendorf's inclusion of guns in his revised text may not have received much attention when he wrote the text in the 1960s. However, today's social and political climate may make this image even more powerful for some than that of nuclear weapons.

Finally, it is clear that Westendorf depended on Psalm 46 as his primary reference point. In doing so, he depicts God as a God of peace rather than of war. The Cuban Missile crisis most certainly influenced Westendorf's thinking. So did the growing enthusiasm and energy for ecumenical efforts that emerged as a result of the Second Vatican Council.[174] There was also keen interest at this time for adopting the robust texts and tunes of the Protestant traditions. The OCP hymnal *Journeysongs* (2012) and GIA's *Worship* (2011) include a translation of Luther's original version of "A Mighty Fortress." However, in their latest hymnal, *One in Faith* (2016), WLP continues to use Westendorf's text.

Below is the NIV translation of Psalm 46. A comparison with Westendorf's text highlights his strong dependence on the psalm. The NIV translation uses the term "fortress" as did the English translation of Luther's text. Other translations, the NRSV for example, translate fortress as "refuge" in verse 11 of the psalm.

---

174 I was able to confirm this interpretation of Omer Westendorf's approach and intentions during a telephone conversation with Alan Hommerding at World Library Publications on Dec. 11, 2013.

Psalm 46 (NIV)[175]

[1] God is our refuge and strength, an ever-present help in trouble.

[2] Therefore we will not fear, though the earth give way
and the mountains fall into the heart of the sea,

[3] though its waters roar and foam
and the mountains quake with their surging.

[4] There is a river whose streams make glad the city of God,
the holy place where the Most High dwells.

[5] God is within her, she will not fall; God will help her at break of day.

[6] Nations are in uproar, kingdoms fall; he lifts his voice, the earth melts.

[7] The Lord Almighty is with us; the God of Jacob is our fortress.

[8] Come and see what the Lord has done,
the desolations he has brought on the earth.

[9] He makes wars cease to the ends of the earth.
He breaks the bow and shatters the spear; he burns the shields with fire.

[10] He says, "Be still, and know that I am God; I will be exalted among the nations,
I will be exalted in the earth."

[11] The Lord Almighty is with us; the God of Jacob is our fortress.

In the twenty-first century, composers of texts and music continue to create new hymns about the gift of redemption won for us in Jesus Christ. However, since the Second Vatican Council, there have been noticeable shifts in the language, metaphors, and theological emphases used to create contemporary hymns on this topic. One such hymn is "Merciful God." Mary Louise Bringle wrote the text. The text of the stanzas follows:[176]

---

175 *The Holy Bible: New International Version* (Grand Rapids, MI: Zondervan Publishing, 2011).
176 "Merciful God," *Worship* (2011), #478. Tony E. Alonso composed the tune, INDIGO, (LM with refrain) that is yoked with the text in *Worship*. However, the text has also been published with the tune, PHOENIX, by William P. Rowan in *Glory to God* (Louisville, KY: Presbyterian Publishing Corp., 2013), #433. See also Kubicki, "Hymn Text Master Class," *GIA Quarterly* 23:1 (2011): 16–17.

Surely, you alone can save us.
You pay our price with precious blood.
Reaching through your great compassion,
You lift up your people with love.

Surely, you alone uphold us.
You give us strength for all our needs.
Shielding with a father's favor,
You bless us with pardon and peace.

Surely, you alone can heal us.
Yours is the will to make us whole.
Soothing with a mother's kindness,
The contrite of heart you console.

Surely, you alone can free us.
You break the bonds of guilt and sin.
Bracing, till we walk uprightly,
You bolster our hope once again.

Surely, you alone refine us.
You give us grace for lives made new,
Forging, through your fire and radiance,
A sacrifice worthy for you.

Surely, you alone redeem us.
You fill our dust with holy breath.
Bursting from the grave in glory,
You rise from the ashes of death.

In six stanzas the hymn provides a series of verbs that unfold the meaning of redemption. They include save, uphold, heal, free, refine, and redeem—all located near the end of the first line of each stanza. Taken together, these verbs offer a holistic understanding of salvation or redemption. Typically, the Christian imagination locates the "winning" of salvation in the death of Jesus Christ on the cross (*Christus Victor*). Often, the prevailing belief is that the individual Christian will experience that salvation only after death. Bringle's text offers a more integrative understanding. Redemption is viewed as a process that begins now, in this life, on this side of the grave. The text describes salvation as lifting us up with loving compassion, strengthening us, offering pardon and peace, soothing and consoling. As the hymn continues, redemption is described as freeing us from the bonds of guilt and sin, bolstering our hope, becoming formed (forged) into new creatures and then finally rising from the dead to share in the glory of God. The text indirectly mentions our Lord's suffering and death on the cross in stanza one when it says that Christ paid our price "with precious blood."

Furthermore, the text of "Merciful God" is more Trinitarian than traditional texts on redemption that tend to have a strong Christological focus. Instead, this hymn provides a perspective that views the work of redemption as the work of the Trinity. The text addresses God using phrases such as "shielding with a father's favor," "you pay our price with precious blood," and "you fill our dust with holy breath." This last phrase suggests a connection with the Trinity's act of creation through its reference to dust and breath. The second creation story in Genesis explains: "Then the Lord God formed man from the dust of the ground and breathed into his nostrils the breath of life; and the man became a living being" (Gen 2:7 NRSV). In Christian theological discourse (and in classic hymn texts), persons of the Trinity have often been assigned specific roles, e.g., Father as creator, Son as redeemer, and Spirit as sanctifier. However, in reality, the one God is active and present in all of these activities. In fact, many theologians would argue that the act of creation and redemption are part of one loving relationship that God has with created reality, and in particular, with humankind. Mary Louis Bringle weaves many of these theological threads throughout her text.

There is one more interesting and helpful aspect about the Bringle hymn. It includes three possible refrains for specific liturgical moments. The first is specific to Ash Wednesday; the other two are for the Lenten season, with one refrain specific to the action of gathering and the other to the communion processional. This type of multiple or optional refrain has become more common since the Second Vatican Council. The practice of providing multiple refrains highlights the contextual nature of the assembly's singing.

Ash Wednesday refrain:

Sign us with ashes, merciful God,

Children of dust, as to dust we return.

Sign us with ashes, merciful God;

Mark us and make us your own.

Lent gathering refrain:

Gather your people, merciful God,

Gather the longing, the lost, the unsure.

Gather your people, merciful God,

Name us and claim us as yours.

Lent communion refrain:

Feed us and guide us, merciful God:

Light, when the shadows of life cloud our view.

Feed us and guide us, merciful God,

People who hunger for you.

Hymns on the topic of redemption or salvation can be found throughout the Church year. The season of Lent, Holy Week, and the Triduum, as well as the season of Easter provide ample opportunities to reflect and sing about this precious gift. These hymns are also used for funeral services. Traditionally, the theological point of these texts is praise for Christ's death and resurrection and its promise of our resurrection "on the last day."

However, the theological notion of salvation or redemption is embedded in many hymns that fall into other topical categories as well. For example, "Come, Join the Dance of Trinity," by Richard Leach is located in the section labeled "Trinity" in Worship (2011). It is also listed in the index under the topic "salvation." The text expands our understanding of the meaning of salvation with its use of the dance metaphor. Of course, the metaphor of the divine dance is not new. It has its roots in the Greek verb *perichorein*. Gregory of Nazianzen (fourth century) introduced the verb into Christological discourse and Maximus the Confessor used the Greek noun perichoresis in the seventh century. John of Damascus (eighth century) popularized their application to Trinitarian language. Twentieth-century theologians such as Catherine Mowry LaCugna and Elizabeth A. Johnson have used the term *perichoresis* to describe the inner life of God whereby the three divine persons share life in an eternal flow of love.[177] In this way, dance imagery is used to capture the dynamic activity that is involved. In his text "Come, Join the Dance of Trinity," Leach expands the traditional notion to include our relationship with the Trinity, a relationship that brings salvation understood as wholeness. Leach grasps the power of the image and uses it as his central metaphor. The dance is not solo dance or even individual group dancing. Rather it is about group dancing similar to the circle dance, contra dance, English country-dance, or the Rueda de Casino.[178] A related Greek word, *perichoreuo*, means to "dance around" or "dance" in a ring. This word adds further light on the meaning of the divine dance since it suggests that the dance image involves dancing together in mutual love and unity. The first two stanzas of "Come, Join the Dance of Trinity" follow:[179]

> Come, join the dance of Trinity,
> Before all worlds begun,
> The interweaving of the Three,
> The Father, Spirit, Son,
> The universe of space and time
> Did not arise by chance,
> But as the Three, in love and hope,
> Made room within their dance.

> Come, see the face of Trinity,
> Newborn in Bethlehem;
> Then bloodied by a crown of thorns
> Outside Jerusalem.
> The dance of Trinity is meant
> For human flesh and bone;

---

177   See Kubicki, *The Presence of Christ*, 150. See also Catherine Mowry LaCugna, *God for Us* (San Francisco: HarperCollins, 1991), 274 and Elizabeth A. Johnson, *She Who Is: The Mystery of God in Feminist Theological Discourse* (New York: Crossroad, 1992), 220.
178   See Kubicki, "Hymn Text Master Class," *GIA Quarterly*, 24:2 (2013), 18.
179   "Come, Join the Dance of Trinity," *Worship* (2011), #554. In *Worship* the text is yoked with Ronald E. Krisman's tune THE FLIGHT OF THE EARLS (CM D). However, the more familiar tune, KINGSFOLD, is used with this text in *Evangelical Lutheran Worship* (Minneapolis, MN: Augsburg Fortress): #412 and *Worship and Song* (Nashville: Abingdon Press, 2011), #3017.

When fear confines the dance in death,
God rolls away the stone.

Everyone is invited to join in the dance. In the first stanza, this dance of God is described as "interweaving" and "making room" for all of creation, not just the human race. Stanza two celebrates the face of the Trinity made visible in Jesus. Beginning with his birth in Bethlehem, continuing through his passion and resurrection, the dance expresses freedom from fear and death is portrayed by the rolling away of the stone. It is clearly a celebration of the mystery of redemption, a mystery that is dynamic and in which we are meant to be active participants.[180] The first two stanzas of "Come, Join the Dance of Trinity" follows:

Come, speak aloud of Trinity,
As wind and tongues of flame
Set people free at Pentecost
To tell the Savior's name.
We know the yoke of sin and death,
Our necks have worn it smooth;
Go tell the world of weight and woe
That we are free to move!

Within the dance of Trinity,
Before all worlds begun,
We sing the praises of the Three,
The Father, Spirit, Son.
Let voices rise and interweave,
By love and hope set free,
To shape in song this joy, this life:
The dance of Trinity.

The text of stanza three holds the freedom of the dance in creative tension with the confinement we endure because of sin and death. But the stanza is a celebration of our freedom in the Spirit given to us at Pentecost.

---

180 See Kubicki, "Hymn Text Master Class," *GIA Quarterly* 24:2 (2013), 18–19.

In stanza four, we sing praise to Father, Spirit, and Son while moving—that is, dancing—within the Trinity's very life. The communal movement that the text conjures up is exhilarating. The experience of salvation is expressed through the freedom of the dance. It is something we can participate in now and it is possible because God gifts us with the Holy Spirit in baptism.

Theological Implications of these Shifts

This sampling of hymn texts is meant to whet the appetite for taking a closer look at the theology expressed through the metaphors and images found in Christian hymn texts. Some general observations, however, can be made. The first is that theological notions of redemption/salvation that use the traditional imagery of the cross are found in great abundance in Christian hymn texts. However, shifts in the theological discourse after the Second Vatican Council have encouraged some hymn text writers to explore new, more dynamic and holistic ways of imagining the faith and describing our experience of it. They have done this through metaphors that engage many of our senses and are deeply rooted in our experience of bodiliness. Such metaphors remind us that our life in God does not exist only in some far off place at some yet-to-be-determined time in the future. Rather, our life in God begins *now*; it is meant to be transformative of our life now. The symbols of the liturgy, including hymns texts, assist us in negotiating this relationship. Furthermore, while metaphors present a comparison between two realities that are unlike, they also present us with ways of imagining our ongoing relationship with the living God—a God who is full of mercy and loves to dance!

CHAPTER 4

IMAGES OF CHURCH IN CLASSIC AND CONTEMPORARY HYMNODY[181]:
HISTORY, RITUAL AND HYMNALS

The introduction to this book noted that this study would consider theological meaning of hymn singing within four contexts: music, ritual, history and space. In this chapter, we will spend some time looking closely at the historical usage of hymns within ritual, that is, liturgy. We will consider both the history of specific hymns, edits that appear in various hymnals, and their potential power to communicate theological meaning within the liturgy. In addition, the unique way in which liturgical singing both shapes and expresses an ecclesiology will also be examined. Ideas developed here are built on an understanding of symbol, metaphor, and imagery covered in earlier chapters.

Liturgy is linked in an integral way to the nature of the Church. This statement affirms a vital connection between the way the Church defines and interprets itself at any given time and the style and substance of its official prayer and its hymns. This assertion likewise affirms the fact that through its ritual prayer, the Church simultaneously expresses its self-understanding and contributes to shaping that self-understanding.[182] So, while ecclesiology (theology of church) may be said to have serious consequences for how we do ritual (celebrate the liturgy), the opposite is also true. That is, how

181 An earlier version of this chapter was first published in *Worship* 84 (2010): 432–452. Thanks to Liturgical Press for permission to use material from that article here.
182 Miriam Therese Winter, *Why Sing? Toward a Theology of Catholic Church Music* (Washington, DC: The Pastoral Press, 1984), 59.

we celebrate the liturgy and the hymns our assemblies sing have serious consequences for our understanding of who we are as church.

The previous chapter examined hymns that sing about eschatology and the mystery of redemption or salvation. The first part of this chapter explores the ecclesial nature of the liturgy as symbolic activity. The second part highlights the link between liturgy and ecclesiology by focusing specifically on singing hymns on the topic of Church. By doing so, these two sections intend to highlight the potential for hymn singing to shape and express an assembly's understanding of itself as Church. The images of Church in three traditional hymns will be examined in order to discover the ecclesiology expressed in the texts, suggested in textual revisions, and enacted through the action of singing. One hymn composed after the Second Vatican Council will also be examined for its particular images of church. Comparisons will be made between traditional and post-Vatican II texts. The third part of this chapter will briefly examine the way in which the pilgrimage site at Taizé, France has consciously employed sung prayer as a means to express and shape a particular ecclesiology.

THE ECCLESIAL NATURE OF THE LITURGY

Since language itself is symbolic, it is not surprising that what we mean by the word "church" often contains multiple levels of meaning. In New Testament usage, the Greek word "ekklesia" referred to "the people gathered for worship." The first and primary meaning of church ("ekklesia") was the gathered assembly. And while the word "church" was also used metaphorically in the New Testament to refer to the church as God's building (*see 1Co 3:9*), it was only much later that the word also referred literally to the *building* that housed the people who gathered for worship. Sometimes, the word "church" is used more narrowly to mean "hierarchy." However, this limited understanding does not reflect the richness of its New Testament roots, nor its link with the assembly's worship. In its "Constitution on the Sacred Liturgy" (*Sacrosanctum Concilium* (SC), 1963), the Second Vatican Council affirmed the fact that the liturgy is an ecclesial action. In other words, it is an action of the church—the whole church, the gathered assembly. Article 2 states that through the liturgy, especially the Eucharist, "the faithful are enabled to express in their lives and manifest to others the mystery of Christ and the real nature of the Church."[183] Commenting on the Second Vatican Council's presentation of the liturgy as the action of the Church, Yves Congar pointed out that this move was a retrieval of an ancient tradition that held that the "ecclesia," the Christian community, is the subject of the liturgical action.[184] This understanding of the assembly as *subject* of the liturgical action was an important principle of the Second Vatican Council. Furthermore, the revised *General Instruction of the Roman Missal* (GIRM 2002) reaffirms these insights when it begins article 19 by quoting SC 41: "The presence and active participation of the faithful bring out more plainly the ecclesial nature of the celebration."[185]

As the subject of the liturgical action, the assembly expresses its beliefs, values, commitments, relationships, memories and hopes that constitute it as a community. And while the assembly communicates its message, the Church is being mediated—that is, becomes more fully what it is—since liturgical assemblies are particular realizations of the Church.[186] All of these comments point to the social nature of the liturgy, since ritual is produced within the ecclesial process, is performed by an assembly, and participates in the ongoing life of the Church—a social reality.[187]

As the hymn text writer Brian Wren so aptly put it,

> when a congregation sings together, its song is an acted parable[188] of community. In the act of singing, the members not only support one another, but [sic] proclaim a community of faith reaching beyond the congregation that sings. Thus, the corporate or communal inclusiveness of congregational song is ecclesial: it declares what the church aims and hopes to be, and reminds the singers of their common faith and hope.[189]

---

183 Austin Flannery, gen. ed., "Constitution on the Sacred Liturgy," (SC), in *Vatican Council II: The Conciliar and Post Consiliar Documents* (Grand Rapids, MI: William B. Eerdmans Publishing, 1984) no. 2.

184 Yves M. J. Congar, "L'Ecclesia ou communauté chrétienne, sujet integral de l'action liturgique," in *La Liturgie après Vatican II*, ed. J. P. Jossua and Y. Congar (Paris: Cerf, 1967), 241 as cited by Margaret Mary Kelleher, "Liturgy: An Ecclesial Act of Meaning" in Worship 59 (November 1985), 482.

185 GIRM no. 41.

186 GIRM nos. 491, 493.

187 Congar, 241.

188 The phrase "parable of community" was also used earlier by Roger Schutz to describe the monastic community he founded in Taizé, France. See Kubicki, *Liturgical Music as Ritual Symbol* for further discussion of the relationship of Taizé chants and the ecclesiology of the community.

189 Wren, *Praying Twice*, 93.

The Symbolic Nature of the Liturgy

Communication is an essential component of the life of any social group. Just as other social groups, the Church has its own language or set of symbols through which its particular meanings are communicated. Knowledge and use of the Church's public language is one of the signs of membership in the Church. The Bible as well as hymns, creeds, preaching, and personal testimony are all significant forms of language for the Christian Church, allowing it to discover and express its social identity.[190] Even in the early days of the liturgical movement that preceded Vatican II, such great leaders as Dom Prosper Guéranger understood the true nature of symbol as something having inevitable social consequences. He knew that both symbol and ritual have everything to do with social formation, cohesion, and survival.[191]

The language of the liturgy is symbolic. This is so because its basic units are ritual symbols: objects, actions, relationships, words, music, gestures, and arrangements of space.[192] Because it can be said to have many layers of meaning, a symbol is both illusive and multivalent (polyvalent). Clusters of symbols in motion constitute ritual. Several Church documents make reference to the power of symbols in the liturgy, specifically to the power of music making as symbolizing activity. In *Music in Catholic Worship*, the United States bishops' first official commentary on liturgical music following Vatican II, they say this about the variety of symbols found in the liturgy:

> Among the many signs and symbols used in the Church to celebrate its faith, music is of preeminent importance. As sacred song united to words it forms a necessary or integral part of the solemn liturgy . . . It should heighten the texts so that they speak more fully and more effectively. . . [and] It imparts a sense of unity to the congregation.[193]

---

190 Margaret Mary Kelleher, "Liturgy as an Ecclesial Act of Meaning: Foundations and Methodological Consequenses for a Liturgical Spirituality," (PhD diss., The Catholic University of America, 1983), 74–75.

191 Aidan Kavanaugh, "Beyond Words and Concerts to the Survival of Mrs. Murphy," in *Pastoral Music 1* (April–May 1977), 17.

192 Margaret Mary Kelleher, "Liturgical Theology: A Task and a Method," in *Worship* 62 (January 1988), 12.

193 Bishops' Committee on the Liturgy, *Music in Catholic Worship (MCW)* Washington, DC: USCCB Publications Office, 1972), no. 23.

The bishops continue:

> In addition to expressing texts, music can also unveil a dimension of meaning and feeling, a communication of ideas and intuitions which words alone cannot yield. This dimension is integral to the human personality and to growth in faith. It cannot be ignored if the signs of worship are to speak to the whole person.[194]

In their latest document on music, *Sing to the Lord: Music in Divine Worship*, the bishops refer to the role of symbols to proclaim Christ's presence in the Church by quoting from the *Catechism of the Catholic Church*. That document speaks of the sacramental principle that believes that the words, gestures, signs, and symbols used in the liturgy express God's gesture toward humanity and humanity's response.[195]

In this way we can say that music wedded to text in the liturgy serves as a preeminent symbol capable of shaping and expressing the faith of the assembly. In other words, this process contributes to the spiritual formation of the assembly.[196] This is a vitally important task. Don Saliers is keenly aware of this power of sung prayer when he says:

> Musical choices take us either toward or away from such deep patterns of emotion which constitute the Christian life, the "Christ-formed" life, if you will. Church music is thus integral to proclaiming and receiving the word and the mystery of the saving reality of the gospel. This is why questions of sung prayer are really questions of congregational spirituality. Over time the community of worship will be shaped by its musical language and forms, for good or for ill. We must be sensitive to this, and to the problems and the opportunities this presents us in thinking through the whole program of parish music.[197]

---

194 MCW, 24
195 Committee on Divine Worship, *Sing to the Lord: Music in Divine Worship (STL)* (Washington, DC: USCCB, 2008), no. 6. See also, *Catechism of the Catholic Church*, 2nd ed. (Washington, DC: *Liberia Editrice Vaticana*—USCCB, 2000), nos. 1146, 1148.
196 See also chapter one for a discussion of the relationship of belief, faith, and celebrating liturgy.
197 Don Saliers, "The Integrity of Sung Prayer," in *Worship* 55 (July 1981), 294.

Indeed, if this is the case, then the choices that we make week by week and year by year concerning the sung prayer we invite our assemblies to perform are not insignificant. Rather we need to recognize their power, over time, to inform the theology and shape the spirituality of our assemblies.

This raises some important questions, then, in regard to ecclesiology. Just what kind of church is being disclosed and expressed in our liturgical celebrations? What kind of information is being presented to the assembly in their ritual celebrations? What are they learning about themselves, about God, about Jesus Christ, about salvation, about life in an ecclesial community? What image of Church is being mediated through ritual?[198] And more specifically, how do the hymns that we place on their lips each week assist (or hinder) their experience and understanding of what it means to be Church? These questions will now be more concretely addressed by examining specific classic hymns on the topic of Church that are sung across denominational lines.

Singing Hymns as an Ecclesial Act of Meaning

We begin by examining three classic hymns for the ecclesiology which they express: "Christ Is Made the Sure Foundation," "O Christ the Great Foundation," and "At That First Eucharist." Each hymn text will be examined for images or metaphors of the Church, as well as for doctrinal or creedal expressions. Original and revised versions of the texts will be traced and compared. To a limited extent,[199] the context in which the hymns are sung will also be examined. For not only is the text of sung prayer a powerful symbol capable of shaping and expressing the Church, but it is also a symbol which, as part of ritual, is experienced *in motion*, that is, in the context of real human beings singing during worship. For it is within the actual performance of the liturgy that meaning is communicated and created by and for the church; it is the actual performance of the rite by an assembly that determines which meanings emerge.[200] As Victor Turner points out in his studies on ritual, "[T]exts not only animate and are animated by contexts

---

198   Kelleher, "Liturgical Theology," 18.
199   Doing a detailed contextual analysis is beyond the scope of this study. Perhaps, however, these observations may inspire further research by other scholars and pastoral practitioners.
200   Margaret Mary Kelleher, "Liturgy: An Ecclesial Act of Meaning," in *Worship* 59 (November 1985), 490.

but are processually inseverable from them."[201] In other words, the texts cannot be separated from the action by which they are "spun out" in a ritual setting. The two mutually influence each other. The poet, the artist, and the musician understand this, even if only intuitively. Indeed, the Church, as a cluster of New Testament images, is of the nature of poetry, of song, and of dance.[202] These interact with each other to create ecclesial meaning.

In addition to situating hymns within the liturgical context, their placement in specific topical categories within a hymnal reveals an implicit ecclesiology operative in the choices made by the hymnal's editors. The hymnal, *Worship* (2011),[203] for example, gives forty-eight titles under the topic of "Church." The three hymns under consideration in this chapter are all included. In *Worship* (1986) the conclusion of the list of hymns under the topic "Church," cross-references "discipleship," "ministry," "mission," and "social concern." Referring to these topics is significant since it implicitly suggests that discipleship, ministry, mission, and social concern are somehow directly related to the topic "Church." Interestingly enough, all of these topics coincide with an understanding of the Church that Avery Cardinal Dulles refers to as the model of Church as servant.[204] This designation reveals a dramatic change of focus in the Church's own self-understanding which occurred at the time of Vatican II, and which finds its articulation in the "Pastoral Constitution on the Church in the Modern World," (*Gaudium et spes*, 1965). Another hymnal, *Journeysongs* (2012), cross-references "Global Family" and "people of God." Here again, the Second Vatican Council's promotion of the church as the people of God is acknowledged as well as the new global vision that has been promoted within the justice and peace activities of church organizations. Of the three hymns, only "O Christ the Great Foundation" is found in the cross-references and it is found in each one of them. Thus even in the simple act of setting up a topic index, the hymnal editors make a number of ecclesiological statements, supporting as they do by their general design, an

---

201 Victor Turner, "Process, System, and Symbol: A New Anthropological Synthesis," *Daedalus* 106 (1977), 61.

202 George H. Travard, *The Church, Community of Salvation: An Ecumenical Ecclesiology*, New Theological Studies I, gen. ed. Peter C. Phan (Collegeville, MN: Liturgical Press, 1992), 93.

203 *Worship: A Hymnal and Service Book for Roman Catholics*, 4th ed. (Chicago: GIA Publications, 2011). The limits of this chapter require that renditions of the three traditional hymn texts in contemporary usage be limited to a few select hymnals. It seems more useful to follow the changes of one or two hymnals through several editions. So, for example, *Worship* (1986) offered only 31 hymns under the heading "Church."

204 Avery Cardinal Dulles, *Models of the Church*, expanded edition (New York: Image Books, a division of Doubleday and Co., 2002), 81–94.

ecclesiology consonant with the statements on Church issued by the Second Vatican Council. Other hymnal editors have acted similarly.

In terms of musical style, the three texts are often set to traditional hymn tunes. This is the case, for example, in *Worship*. The tunes of "O Christ the Great Foundation" (tune: AURELIA) and "At That First Eucharist" (tune: UNDE ET MEMORES) are written in simple meter (four/four or common time). This creates a solid sense of rhythm in a processional or marching style with subdivisions of the beat into two. The music for "Christ Is Made the Sure Foundation" (tune: WESTMINSTER ABBEY) is written in compound meter (six/four time), providing a more flowing sense of rhythm because the beat subdivides into three rather than into two. In any case, the regular shape of the phrases of each hymn tune, as well as the recurring rhythmic and melodic motifs, creates a strong and clear melody that invites confident participation. This is significant because in most cases the entire congregation sings these hymns while they are standing or walking. "Christ Is Made the Sure Foundation" and "O Christ the Great Foundation" serve well as gathering (entrance) or recessional hymns. "At That First Eucharist" is perhaps most often chosen as a communion processional although it could also serve as a post-communion hymn. Two of these three liturgical moments—the gathering song and the communion song—play a critical role in creating and sustaining an awareness of community.[205] It is important, then, that the genre of music chosen be capable of enabling the assembly to participate easily and wholeheartedly. Keeping these general observations on the three hymns in mind, let us proceed to a more detailed analysis of the text of each. The first is the eleventh-century text, "Christ Is Made the Sure Foundation."[206]

> Christ is made the sure foundation
> and the precious cornerstone,
> who the twofold wall surmounting
> binds them closely into one:
> holy Sion's help for ever
> and her confidence alone.

---

205 GIRM, no. 46 and no. 86. See also, MCW, no. 60.
206 Erik Routley, *A Panorama of Christian Hymnody* (Collegeville, MN: Liturgical Press, 1979), 68.

All that dedicated city
dearly loved by God on high,
in exultant jubilation
pours perpetual melody;
God the One and God the Trinal
singing everlastingly.

To this temple, where we call thee,
Come, O Lord of hosts, today!
With thy wonted loving kindness
hear thy people as they pray;
and thy fullest benediction
shed within its walls for ay.

Here vouchsafe to all thy servants
that they supplicate to gain:
here to have and hold for ever
those good things their prayers obtain;
and hereafter in thy glory
with thy blessed ones to reign.

Laud and honour to the Father,
laud and honour to the Son;
laud and honour to the Spirit;
ever three and ever one:
consubstantial, co-eternal,
while unending ages run.

The text of this hymn, "Angularis fundamentum" ("Christ Is Made the Sure Foundation"), is an eleventh-century Latin hymn that some scholars suspect may go back as far as the sixth century.[207] Actually, the text as it is most frequently used today is the second part of a much longer hymn entitled "Urbs beata Jerusalem" ("Blessed City, Heavenly Jerusalem"). Dividing

---

207   Erik Routley, *An English-Speaking Hymnal Guide* (Collegeville, MN: Liturgical Press, 1979), 109.

this hymn after stanza four goes back to medieval liturgical custom.[208] In practice, each section ended with a doxology that appeared as stanza five and stanza ten. Modern hymnals offer different combinations of stanzas, some printing all nine. Many use only the second part, "Christ Is Made the Sure Foundation," which is the subject of our consideration here. In *Worship* (1986 and 2011) and *Journeysongs* (2012) the text is set to the tune WESTMINSTER ABBEY, an adaptation of a seventeenth-century anthem by Henry Purcell. In *RitualSong* (1996, 1998),[209] a version of the text closer to the original is set to a new hymn tune, EDEN, by O. M. Feilden. The second edition of *RitualSong* (2016) reverts back to using the tune WESTMINSTER ABBEY. *Gather* (2011) includes the hymn, but uses the tune ST. THOMAS instead. *One in Faith* (WLP 2016) uses the tune REGENTS SQUARE.

The text of the hymn, translated from the Latin in the nineteenth century by John M. Neale, contains many concrete images for the Christian church. These include "foundation," "cornerstone," "temple," and "Sion." They suggest security, strength, protection, and dependability. *The Dogmatic Constitution on the Church* (*Lumen gentium*, 1964) discusses the long tradition of using these images to describe the Church and points to their roots in Sacred Scripture:

> Often, too, the church is called God's building (see 1 Cor 3:9). The Lord compared himself to the stone which the builders rejected, but which was made into the cornerstone (see Mt 21:42 and parallels; Acts 4:11; 1 Pet 2:7; Ps 117:22). On this foundation the church is built by the apostles (see 1 Cor 3:11) and from this it receives stability and cohesion. This edifice is given various names: the house of God (see 1 Tim 3:15) in which his family lives; the household of God in the Spirit (see Eph 2:19–22); "the dwelling-place of God among mortals" (Apoc 21:3); and, especially, the holy *temple*. This temple, represented in sanctuaries built of stone, is praised by the Fathers and is rightly compared in the liturgy to the holy city, the new Jerusalem. As living stones we here on earth are built

---

208 Routley, *Panorama*, 68.
209 *RitualSong* (Chicago: GIA Publications, 1996, 1998).

into it (1 Pet 2:5). It is this holy city which John contemplates as it comes down out of heaven from God when the world is made anew, "prepared like a bride adorned for her husband" (Apoc 21:1f.).[210]

In addition to the imagery contained in the text, there are also significant creedal statements. The last two lines of stanza two profess faith in a God who is both one and triune. This is reaffirmed in the doxology in the last stanza that mentions each person of the Blessed Trinity separately and then reiterates belief that they are three in one. In addition, the last stanza of the original text closes the doxology by professing the three persons of the Trinity "consubstantial and co-eternal."

Thus, strong images of the Church as "building" and "city" are intertwined with creedal statements that proclaim that the Church's faith is its source of unity—The Triune God. This faith, furthermore, is built on Christ on whom it depends as its "sure foundation." The third stanza portrays the Church in the traditional role of Church "militant," striving to achieve beatitude after a time of struggle.

The revised text of "Christ Is Made the Sure Foundation,"[211] as it appears in *Worship* (1986), is attributed to the translator John M. Neale, but with several alterations.

Christ is made the sure foundation,
Christ the head and cornerstone;
Chosen of the Lord, and precious,
Binding all the Church in one;
Holy Zion's help forever,
And her confidence alone.

To this temple where we call you,
Come, O Lord of hosts, today;
With your wonted loving kindness

---

210 Austin Flannery, gen. ed., "Dogmatic Constitution on the Church," in *Vatican Council II: Constitutions, Decrees, Declarations: A Completely Revised Translation in Inclusive Language* (Northport, NY: Costello Publishing Company, 1996), no. 6.
211 "Christ is Made the Sure Foundation," *Worship* (1986), #617.

Hear your servants as they pray,
And your fullest benediction
Shed in all its bright array.

Grant, we pray, to all your people,
All the grace they ask to gain;
What they gain from you for ever
With the blessed to retain,
And hereafter in your glory
Evermore with you to reign.

This 1986 version includes only three stanzas and a number of changes in the use of imagery and articulation of creedal statements. There are fewer images and they are less homogeneous. Although Zion is mentioned, the words "city" and "wall" are not included. The image of "head" in stanza one, line two, did not appear in Neale's original translation. Perhaps Pius XII's encyclical, *Mystici corporis*, (1943) may have influenced this insertion in the *Worship* (1986) version.[212] The subject of that papal document was the notion of church as mystical body, with Christ as head of the body. This addition works to broaden the richness of the imagery by introducing a new metaphor. Likewise, the mention of "grace" in the third stanza of the text supports the imagery of Christ as "Head" and thus further develops the notion of Church as mystical communion. In this way, the new translation appears to move from an understanding of Church that focuses strongly on the institutional model, to one that includes the notion of mystical communion.

When GIA published *RitualSong* (1996) ten years after *Worship* (1986), the editors returned, for the most part, to the original text that was altered in the 1986 edition. This is the text of "Christ Is Made the Sure Foundation"[213] published in 1996.

Stanza 1: same as 1986 text above

Stanza 2: same as 1986 text above

---

212 *Worship II*, published by GIA in 1975, already had the insertion of the word "Head" in the first stanza.
213 "Christ Is Made the Sure Foundation," *RitualSong* (1996), #778.

Here vouchsafe to all your servants
What they ask of you to gain;
What they gain from you for ever
With the blessed to retain,
And hereafter in your glory
Evermore with you to reign.

Laud and honor to the Father,
Laud and honor to the Son,
Laud and honor to the Spirit,
Ever three and ever One,
One in might and One in glory,
While unending ages run.

The 1996 hymn contains four stanzas rather than three, the first two of which are identical to the 1986 edition. The interesting changes occur in stanzas three and four. Here stanzas revert back to stanzas four and five of the original with a few alterations. Archaic language such as "thy" is dropped, but "vouchsafe" returns in 1996 after having been replaced in 1986 by "grant." Technical theological terms such as "consubstantial" and "co-eternal" are not retained, but the less familiar "laud" is. In terms of church imagery, key images such as foundation, cornerstone, Zion, and temple are retained. The eschatological dimension of the original fourth stanza returns as does the doxology in the final stanza.

Other recent hymnals published by Oregon Catholic Press (OCP) and World Library Publications (WLP) have observed similar editorial changes. *Journeysongs* (2010) uses "praise" in place of "laud" and replaces "vouchsafed" with "grant." *One in Faith* (2016) follows the text also used by *Worship* (2011) with the exception that "laud" is replaced by "praise." What seems to have been at issue was which language would both speak most easily to the assembly and allow them to speak through the hymn text.

Creedal statements regarding the afterlife and the three in one nature of God in *RitualSong* (1996) are stronger than the 1986 text and clearer than the original nineteenth-century translation. At least one of the effects of these changes is to create a text that speaks of church in more explicitly eschatological and Trinitarian terms. On the other hand, the changes also revive the use of language that is not common parlance outside the context of worship, e.g., "vouchsafe" and "laud."

Finally, *Worship* (2011) and *RitualSong* (2016) include further changes to the text of "Christ Is Made the Sure Foundation."[214]

Christ is made the sure foundation,
Christ our Head and cornerstone,
Chosen of the Lord and precious,
Binding all the Church in one;
Holy Zion's help forever
And our confidence alone.

To this temple, where we call you,
Come, O Lord of hosts, today;
With your steadfast loving kindness,
Hear your servants as they pray;
And your fullest benediction
Shed in all its bright array.

Here bestow on all your servants
What they ask of you to gain;
What they gain from you, forever
With the blessed to retain;
And hereafter in your glory
Evermore with you to reign.

Praise and honor to the Father,
Praise and honor to the Son,
Praise and honor to the Spirit,
Ever three and ever one:
One in might and one in glory
While unending ages run!

---

214 "Christ Is Made the Sure Foundation," *Worship* (2011), #732 and *RitualSong* (2016), #852.

The changes are significant improvements in language usage rather than imagery or creedal statements. Nevertheless they are important since the editors appear to have more seriously taken into account the actual assembly singing the text. The word "our" appears twice in stanza one for the first time. This provides a more personal, relational tone to the text and also eliminates the use of the traditional feminine for Church. Not everyone will see that as an improvement, but many will. The second stanza updates the text by changing "wonted" to "steadfast."[215] Stanza three is significantly rewritten, eliminating unfamiliar and dated usage. It returns to using the word "servants" rather than "people" as was the case in the nineteenth-century translation. The fourth stanza, including Trinitarian doxology and eschatological focus, is reinstated almost as it was in *RitualSong* (1996). The one update is changing the word "laud" to "praise." This last revision appears to achieve a good balance between fidelity to the original text and attentiveness to the evolution in language usage. Potentially, these changes enable theological meaning to be more accessible and inspiring.

"THE CHURCH'S ONE FOUNDATION"[216]

Hymnologists consider this hymn to be one of the most theologically substantial of all the Victorian hymns. Samuel John Stone wrote it in 1866 when he was a young priest reacting to the Colenso controversy.[217] Gradually it became a universal hymn of celebration for great church occasions. Since, within the author's lifetime those occasions became more frequent and the processions longer, Stone inflated the text to eleven stanzas. However, as the additional stanzas never fitted the original text properly in the first place, they have appropriately fallen away.[218]

> The Church's one foundation
> Is Jesus Christ, her Lord
> She is His new creation

---

215 *One in Faith* translates the third line of stanza two as "steadfast" and the last line of that same stanza as "shed within its walls always." Otherwise the text is the same.

216 Routley, *Panorama*, 95

217 The Colenso controversy was a heresy-hunt in the Church of England that concerned removing a South African bishop from his see for saying that Moses did not write Deuteronomy because it contains an account of his own funeral.

218 Routley, *Panorama*, 95.

By water and the Word:
From heav'n He came and sought her,
To be His holy Bride;
With His own Blood He bought her,
And for her life He died.

Elect from every nation,
Yet one o'er all the earth,
Her charter of salvation
One Lord, one faith, one birth,
One holy Name she blesses,
Partakes one holy Food,
And to one hope she presses
With every grace endued.

Though with a scornful wonder (OCP omits this stanza)
Men see her sore opprest, (The world sees her oppressed (WLP))
By schisms rent asunder,
By heresies distrest, (distressed)
Yet Saints their watch are keeping,
Their cry goes us, "How long?"
And soon the night of weeping
Shall be the morn of song.

'Mid toil, and tribulation,
And tumult of her war,
She waits the consummation
Of peace for evermore;
Till with the vision glorious
Her longing eyes are blest,
And the great Church victorious
Shall be the Church at rest.

Yet she on earth hath union
With God the Three in One,

> And mystic sweet communion (And with the saints,
>
> communion (OCP))
>
> With those whose rest is won:
>
> O happy ones and holy!
>
> Lord, give us grace that we,
>
> Like them the meek and lowly,
>
> On high may dwell with Thee. Amen. (May live eternally (WLP))

Samuel John Stone first published the hymn in his *Lyra Fidelium* in 1866. The text has been consistently set to the tune AURELIA by Samuel S. Wesley which was, however, originally composed for another hymn text entitled "Jerusalem the Golden."[219]

The text is rich in imagery and theology. In addition to beginning with the image of "foundation," the first stanza includes such baptismal images as "new creation" and "water." Further images such as "Word," "Bride," and "buying or redemption" are all contained in the first six lines.

Although the second stanza contains images such as "charter," "food," and "grace," the creedal notions of unity predominate with seven repetitions of the word "one" in the space of the six-line stanza. Notions of Church as institution (charter) are juxtaposed with notions of Church as mystical communion (grace), as well as Church as sacrament. Strong language characterizes stanza three. Such vivid images as "oppression," "rending asunder," "watching," "night," "crying out," "weeping," and "morning" describe an experience of the Church torn apart by heresy.[220] The fourth stanza begins by depicting the Church Militant with more abstract metaphors such as "toil," "tribulation," "war," "peace," "victory," and "rest." As the stanza develops, the eschatological notion of the Church comes through in lines three and four with the verbs "waiting" and "longing." The stanza closes with a picture of the Church Triumphant gazing at the vision glorious. The final stanza comes back to notions of unity and mystical communion, based again on faith in the God who is Three in One. The ultimate goal

---

219 W. H. Frere, ed., *Hymns Ancient and Modern: Historical Edition* (London: William Clowes and Sons, Limited, 1909), 494.

220 This stanza is omitted in *Journeysongs* (2012). *One in Faith* (2016) edits the second line to read "the world sees her oppressed," thus eliminating an archaic and an exclusive expression. *Journeysongs* (2012) edits line three of the final stanza to read "and with the saints, communion." The final line of the hymn is changed to "may live eternally" in *One in Faith* (2016). *Journeysongs* (2012) publishes the last line unchanged.

of the Christian life is expressed through such images as "unity," "rest," "happiness," "grace," and "dwelling on high."

Worship (1986) attributes its version of the text to Timothy T'ingfang Lew. It would seem he is responsible for the very significant reworking of the text. The same version is published in RitualSong (2016).[221]

> O Christ the Great Foundation
> On which your people stand
> To preach your true salvation
> In ev'ry age and land:
> Pour out your Holy Spirit
> To make us strong and pure,
> To keep the faith unbroken
> As long as worlds endure.
>
> Baptized in one confession,
> One church in all the earth,
> We bear our Lord's impression,
> The sign of second birth:
> One holy people gathered
> In love beyond our own,
> By grace we were invited,
> By grace we make you known.
>
> Where tyrants' hold is tightened,
> Where strong devour the weak,
> Where innocents are frightened
> The righteous fear to speak,
> There let your church awaking
> Attack the pow'rs of sin
> And, all their ramparts breaking,
> With you the victory win.
>
> This is the moment glorious
> When he who once was dead

---

221 "O Christ the Great Foundation," Worship (1986), #618 and RitualSong (2016), #854.

Shall lead his church victorious,

Their champion and their head.

The Lord of all creation

His heav'nly kingdom brings

The final consummation,

The glory of all things.

The strongest link between this 1986 version and the original 1866 version is the use of the same hymn tune. The five stanzas of the original have been conflated into four. The general focus in terms of imagery and creedal statements is similar, but there are clear changes of emphasis. Instead of the simple mention of "Word" in stanza one, the revised text speaks of preaching salvation. And although the Holy Spirit was implicit in the activity described in the original version, there is an explicit invocation to the Holy Spirit in the revised text. The traditional image of church as "bride" is omitted[222] and the new text lacks the strong relational quality of the original. There seems to be a stronger leaning toward an understanding of Church as herald in the second text. This idea is reiterated at the end of the second stanza where it again speaks of making the Lord known.

The third stanza uses military imagery as did the original, but this time the Church is not fighting heresy, but the evil powers of oppression. Images such as "tyrants," "weak," "innocents," and "ramparts," provide a certain power to the text as does the use of such strong verbs as "tightened," "devour," "frightened," "awaking," and "breaking."

The final stanza again pictures the Church as herald of Christ's lordship and of the future kingdom. Neither a doxology nor creedal statements about the Trinity are included. Rather, images of "champion," "head," "kingdom," and "glory" recapitulate the metaphors of the entire text. Clearly the hymn is rich in multiple images that correspond to the various models of the Church as Avery Cardinal Dulles[223] outlines them. The revised (some might argue, the new) text holds up the importance of keeping the faith unbroken (stanza one), but de-emphasizes the role of the Church as battling heresy.

---

222 The use of the image "bride" was beginning to be viewed as sexist at the time when many denominations were revising their hymnals in the 1970s and 1980s. See Gracia Grendel, "Inclusive Language in Hymns: A Reappraisal" in Currents in Theology and Mission 60 (June 1989): 187–193.

223 See note 204.

This omission may well reflect the new ecumenical spirit that emerged after the Second Vatican Council. Instead, the *Worship* (1986) text portrays the Church as devoting its energy to preaching and righting wrong—this time social ills rather than heresy.

Worship (2011) and *Gather* (2011) return with a few updates to the original nineteenth-century text by Samuel John Stone.[224]

> The Church's one foundation
> Is Jesus Christ, her Lord;
> She is his new creation
> By water and the Word.
> From heav'n he came and sought her
> To be his holy bride;
> With his own blood he bought her,
> And for her life he died.
>
> Elect from ev'ry nation,
> Yet one o'er all the earth;
> Her charter of salvation:
> One Lord, one faith, one birth.
> One holy name she blesses,
> Partakes one holy food,
> And to one hope she presses
> With ev'ry grace endued.
>
> (omits original stanza 3)
>
> Through toil and tribulation
> And tumult of her war
> She waits the consummation
> Of peace forevermore
> Till with the vision glorious
> Her longing eyes are blessed,
> And the great Church victorious
> Shall be the Church at rest.

---

224 "The Church's One Foundation," *Worship* (2011), #736 and *Gather* (2011), #742.

> Yet she on earth has union
> With God, the Three in One,
> And mystic sweet communion
> With those whose rest is won.
> O blessed heav'nly chorus!
> Lord, save us by your grace
> That we, like saints before us,
> May see you face to face.

Stanzas one and two return to the original 1866 text. Stone's third stanza, referring to schisms and heresies, is omitted. Instead of beginning the next stanza with "mid" the 2011 hymnals use the word "through." The last stanza eliminates archaisms by changing "hath" to "has" and "Thee" to "you." The last four lines involve more creative and extensive editing that make the text more accessible to a contemporary assembly and highlight eschatological hope and vision with greater clarity. In the 2011 hymnals, the theological foci of baptism and the Word return, as does the image of Church as bride.

WLP's *One in Faith* (2016) includes stanza three that is omitted in the two GIA 2011 hymnals. OCP's *Journeysongs* (2010) omits the original stanza three. Both publishers include very minor edits.

"At That First Eucharist"

William H. Turton composed the text in 1881 at St. Mary Magdalene, Munster Square in London for the English Church Union. The original first line began "O Thou who at thy Eucharist didst pray." It was first published in the *Altar Hymnal* in 1884. Later, the opening line was altered to read "Thou who at thy first . . ." when it was included in the 1889 edition of *Hymns Ancient and Modern.* Later, it was again altered to begin "At that first Eucharist . . ."[225]

> O Thou who at thy Eucharist didst pray,
> That all thy Church might be forever one,
> Grant us at every Eucharist to say

---

225 Routley, *An English-Speaking Hymnal Guide*, 70.

With longing heart and soul, 'Thy will be done:'
O may we all one Bread, one Body be,
Through this blest Sacrament of unity.

For all thy Church, O Lord, we intercede;
Make all our sad divisions soon to cease;
Draw us the nearer each to each we plead,
By drawing all to thee, O Prince of Peace.
Thus may we all one Bread, one Body be,
Through this blest Sacrament of unity.

We pray thee too for wanderers from thy fold;
O bring them back, Good Shepherd of the sheep,
Back to the faith which saints believed of old,
Back to the Church which still that faith doth keep.
Soon may we all one Bread, one Body be,
Through this blest Sacrament of unity.

So, Lord, at length when sacraments shall cease,
May we be one with all thy Church above,
One with thy saints in one unbroken peace,
One with thy saints in one unbounded love:
More blessed still, in peace and love to be,
One with the Trinity in Unity.

From the beginning, the text was set to the tune UNDE ET MEMORES although that tune was actually first used with a hymn text beginning "And now, O Father, mindful of the love. . . ." William H. Monk composed the tune for inclusion in *Hymns Ancient and Modern* (1875, a hymnal he edited).

The primary focus of this hymn is different from the previous two in that the Eucharist, rather than the Church, is its primary focus. Nevertheless, a theological axiom states that the Eucharist makes the Church and the Church makes the Eucharist. This hymn expresses that insight in a direct way.[226] The two previous hymns discussed are particularly appropriate during the entrance

---

226 Henri de Lubac, *Corpus Mysticum: The Eucharist and the Church in the Middle Ages*, trans. by Gemma Simmonds (South Bend, IN: University of Notre Dame Press, 2007), 88.

processional or the recessional; this third hymn is usually designated as a hymn for the communion processional. In both *Hymns Ancient and Modern* (1881) and *Worship* (1986), the hymn is listed as a song for Eucharist. This indeed works well since the imagery of the hymn characterizes the Church as mystical communion and sacrament.

The 1881 text includes the scriptural images of "one bread, one body" (1Cor 11:17) in the first two stanzas. Unity is the primary focus. The third stanza moves into the scriptural imagery of the Church as "sheepfold" with Christ the "Good Shepherd." Faith is characterized as an ancient tradition preserved by the Church. Finally, in the last stanza, the unity of the church is associated with the unity of the Trinity when, in the end, the Church Militant will be joined with the Church Triumphant.

In addition to comparing the original text of the hymn and the version found in *Worship* (1986), an intermediary version of the text was published in *Our Parish Prays and Sings* (1959),[227] at the time when the dialogue Mass was being promoted just before the Second Vatican Council. Stanzas 1–4 below are found in *Our Parish Prays and Sings* (1959); stanzas 1–3 are found in *Worship* (1986).[228]

> At that first Eucharist before you died,
> O Lord, you prayed that all be one in you;
> At this our Eucharist again preside,
> And in our hearts your law of love renew.
> Thus may we all one Bread, one Body be;
> Through this blest Sacrament of Unity.
>
> For all your church, O Lord, we intercede;
> O make our lack of charity to cease;
> Draw us the nearer each to each we plead,
> By drawing all to you, O Prince of Peace.
> Thus may we all one Bread, one Body be;
> Through this blest Sacrament of Unity.

---

227 *Our Parish Prays and Sings: Dialogue Mass, Hymns, Chants* (Collegeville, MN: Liturgical Press, 1959), pp. 61–62 (mass hymn #11).
228 "At That First Eucharist," *Worship* (1986), #733.

We pray for those who wander from the fold;
O bring them back, Good Shepherd of the sheep,
Back to the Faith which saints believed of old,
Back to the church which still that Faith does keep.
Thus may we all one Bread, one Body be,
Through this blest Sacrament of Unity.

So, Lord, at length when Sacraments shall cease,
May we be one with all your Church above,
One with your saints in one unending peace,
One with Your saints in one unbounded love.
Thus may we all one Bread, one Body be,
Through this blest Sacrament of Unity.

The inclusion of this text is significant—and perhaps even surprising—because it is of Protestant origin and occurs in a Roman Catholic hymnal before the Second Vatican Council was convened.[229] The text preserves the characterization of Church as sacrament of unity. It also includes the shepherd imagery. However, some alterations should be noted. Instead of "longing with heart and soul" that God's will be done, Christians are asking that the Lord renew in their hearts the "law of love." This highlighting of love continues in the second stanza where, instead of praying that "our sad divisions cease"—presumably the divisions caused by heresy or schism—Christians are praying that their "lack of charity may cease." May we assume that this "lack of charity" also refers to Roman Catholic attitudes toward their Protestant brothers and sisters? Nevertheless, unity remains the underlying motif and the Eucharist is celebrated as the sacrament of unity. The final stanza of the hymn is retained as it was published in the 1881 version.

The *Worship* (1986) version of this hymn follows the rendering of the text as published in the 1959 hymnal with one exception. Whereas *Our Parish Prays and Sings* includes the fourth stanza of the hymn intact, *Worship* drops it (see above). The text is eschatological, looking forward as it does to the final age when sacraments themselves will cease to exist. It includes a

---

229   On the other hand, this forward-looking editorial decision is less surprising when one considers that the hymnal was published by Liturgical Press in Collegeville, MN, the center of the Liturgical Movement in the United States.

creedal statement on the Trinity and so concludes with the traditional ending to Christian prayer. Omitting that stanza leaves the *Worship* (1986) version unfinished or incomplete at best. Without singing about the eschatological fulfillment, the text fails to acknowledge that indeed sacraments and the church itself are a means while on the journey, but not the final resting place.

The 2011 hymnals, *Worship* and *Gather*, return to a closer rendering of the original 1881 text.[230]

> Lord, who at your first Eucharist did pray
> That all your Church might be forever one,
> Help us at ev'ry Eucharist to say
> With longing heart and soul, "Your will be done."
> Thus may we all one Bread, one Body be,
> Through this blest Sacrament of Unity.
>
> For all your Church, O Lord, we intercede;
> O make our lack of charity to cease.
> Draw us the nearer each to each, we plead,
> By drawing all to you, O Prince of Peace.
> Thus may we all one Bread, one Body be,
> Through this blest Sacrament of Unity.
>
> We pray for those who wander from your fold;
> O bring them back, Good Shepherd of the sheep,
> Back to the faith which saints believed of old,
> Back to the Church which still that faith does keep.
> Thus may we all one Bread, one Body be,
> Through this blest Sacrament of Unity.
>
> So, Lord, at length when sacraments shall cease,
> May we be one with all your Church above,
> One with your saints in one unbroken peace,
> One with your saints in one unbounded love.
> More blessed still, in peace and love to be
> One with the Trinity in unity.

---

230 "Lord, Who at Your First Eucharist," *Worship* (2011), # 954 and *Gather* (2011), #914.

In comparing this 2011 text with previous renditions, we observe that the first line is rendered more euphonic and archaic language is replaced. The second stanza retains the focus on "lack of charity" from the 1959 text. The most significant change between 1986 and 2011 editions of *Worship* is the return of stanza four. This is a positive move since it once again includes the eschatological vision that in the final age, sacraments shall cease as the Church enters into full unity with the Trinity. Inexplicably, *RitualSong* (2016) omits the fourth stanza once again.

One in Faith (2016) publishes all four stanza of this hymn, using the 1959 version of the first line. *Journeysongs* (2010) includes the fourth stanza and includes two different versions of stanza one. The first is close to the original version, maintaining even the use of the archaic "thy." The alternate is very close to the 1959 version.

"SING A NEW CHURCH"

In addition to the revisions of classic texts, the period following the Second Vatican Council witnessed a resurgence of writing of new texts. One hymn that appears to have caught the imagination of local churches in Roman Catholic communities (and to have incited some controversy) is a text by Delores Dufner, O.S.B., set to the tune NETTLETON. The text was composed in 1991. NETTLETON is a popular American hymn tune in 87 87 D meter in three/four time. It first appears in *Repository of Sacred Music* published by John Wyeth in 1813.

"Sing a New Church" was originally published by Oregon Catholic Press (OCP)[231] and now is also included in *Gather Comprehensive*, 2nd edition (2004),[232] *Gather* (2011), and *Worship* (2011), and *RitualSong* (2016), all published by GIA, and *Journeysongs* (2012) published by OCP. Dufner composed the text at the request of the National Association of Pastoral Ministers (NPM) for the Pittsburgh Convention in 1991. When it was sung for worship at the convention, the assembly sang a tune by composer Peter Jones. Nevertheless, even as she was creating the text, Dufner imagined it sung to the tune NETTLETON. So for the hymn fest scheduled during that

---

231 Since 1991, "Sing a New Church" has appeared regularly in the annual editions of the *Music Issue* and *Breaking Bread*, both published by OCP. However, it was not included in the 2003 edition of *Journeysongs*, 2nd edition. It is now included in *Journeysongs*, 2012.

232 *Gather Comprehensive*, 2nd edition (Chicago: GIA Publications, 2004).

same convention, "Sing a New Church"[233] was sung to NETTLETON at Dufner's request. She believed that NETTLETON communicated a sense of vitality, resilience, and strong commitment that suited her text. It had the additional benefit of being familiar.

Summoned by the God who made us
Rich in our diversity,
Gathered in the name of Jesus,
Richer still in unity:

Refrain:
Let us bring the gifts that differ
And, in splendid, varied ways,
Sing a new church into being,
One in faith and love and praise.

Radiant risen from the water;
Robed in holiness and light,
Male and female in God's image,
Male and female, God's delight; *Refrain*

Trust the goodness of creation;
Trust the Spirit strong within.
Dare to dream the vision promised
Sprung from seed of what has been. *Refrain*

Bring the hopes of ev'ry nation;
Bring the art of ev'ry race.
Weave a song of peace and justice:
Let it sound through time and space. *Refrain*

Draw together at one table
All the human family;
Shape a circle ever wider
And a people ever free. *Refrain*

---

233 "Sing a New Church," *Gather Comprehensive* 2nd edition (2004), #743, *Worship* (2011), #727, *Journeysongs* (2012), #830, and *RitualSong* (2016), #848.

Since Dufner created the text after the Second Vatican Council, it is not surprising that its images of Church are different from those we have looked at earlier in this chapter. Nevertheless, they are rooted firmly in the tradition. A brief review of the primary images in the three hymns already analyzed will serve as an introduction to the differences in the Dufner text.

"Christ Is Made the Sure Foundation" includes images of cornerstone, foundation, and building in its original version. The twentieth-century revision adds the image of Christ as "head" and mentions "grace" in that context. The new version thus moves from a more institutional model to one that includes images of mystical communion. "The Church's One Foundation" is rich in multiple images that correspond to several models of the Church as outlined by Avery Cardinal Dulles. The revision moves away from focusing on the Church's role in fighting heresy to its role as preacher and righter of social ills. "At That First Eucharist" makes the Eucharist rather than Church its primary focus. Unity is the underlying motif and Eucharist is celebrated as *the* sacrament of unity. Images of Church as mystical communion and sacrament are present both in the original and the revisions. However, some revisions omit the eschatological theme as it is expressed in the final stanza.

"Sing a New Church" does not explicitly employ traditional images or models of the Church. The primary metaphor for Church is, in fact, an entity created not out of bricks and stone (foundation), but through the action of singing. The Church is thus portrayed more as a verb than as a noun since it exists as the singing people of God more than a building or city. Perhaps this text at least partially inspired the United States Catholic Conference of Bishops to use this image in their latest document, "Sing to the Lord: Music in Divine Worship," in this way:

> God has bestowed upon his people the gift of song. God dwells within each human person, in the place where music takes its source. Indeed, God, the giver of song, is present whenever his people sing his praises.[234]

---

234 STL, #1.

Immediately after this article, the bishops speak more directly of the role of singing in worship:

> Music is therefore a sign of God's love for us and of our love for him. In this sense, it is very personal. But unless music sounds, it is not music, and whenever it sounds, it is accessible to others. By its very nature song has both an individual and a communal dimension. Thus it is no wonder that singing together in church expresses so well the sacramental presence of God to his people.[235]

The article claims—and rightly so—that singing together, not only *in* church, but *as* Church, is an action that possesses sacramental power, a power it possesses because it is symbolizing activity.

While "singing" is the primary metaphor for church, this action verb is part of a larger array of strong verbs in the Dufner text. The presence of these strong verbs gives the text an energy that is not easy to replicate with nouns or even adjectives. Some of the verbs are passive since they describe God's action on the Church: "summoned," "gathered," "robed." The first two describe our call to be Church and the third makes reference to baptism, our initiation into the Church. Other verbs include the call to "bring" gifts, "trust," "dream," "weave," and "sound." There is a play on the alternating experiences of diversity and unity, varied and one, maleness and femaleness. Other, more traditional images include water, light, and seed. The image of weaving a song brings two dimensions together, sight and sound, tapestry and music. The movement of the text finally reaches its climax when the singing draws everyone together at the one table, characterizing the Church as a circle that encompasses all the human family.

This energy and activity depicts the Church as dynamic rather than static. It is what enables Dufner to describe the Church as "new." It is a breathing, growing body of people, living in the Spirit. The eschatological vision she poetically depicts echoes the language of the Book of Revelation (21:1–5a) when it declares:

---

235 STL, #2.

Then I saw a new heaven and a new earth; for the first heaven and the first earth had passed away, and the sea was no more. And I saw the holy city, the new Jerusalem, coming down out of heaven from God, prepared as a bride adorned for her husband. And I heard a loud voice from the throne saying, "See, the home of God is among mortals. He will dwell with them; they will be his peoples, and God himself will be with them; he will wipe every tear from their eyes. Death will be no more; mourning and crying and pain will be no more, for the first things have passed away." And the one seated on the throne said, "See, I am making all things new."

The church that sings this song and which is described in this text is itself a part of this prophetic vision. The Spirit continually makes all things new so that in the final eschatological consummation of all things, rising from the waters of baptism and robed in God's light, the entire human family, seated at the final banquet, will truly be one and free.

THE ECCLESIOLOGY OF TAIZÉ

Any discussion of how singing expresses and shapes an ecclesiology needs to include at least a brief consideration of the singing at the pilgrimage site in Taizé, France.[236] Many parish communities are familiar with such pieces as "Jesus, Remember Me," "Eat This Bread," "Ubi Caritas," and "Veni, Sancte Spiritus" by Jacques Berthier. Some may have even participated in a "Taizé Prayer around the Cross." However, most may be unfamiliar with the history and theology of this well-crafted, but highly accessible, music.

In order to understand the significance of the ministry of the Taizé community and their unique worship music, we begin by reviewing a brief history of their beginnings. Taizé is a small village nestled in the Burgundian Hills of eastern France. Jacques Berthier (1923–1994), Parisian organist and composer, originally composed the music that is sung at this pilgrimage site. Today, other members of the community have anonymously created new

---

236 See Kubicki, *Liturgical Music as Ritual Symbol*, for a fuller treatment of the history, music, and theology of Taizé music.

chants[237] in the style of Berthier. A limited number of works by other outside composers, including Joseph Gelineau, are also sung for worship. While the ecumenical community began shortly after World War II, Taizé as a pilgrimage site developed slowly after the Second Vatican Council. In fact, Brother Roger Louis Schutz-Marsauche (1915–2005) and a few of his brothers were observers at the council and enthusiastically embraced both its liturgical theology and its ecclesiology. They also participated in several assemblies of the World Council of Churches and engaged in several dialogues with Athenagoras, Patriarch of the Ecumenical Orthodox Church from 1948–1972. The community itself is ecumenical and includes brothers from Protestant, Roman Catholic and Orthodox backgrounds. Their worship incorporates Sacred Scripture, Eucharist, and Orthodox iconography in an effort to symbolize the Christian unity for which they prayer and work each day.

When the community initially began, Brother Roger's intention was to offer reconciliation and hospitality to a war-torn Europe. While ecumenism was an important aspect of the brothers' mission, reaching out in reconciliation and hospitality to all who were isolated and alienated in society was also a priority. At first, small groups of visitors joined the brothers for prayer in their small church. Eventually, however, the number of visitors grew and could not be accommodated in the tiny worship space. A German organization called *Sühnezeichen* (sign of reconciliation) assisted in the building of a new church, the great Church of Reconciliation. The building itself is designed to accommodate small and large groups of visitors. Centrally located, it serves as the heart and center of life at the pilgrimage site.

In addition to welcoming visitors to prayer at the Great Church of Reconciliation, the community also began sponsoring global gatherings called "councils of youth." After the first such meeting (1974), Brother Robert Giscard (1922–1993), at the recommendation of Joseph Gelineau, S. J. (1920–2008), approached Jacques Berthier for assistance in creating music that would serve large polyglot groups of youth. True to the inspiration of

---

237 The French publication *Célébrer* has referred to Taizé music as "*les chants de Taizé.*" For this reason, I refer to Berthier's music as chants rather than songs (*chansons*). However, the use of "chants" is not intended to equate his metered style with the unmetered monophonic style often referred to plainsong or Gregorian chant. However, chant was a significant aspect of Berthier's education in church music. He explicitly acknowledged it as the inspiration for his own compositions. Perhaps the designation of Berthier's Taizé music as chants aptly links his work to the chant-like mantras of the East because of their brevity and repetition.

Vatican II, the brothers' priority was the active participation of all their guests in their sung prayer. This was a serious challenge given the diversity of languages, cultures, and religious traditions of the young pilgrims.

Since the days of collaboration between Giscard and Berthier, the community has sought to provide sung prayer that would invite pilgrims to participate wholeheartedly—with both heart and voice—in its worship. No one chant expresses this overarching mission. Rather, the entire corpus of music that was created specifically for this worship experience, structures the prayer and daily life of the pilgrims. How does it do this?

First of all, the liturgical songs of Berthier and Giscard consist of both quality texts and quality music. Berthier was a classically trained church musician. Giscard worked with him and with the community that actually sang the songs to ensure that the texts were not only of the highest quality, but also accessible to the worshipers and ecumenically sensitive. In this sense, the music was provisional. Often a piece of music would undergo several revisions before a suitable version was achieved. Even after it was published, revisions were possible down the road when new insights were received.[238] In a significant way, the assembly is the foundation of the sung prayer—not the instruments, the cantors, or choir.

The singing of Jacques Berthier's Taizé music serves as symbolizing activity for the pilgrimage experience. As symbolic activity, it negotiates identity and relationships by breaking down barriers of language, nationality, race, economic status, social status, and denomination. The specific texts are scripturally based, devoid of denominational associations, and hospitable. These characteristics, as well as their brevity and repetitive nature, invite participation. All of this embodies, expresses, and shapes a theology of church that supports Christian unity, promotes reconciliation, and models a discipleship of equals. It happens because of the quality of the traditional texts chosen, the accessibility of the music, and focus on enabling participation.

The music of Taizé falls into one of four categories: ostinato chorales, litanies, acclamations, and canons. Perhaps one of the clearest examples of

---

238 A good example of a text that was amended even after its first publication is "Bless the Lord." The original text was "Bless the Lord my soul and bless his holy name. Bless the Lord my soul, who rescues me from death." Later, the text read "Bless the Lord my soul and bless God's holy name. Bless the Lord my soul, who leads me into life."

the ecumenical focus and reconciliatory intent of Taizé sung prayer is the quiet, but insistent ostinato:

> There is one Lord, one faith one baptism;
> there is one God, who is Father of all.[239]

This text, based on Ephesians 4, highlights the common unity rather than divisions that exist among the various Christian churches. The singers voice the words "Lord," "faith," "God," and "all" on the longest notes (half or dotted half notes) of the melody. None of the voices moves when these notes are sung. The rhythmic movement is, so to speak, in unison. Repeating this ostinato for several minutes of prayer does not appear to create boredom or agitation.[240] Rather, the singing creates a sonic environment in which worshipers have a tangible experience of unity in the act of singing and in the expression of what they believe makes them one. The word "one" is sung four times. God is Father of all. In other words, in the essentials of Christian faith, all are one in God.

In the early days of Christian worship, the language was Latin.[241] Since almost no one knew Latin, it seemed to put everyone on an equal footing. Short, familiar phrases such as "Gloria in excelsis" and "dona nobis pacem" were used. Eventually, however, the community chose instead to employ multiple languages in its worship, now more than twenty! The effort to sing in another person's language can be an act of reaching out to the stranger and an attempt to walk in his/her shoes. In any hour of worship, many languages are sung, thereby offering hospitality over a short time to many language groups. Since there has always been an effort to respect and observe the rhythmic flow of each language, some chants are not set in multiple languages although free translations are sometimes provided. This is particularly true is the latest publications used for prayer at the pilgrimage site itself.

---

239   Music from Taizé, volume II (Les Presses de Taizé, France: GIA Publications, 1982, 1983, 1984), #76.
240   I visited Taizé twice and have also experienced Taizé prayer many times in the United States, sometimes led by one of the Brothers of Taizé, but more frequently led by local communities of various denominations. My own experience and the comments of other participants are reflected in these comments.
241   In the first volume of Taizé music made available in the United States through GIA, only one in a collection of 115 chants was in English. This was "Jesus, Remember Me," an ostinato that was composed originally in English. The great majority of the chants were in Latin, with a few familiar Hebrew of Greek phrases such as Amen, Alleluia, or Kyrie eleison.

Taizé's ecclesiology has consistently informed its efforts to enable the active participation of its pilgrims and promote Christian unity. In this it is a model for how intentional effort can make a difference in the worship life of a community and its visitors. The very act of singing together becomes a vehicle for unity and acceptance of the other. This, indeed, can occur on both the personal and the communal level. Brother Giscard once wrote:

> Using few notes and words, the continuous flow of the refrain expresses something essential: it constantly penetrates further and further into the depth of a person. Early Christianity, it is true, experienced a type of prayer comprised of a few words repeated over and over again as the name of Jesus was invoked to give peace and unity to the depths of one's being. But it is *through singing* (emphasis added), for pastoral reasons, and in a manner we could not have foreseen at the beginning, that we have rediscovered a similar path. What once mediated individual prayer is now experienced as means of communion with others.[242]

Without attempting to mimic what happens at Taizé, every local assembly that examines the actual dynamics of its sung prayer, its goals and motivation, might learn much about its own theology of church. Indeed, such an exercise might be a creative and enlivening way to re-energize a parish's spirituality through its music program. Efforts to work intentionally to be ecumenically sensitive and open to diversity begin not only with an individual hymn, but also with the contents of the repertoire as a whole. It is also determined by the way the assembly is invited to take up their baptismal responsibility to raise up the world to God in prayer.

Observations

Perhaps the detailed analysis of this chapter has left the reader dizzy or at least wondering about the purpose of all of this close textual reading. Although it would be impossible to make generalizations regarding hymnody on the topic

---

242 Brother Robert, "Taizé Music...A History," *Pastoral Music* (February–March 1987), 21.

of Church from the small sampling included here, there are some significant observations that may be made concerning the materials covered. Firstly, the singing of hymns by the assembly is part of the ritual activity that constitutes the singers as Church. This is important and integral activity and it is rooted in baptism. It is not icing on the cake. Secondly, hymnody on the topic of church is a venerable and ancient tradition in the Church. It is part of our history and provides rich insights into understanding who we are. Thirdly, those hymns that have been an important part of our tradition draw their inspiration both from Scripture and from the Church's professions of faith. In every age, however, they may need some dusting off and tuning up so that they continue to speak to us and to the world. Fourthly, questions of dogma or shifts of emphasis in theology are reflected in hymn texts and the editorial decisions of hymnal publishers. Many of these shifts are responses to the signs of the times and require careful discernment. Fifthly, those hymns that possess the richest imagery and reflect a variety of images for church provide for a broader usage and versatility. Our spirituality and our theology need such richness. Sixthly, that very variety and versatility signals the fact that no one image or symbol has the power to capture the nature of the Church in its totality. After all, there are four Gospels of Jesus Christ. No one of them tells the entire story. Finally, the Taizé corpus teaches us that we do not necessarily become one by singing about unity. Rather, the very act of singing together, attentiveness to the other, a willingness to walk in another shoes (or sing in another's native tongue) can be far more effective vehicles for promoting unity, reconciliation, and respect.

We are, in the final analysis, caught up in symbols and images set in motion within ritual activity—symbols and images that are essentially open. As cited above, the closing chapters of the Book of Revelation set out the nature and structure of the Church in images of the New Jerusalem. Its poetry escapes the categories of any single theological system or legislative code. For both rational speculation and law reach their limit before the openness of images. Indeed, past and present images can generate fresh images into the future. The reality is that trying to capture mystery in images can never be fully achieved.[243] What we, as Church, can only hope to do in the face of

---

243 Tavard, *The Church*, 93.

this mystery is to continue to sing. In this way, we offer our humble, but confident assent to mystery with a resounding "Amen!" This we continue to do, even when it is not always easy.

Perhaps not every hymn is up to the task, but certainly the classics enable us to engage in divine and human mystery. The next chapter will begin by exploring what it means to claim that a hymn is a classic. It will also examine how hymn singing has the power to actually accomplish an action, disclose reality, and transform the assembly both on an individual and communal level.

CHAPTER 5

PERFORMATIVE AND TRANSFORMATIVE POWER
OF CLASSIC HYMN TEXTS

WHAT IS A CLASSIC?

Thus far we have been looking at what might be referred to as "traditional" hymn texts. However, we have not yet explored the meaning of the word "classic" that is often closely associated with the characteristic label "traditional." In this chapter, we will focus on the performative and transformative power of classic hymn texts within liturgical celebrations. We often have an intuitive grasp of what we mean when we call a movie, a song, a novel, or a play "classic." However, it is helpful to identity specific qualities or characteristics so that we have common ground or criteria for judging whether or not a hymn might be a classic.

The writings of twentieth-century thinkers Hans-Georg Gadamer and David Tracy can assist our exploration of the meaning of the term "classic." Gadamer defines a classic as that which transcends changing times and changing tastes. It is therefore something enduring, something whose significance cannot be lost, a kind of timeless present. Perhaps one of the most important aspects of a classic is its normativity. It sets the standard for others in its category, is self-significant and hence self-interpretive. A classic speaks in such a way that it is not simply a statement about the past, but rather has something to say to the present. It can do this because of a timeless quality that has to do with the fact that a classic, because it touches the heart of the human experience, transcends generations, cultures, changing tastes, and the vicissitudes of time. Furthermore, in its category or class, it represents excellence of its kind.[244]

Tracy explains classic in this way: "We all find ourselves compelled both to recognize and on occasion to articulate our reasons for the recognition that certain expressions of the human spirit so disclose a compelling truth about our lives that we cannot deny them some kind of normative status. Thus do we name these expressions, and these alone, 'classics.'"[245] By using the term "classic" we acknowledge that there is such a thing as a normative element in our cultural experience, experienced as a realized truth. When we name certain texts, events, persons, music, art, movies, rituals, or symbols "classic," we recognize nothing less than the disclosure of a reality we cannot but name truth. When this happens, there is a moment of recognition that surprises, provokes, challenges, even shocks and eventually transforms us. Such an experience can turn conventional opinions upside down and expand our sense of the possible.[246] The classic, with its two notes of permanence and excess of meaning, always demands interpretation, never mere repetition nor simplistic rejection. The interpreter must risk being caught up in, even being played by, the questions and answers—the subject matter—of the classic. And, where both form and subject matter are of major significance—where the truth of existence is engaged, indeed is at stake—the risk is greater, and the result will prove not so much refreshing as transformative.[247]

Before moving on to a consideration of a "religious" classic and specifically, a classic hymn, it may be helpful to explore some examples of classics that might embody some of the characteristics of which Gadamer and Tracy speak. When it comes to works that transcend changing times and tastes, the plays of William Shakespeare come to mind. The story of the star-crossed lovers in *Romeo and Juliet* and the fall of such tragic heroes as Hamlet and Macbeth continue to speak to new generations because they speak to the heart of human experience. The same can be said for Victor

---

244 Hans-Georg Gadamer, *Truth and Method*, second revised edition (New York: Continuum, 1993), 286–290. See also Webster's Dictionary.
245 Tracy, 108.
246 David Tracy, *The Analogical Imagination: Christian Theology and the Culture of Pluralism* (New York: Crossroads, 1981),108–110.
247 Tracy, 154.

Hugo's *Les Misérables* and Charles Dickens' *A Christmas Carol* or L. Frank Baum's *The Wizard of Oz*. Classics also possess the qualities of excellence and normativity. That means that within their class or category, they have consistently been judged excellent or outstanding so much so that they set the standard that other works in that category strive to measure up to or emulate. In the field of classic music, the works of J. S. Bach, Beethoven, Mozart, Leonard Bernstein, and Benjamin Britten come to mind. In the category of popular music, we think of the songs of the Irving Berlin, Frank Sinatra, Elvis Presley, the Beatles, Carole King, and Bruce Springsteen. In the field of the visual arts, we think of Leonardo Da Vinci, Rembrandt, Vincent Van Gogh, Henry Moore, Frank Lloyd Wright, Claude Monet, Georgia O'Keefe, and Ansel Adams. In the field of movies, many of the great classics are movies based on classic novels. A few others worth mentioning include *It's a Wonderful Life, Citizen Kane, Going My Way*, and *The Sound of Music*. We could go on naming classic works and those who created them. The point is that every classic, no matter when it was created, has something to say to the present about what it means to be human and does it in an excellent way. When we encounter such classics, we experience the disclosure of a compelling truth that surprises, provokes, challenges, shocks, and even changes us.[248] Perhaps most of us can personally attest to this about some of the classics mentioned above.

For the Christian, the person of Jesus Christ is a classic and the event of his birth, death, and resurrection are all classic events. Because of their classic status, we are able to celebrate such holydays as Christmas and Easter every year. Throughout the centuries, poets, composers, artists, and storytellers do not simply repeat the narrative details of these events in Christian history. Rather, they strive to reinterpret and re-engage their meaning for us in the present moment. In fact, the history of the interpretation of these events is the way Christians continue to wrestle with the meaning and implications of these classics.

The Bible is the religious classic *par excellence* for Christians. Arranged and excerpted to celebrate the liturgical feasts and seasons, its readings are contained in the Lectionary used for the celebration of the Eucharist. Many

---

248 See Tracy, 108–110.

Christian churches follow the Sunday readings arranged in a three-year cycle while daily readings are arranged in a two-year cycle.[249] For some major solemnities such as Christmas, the Triduum, and Easter the assigned readings are the same for all three cycles. The point is that over a lifetime, we listen to biblical texts proclaimed year in and year out. Nevertheless, while the readings may become very familiar, we are different each time we hear them. Each proclamation addresses a unique moment in the history of our life in relationship with God, other people, and our own selves. In a similar way, the local church proclaiming and breaking open the Scriptures continues to grow and change and understand the Word of God within new horizons of life experience and growth in the Spirit. So yes, the story of the raising of Lazarus is heard in a new way after the death of a loved one and Advent readings resonate more deeply with a woman who is pregnant. That is the power and richness of classic biblical texts.

When we speak of a religious classic, whether a lectionary reading or a classic hymn text, it discloses that which appears to exist beyond the limits or horizon of human experience. In this case, the classic hymn text involves a claim to meaning and to truth that is simultaneously an event of disclosure and concealment of the reality of lived existence. We sense there is more to discover, yet the mystery is never completely grasped.[250] Unlike classics in other areas such as art, science, and politics, religious classics involve a claim to truth *by the power of the whole*. That claim to truth discloses, in some sense, a radical and ultimately gracious mystery.[251] Thus religious classics, like classics in general, speak to the experience of being human. But in the case of the religious classic, the focus of that human experience is on those elements that nudge us (sometimes impel us) to look, feel, and desire beyond our day-to-day human existence. That is what we mean when we speak of "limit," "horizon," or "ground" side of religion. Furthermore, there are classics that some might not label "religious" but also have the potential speak to us about ultimate reality. In this way, we can say that any

---

249 I am speaking here specifically about the lectionary practices of the Roman Catholic Church. However, many Christian churches observe the common lectionary that was created after the liturgical reforms of the Second Vatican Council. In the three-year cycle, Sunday readings appear every three years, except for some solemnities. The years are designated "A," "B," and "C." The two-year weekday cycle is designated "I" and "II." This allows for the use of more Scripture in the Lectionary.
250 Tracy, 163.
251 Tracy, 163.

classic may have some religious dimension if, in fact, a classic, by definition, discloses some aspect of realized truth that changes us.

Both Gadamer and Tracy offer important insights for exploring the transformative power of classic Christian hymns. However, before developing this insight further, we will consider the implications of performative language theory and its contribution to understanding not only the power of the Christian hymn, but also the power of *singing* the Christian hymn.

Hymn Singing as a Performative Speech Act

Under ordinary circumstances, classic Christian hymns are part of a larger event we call ritual or more specifically, liturgical worship. The anthropologist Victor Turner describes ritual as a combination of articulate speech and purposeful action.[252] His definition will assist in considering hymn singing an example of a ritual speech act. In this section, let us consider two questions: (1) How does the singing of hymn texts within the liturgy possess performative power? and (2) How does this performative power potentially enable hymn singing to be transformative?

In his groundbreaking work in performative language theory, J. L. Austin makes the bold claim that the uttering of a sentence can be the doing of an action.[253] His point is that saying something could actually accomplish something. Others after Austin, including G. J. Warnock and John R. Searle, further examined Austin's theory and nuanced his claims. So, for example, Warnock's own analysis concludes that "*sometimes* saying is doing."[254] This would support the assertion that, in certain instances, language as action takes precedence over language as assertion. In other words, meaning can be found, not only in assertion, but also embedded in a field of humanly significant actions.[255] John Searle's research on performative language theory led him to acknowledge that in certain instances utterances possess the power to effect what has been stated. Furthermore, this "power to effect" is produced not simply by words or word order, but also by deep

---

252 Victor Turner, "Process, System, and Symbol: A New Anthropological Synthesis," *On the Edge of the Bush: Anthropology as Experience*, ed. Edith L. B. Turners (Tucson: The University of Arizona Press, 1985), 151.
253 John Langshaw Austin, *How to Do Things with Words* (Cambridge, MA: Harvard University Press, 1962), 5.
254 Geoffrey James Warnock, "Some Types of Performative Utterance," in *Essays on J. L. Austin*, ed. Isaiah Berlin, et al. (London: Oxford University Press, 1973), 69.
255 Lawrence Kramer, *Music as Cultural Practice, 1800–1900* (Berkeley: University of California Press, 1990), 6.

syntactic structure, stress, and intonation contour.[256] This insight opens up the possibility for a discussion of the performative power of hymn singing. The musical setting in combination with words heightens the power of the words to *do something* in the singing of the hymn because of the presence of melody or pitch, rhythm, and meter. For this reason, the performative power of congregational singing is uniquely positioned since the combination of words and music provide the possibility of accomplishing something in the very act of singing. This is a perfect example of what Searle is referring to when he speaks of deep syntactic structure, stress, and intonation contour. When music is combined with text in the case of a hymn, the performative power and theological meaning is potentially enhanced.

Finally, Jacques Derrida's critique of Austin's speech act theory adds an important corrective when he points out that, in order to function at all, a speech act must be iterable, that is, repeatable This means that a speech act is capable of functioning in a new situation, different from the occasion of its original production, and with new persons not originally involved. Our earlier consideration of the definition of a classic reminds us that this repeatability is always a new event of insight and interpretation. Since by its very nature ritual functions as a repeatable event, it is possible to say that hymn singing within ritual has the potential to be a performative speech act.

Because J. L. Austin's work acknowledges that the purpose of language goes beyond the simple utterance of propositions, it has contributed significantly to ritual studies. Wade T. Wheelock has taken Austin's theory and Searle's development of it and applied it specifically to the study of ritual language. Recall that, by definition, propositional statements communicate information. Ritual utterances, on the other hand, are speech acts that usually contain little or no information. Rather, they are meant to create and allow participation in a known and repeatable situation. Instead of information, repetition is the norm and metaphors and ambiguity abound. Because of this, we can conclude that the language of ritual must be primarily understood and described as *situating* rather than *informing* speech. In other words, speaking or singing the texts presents the situation, expresses and actually helps to create the situation, and/

---

256 John R. Searle, "Austin on Locutionary and Illocutionary Acts," in *Essays on J. L. Austin*, ed. Isaiah Berlin, et al. (London: Oxford University Press, 1973), 151.

or facilitates the recognition of the situation. This is the case with the Taizé repertoire, particularly the original music composed by Jacques Berthier.[257] At the pilgrimage site in Taizé, France, participants sing brief ostinati, chorales, acclamations, or litanies in a repetitive manner, often lasting several minutes. This practice enables the singers themselves to create the sonic environment in which they are situated. The sonorous harmonies delineate the space of prayer and express attitudes of praise, thanksgiving, petition, contrition, and reflection. The ostinato entitled "Wait for the Lord"[258] by Jacques Berthier is a good example. The brief text is simple, easily learned and memorized:

> Wait for the Lord, whose day is near.
> Wait for the Lord: be strong, take heart!

The text captures one of the fundamental postures of the Christian in the Advent season—patient waiting. The assembly repeats the ostinato for several minutes, while a cantor may sing stanzas over the assembly's song. The expansiveness of the harmonies opens up the actual physical space and also the space within the singer so that waiting for the Lord may be experienced in its fundamental openness and emptiness. In other words, the singing of "Wait for the Lord" situates the singers in a space of waiting and openness that is both physical and spiritual.

Furthermore, as Derrida points out, situating speech has the capacity to be repeated. That is why the ritual music sung at Taizé can be sung in new situations or contexts. The purpose is not to replicate the experience at the pilgrimage site, but to experience the Taizé repertoire in new ways in new places. In fact, every time we gather for worship, we are entering a new situation and experiencing a new event. So it is important that the ritual music, in this case hymnody, be iterable or repeatable. Some examples may help clarify this point.

Recall that we are looking at the act of hymn singing as a ritual speech act. When we sing the "Gloria" at Sunday Mass (a grand and ancient classic doxology), the purpose of singing it is not to provide information. We all know the text and embrace the tenets of faith that it expresses about the

---

257 See chapter four for a fuller discussion of Taizé music.
258 "Wait for the Lord," *Worship* (2011), #410.

Trinity. The 2002 translation of the "Gloria"[259] from the Roman Missal is offered here for review:

> Glory to God in the highest,
> And on earth peace to people of good will.
> We praise you, we bless you, we adore you, we glorify you,
> we give you thanks for your great glory,
> Lord God, heavenly King, O God, almighty Father.
> Lord Jesus Christ, Only Begotten Son,
> Lord God, Lamb of God, Son of the Father,
> you take away the sins of the world, have mercy on us;
> you take away the sins of the world, receive our prayer;
> you are seated at the right hand of the Father, have mercy on us.
> For you alone are the Holy One, you alone are the Lord,
> you alone are the Most High, Jesus Christ,
> with the Holy Spirit, in the glory of God the Father. Amen.

As a speech act, the singing of the "Gloria" is repeated on most Sundays. The singing of the text situates the assembly in a sonic environment of praise into which we are caught up or drawn into. Somehow, we find ourselves capable of doing this over and over again. Nothing new is really learned, but the singing of the "Gloria" creates the situation of praise and also facilitates our ability to perceive what we are doing as an act of praise. The singing of the "Gloria" is performative. By repeatedly singing the "Gloria," the assembly, and each individual member of it, is transformed into a people of praise. We become people of praise in the act of praising. Furthermore, we can say that another outcome of the performance is that the Trinitarian God is indeed praised.

Let us take a look at a classic Easter carol as another example. "The Strife Is O'er" is a translation of a twelfth-century Latin text that is usually sung today to the tune VICTORY (888 with refrain) adapted from Palestrina's music written in the sixteenth century. What is immediately apparent is the repetition of the word "Alleluia!" The hymn includes a total of twenty-three

---

259 From the *Roman Missal*, English Translation According to the Third Typical Edition, 2011. (Collegeville, MN: Liturgical Press, 2011).

repetitions of that one word! Certainly if one were looking for economy of words to communicate information, this would not be the ideal text. But the text is not propositional. Rather, it is performative and situating. Let us take a close look at "The Strife Is O'er" to see how this occurs.[260]

Refrain:
Alleluia, alleluia, alleluia!

The strife is o'er, the battle done;
Now is the Victor's triumph won!
Songs of rejoicing have begun. Alleluia! *Refrain*

The pow'rs of death have done their worst;
But Christ their legions has dispersed.
Let shouts of holy joy outburst. Alleluia! *Refrain*

On the third day Christ rose again,
Glorious in majesty to reign.
O let us swell the joyful strain. Alleluia! *Refrain*

He closed the yawning gates of hell;
The bars from heav'n's high portals fell.
Let hymns of praise his triumph tell. Alleluia! *Refrain*

Lord, by the stripes which wounded you.
Free from death's sting your servants too,
That we may live and sing to you. Alleluia! *Refrain*

Notice that the text includes similar battle imagery to that found in "A Mighty Fortress," examined in chapter three. Again, the *"Christus Victor"* motif is a strong theme often found in classic Christian texts. But what exactly happens when a hymn such as this is sung at the Easter Vigil, on Easter Sunday morning, one of the Sundays of Easter, or at a funeral? Certainly the text is not *informing* the singing assembly that Christ is risen from the dead. Neither is its purpose to convince doubters that Christ's resurrection really

---

260   "The Strife Is O'er," *Worship*, 2011, #511.

happened. For the most part, the assembly knows and believes the story of the Resurrection; they have come to celebrate it. Within the ritual event of the liturgy, the hymn is not experienced as propositional or informational. It is, rather, a ritual act whereby the assembly expresses its joy and its faith in the resurrection of Christ, in the fact that Christ's death and resurrection conquered death forever, and that our own resurrection has been sealed with the re-opening of the gates of heaven. The claim that the assembly is familiar with the Easter Mystery, however, does not diminish the hymn's role as a reminder or act of remembrance. In the midst of our busy lives, even the most committed Christian occasionally needs reminding of the centrality and foundational aspect of the Paschal Mystery to the Christian faith. Easter brings this sacred mystery to mind in "bold print, large font." Remembrance is an integral aspect of liturgical worship. We need to pause and remember what Christ has done and continues to do in our daily lives. We need to remember Christ's promise of our own resurrection in light of his own.

Therefore, if done well, the singing of this song "performs" or expresses the joy that is experienced in this knowledge and in this remembrance. It is not the knowledge that comes from a book. Instead, it is the knowledge that comes from deep faith and deep emotion that is felt and expressed through one's very breath and in one's very bones. It is appropriately expressed by repeating, over and over again, to a tune that soars and harmonies that resound with depth, the joy of being saved by Jesus Christ. The melody, the rhythm, and the meter all contribute to the sonic environment within which the assembly is worshiping. That sonic environment is further delineated by repetition of the word "alleluia." Indeed, this repetition is a key aspect of the hymn's power for expressing joy and celebration. Because singing the alleluia requires neither memorization nor the use of a hymnal, it can draw the assembly into the hymn almost irresistibly.

Jean Ladrière speaks of this as an important aspect of the performativity of liturgical language. He explains that a performative activity (e.g., singing the "Gloria" or "The Strife Is O'er,") awakens in the person singing a certain affective disposition that opens up existence to a specific field of reality. An effect is produced. We speak an attitude. In the case of the hymns examined above, the attitude is one of joyful praise. The same can be said for such hymns as "Joyful, Joyful We Adore You," "Hark! The Herald Angels Sing," "Jesus Christ Is Risen Today," "Holy God We Praise Thy Name," "The Canticle of the Sun," and countless others. This is not to say that an individual is always disposed to the attitude that is being sung. Everyone is a congregation may not be joyful on a particular Sunday morning when a joyful hymn of praise is the gathering or entrance hymn. Nevertheless, like the small child who is repeatedly reminded by his parents to say "thank you," the Christian disposition of joyful praise is learned over time until it becomes a fundamental Christian affection.[261]

Secondly, the effect of singing the hymn not only disposes individuals, but also constitutes a community. That is, singing the hymn is the activity whereby the community is constituted. This is specifically one of the purposes of an assembly's singing the gathering and the communion processional. The *General Instruction of the Roman Missal* (GIRM 2002) makes this clear when it states in article 47: "The purpose of this chant [entrance chant or hymn] is to open the celebration, foster the unity of those who have been gathered, introduce their thoughts to the mystery of the liturgical season or festivity, and accompany the procession of the priest and ministers." Regarding the communion procession GIRM 2002, article 86 states: "Its [communion chant's or hymn's] purpose is to express the communicants' union in spirit by means of the unity of their voices, to show joy of heart, and to highlight more clearly the 'communitarian' nature of the procession to receive Communion." One of the underlying understandings of both of these articles is the fact that *the singing itself* aids in situating the assembly in an experience of unity during the entrance and communion processions.

Notice also that the documents quoted above make reference to the unity of spirit, mind, heart, and voice. In other words, the experience is not only spiritual or mental, but also physical. Through the participation of our bodies, whether it is singing or listening, or moving to the rhythms of the hymns, we have a concrete (physical) and real (mental or spiritual) experience of unity. Both processional hymns are meant to bring the assembly together in a common sentiment whether praise, petition, contrition, thanksgiving, etc.

---

261   This point will be addressed more fully at the close of this chapter in Don Saliers' discussion of the value of repetition.

That is, the language makes present for the participants, the assembly, that about which it speaks and also affects in diverse ways. Again, this is done not as spectacle, but as a tangible reality.[262]

To summarize, we can say that the focus of performative language theory is on language as an activity, not on language as an object. Liturgical singing—as a combination of language and speech—is doing an action, it is situating speech in a unique and powerful way.

The hymn "Come, You Sinners, Poor and Needy"[263] is a good example of this phenomenon. Joseph Hart wrote the stanzas in the eighteenth century. The author of the refrain, however, is anonymous. In the twentieth century, George E. Mims arranged the tune, RESTORATION, originally from *Southern Harmony*.

> Come, you sinners, poor and needy,
> Weak and wounded, sick and sore,
> Jesus, Son of God, will save you,
> Full of pity, love, and pow'r.
>
> *Refrain:*
> *I will arise and go to Jesus,*
> *He will embrace me in his arms;*
> *In the arms of my dear Savior,*
> *Oh, there are ten thousand charms.*
>
> Come, you thirsty, come and welcome,
> God's free bounty glorify;
> True belief and true repentance,
> Ev'ry grace that brings you nigh. *Refrain*
>
> Come, you weary, heavy laden,
> Lost and ruined by the fall;
> If you tarry till you're better,
> You will never come at all. *Refrain*

---

262 Jean Ladrière, "The Performativity of Liturgical Language," *Liturgical Experience of Faith*, ed. H. Schmidt and David N. Power, Concilium series, no. 82 (New York: Herder and Herder, 1973), 55–59.
263 "Come, You Sinners, Poor and Needy," *Worship* (2011), #962.

Performance or movement is an inherent quality of this text. The stanzas are an invitation to come, to approach God's throne of grace through Jesus Christ. The refrain is a response in the positive that replies "yes, I am coming," "yes, I trust," "yes, I believe." The tune is set in common meter so that the singers are physically situated in a rhythm of walking by means of their singing. In addition, the use of alliteration creates another dimension to the sonic environment. The repetition of the "w" in "weak and wounded," of "s" in "sick and sore," of "p" in "pity, love, and pow'r" contribute to a heightened sense of the poetry. The use of repetition of the word "come" at the beginning of each stanza creates a sense of encouragement and longing on the part of Jesus, while the refrain's affirmative response "I will arise and go to Jesus" situates the singers in a sonic environment that has positive responsive energy.

Some might be tempted to criticize the text for the use of "I" instead of "we" at the beginning of the refrain. However, the sum total effect of the text is clearly communal even though each individual makes his or her own response. Lastly, the images in the hymn text speak to our common human experience. The poor and needy anticipate the Lord's embrace, the thirsty are offered God's bounty, the weary, heavily laden, lost, and ruined are invited to come as they are. Thus, by performing the Lord's invitation in the singing of the hymn, and by repeatedly performing a positive response in the refrain, the singing assembly is enabled to express the religious sentiments of the song and experience their faith in God's mercy both individually and communally. Indeed, the assembly is actively engaged in the tensive energy created by what the hymn performs: Christ's persistent invitation, the acknowledgement of need for Christ's restorative mercy, and the confident response of the sinner.

We have briefly discussed how performative language theory might assist in interpreting the dynamic that occurs when a singing assembly wholeheartedly engages in singing and how this singing actually accomplishes the doing of an action. In the next section, we will explore how the insights of phenomenology can assist us in understanding the dynamic of "disclosure" that occurs when the assembly sings.

Disclosure

When we try to perceive reality from within a phenomenological attitude, we look at things as they are manifested or *disclosed* to us. In other words, we begin to look at things in their truth and in their evidencing. At the same time we begin to experience our own person as the self to whom beings or truth are disclosed. In his book, *Introduction to Phenomenology*, Robert Sokolowski describes human beings as "datives of manifestation."[264] By this he simply means that we as human beings are the ones "to whom the world and all the things in it can be given" the ones "who can receive the world in knowledge." In another place, Sokolowski asserts the importance of allowing "a thing to manifest itself to us."[265]

In the context of phenomenology, the word "evidence" is understood, not so much as proof of innocence or guilt, truth or falsehood, but as a verb—evidencing. Evidencing here means to bring about the truth or bring forth a presence. It can be understood as both performance and articulation of a state of affairs. In other words, it is a veritable "event" in the life of human beings. This "eventing" enables a person or persons to "get the point" or "see what is going on."

On the theological level, of course, we know that when the community gathers for worship, one of its primary roles is to "evidence" the presence of Christ in the assembly. This dynamic belongs to the assembly as gathered, even apart from the presence of Christ in the sacred elements. As article 7 of *Sacrosanctum Concilium* (Constitution on the Sacred Liturgy) makes clear,

> To accomplish so great a work Christ is always present in his church, especially in liturgical celebrations. He is present in the sacrifice of the Mass both in the person of his minister, "the same now offering, through the ministry of priests, who formerly offered himself on the cross," and most of all in the eucharistic species. By his power he is present in the

---

264   When Sokolowski uses the term "dative" he is observing its grammatical meaning. The dative is a grammatical case of a word that is either the indirect object of a verb or the object of a preposition. For example, something is manifested, shown, or revealed "to" us.

265   Robert Sokolowski, *Introduction to Phenomenology* (Cambridge, UK: Cambridge University Press, 2000), 44, 64–65, 93. See also Kubicki, *The Presence of Christ*, 29–30.

sacraments so that when anybody baptizes it is really Christ himself who baptizes. He is present in his word since it is he himself who speaks when the holy scriptures are read in church. Lastly, he is present when the church prays and sings, for he has promised "where two or three are gathered in my name there am I in the midst of them" (Mt 18:20).[266]

Thus the gathered assembly manifests the presence of Christ while at the same time it receives or is the dative of manifestation of that presence. Likewise, the singing assembly manifests the presence of Christ through the particulars of the hymn while also receiving a manifestation of Christ by means of the hymn singing.

A good hymn, whether it is ancient or modern, has this ability to disclose truths about God, our community of faith, or us as individuals. The fourth-/fifth-century hymn by Aurelius Prudentius, "Corde natus ex Parentis" is another example of the disclosure that can occur in the singing of a classic hymn. The English translation is "Of the Father's Love Begotten" and it is generally sung to a twelfth-century tune, DIVINUM MYSTERIUM, a chant in Mode V. There is no way to know what the original music may have been. Here is an updated English translation:[267]

> Of the Father's love begotten
> Ere the worlds began to be,
> He is Alpha and Omega,
> He the source, the ending he
> Of the things that are, that have been,
> And that future years shall see,
> Evermore and evermore!
>
> O that birth forever blessed,
> When the Virgin, full of grace,
> Overshadowed by the Spirit,
> Bore the Savior of our race;

---

266   SC no. 7.
267   "Of the Father's Love Begotten," *Worship* (2011), #415.

And the babe, the world's redeemer,
First revealed his sacred face,
Evermore and evermore!

This is he whom seers and sages
Sang of old with one accord,
Whom the voices of the prophets
Promised in their faithful word;
Now he shines, the long-expected;
Let creation praise its Lord
Evermore and evermore!

Let the heights of heav'n adore him;
Angel hosts, his praises sing;
Pow'rs, dominions, bow before him
And extol our God and King;
Let no tongue on earth be silent,
Ev'ry voice in concert ring
Evermore and evermore!

Christ, to you with God the Father,
And the Spirit, One in Three,
Hymn and chant and high thanksgiving
And unwearied praises be:
Honor, glory, and dominion,
And eternal victory,
Evermore and evermore!

One of the keys to the theological meaning of the text is the repetition of the phrase "evermore and evermore." It highlights the notions of time and eternity that are part of the focus of the hymn and introduced in stanza one. As singers or listeners we stand in awe and wonder at what is disclosed to us: God the Father's love, existing from the very beginning and forever. The image of the first and last letter of the Greek alphabet, the alpha and omega, capture this expanse; this love is the source and ending of everything that exists. The hymn's poetry echoes, in part, John's Prologue (Jn 1:1–18): "In the beginning was the Word, and the Word was with God and the Word was God" (Jn 1:1).

Stanza two continues the story. The Father's love becomes incarnate of the Virgin Mary through the power of the Spirit. This babe is Savior or Redeemer of the entire human race. The focus shifts to the mystery of the Incarnation: the face of God's love is revealed in the face of a baby. God's love is disclosed in a way that we can see and experience it in our own human flesh.

The third stanza reminds us that this "eventing" of God's love in human flesh was foretold and sung by prophets from of old. The long-expected savior is now manifested to humankind and all creation responds in praise. The fourth stanza describes unending praise that includes the heavenly hosts of angels who adore, sing praise, bow, and extol our God and King. What is our response to this disclosure? We join them. No human tongue can be silent. Every human voice, together, sings God's praise evermore and evermore.

The final stanza is a doxology that directly addresses Christ, the incarnation of the Father's love. The address is Trinitarian in its scope: our hymn and chant and thanksgiving are unending praise. We acclaim, honor, and attribute glory, dominion, and victory to our Trinitarian God for all eternity. We are able to do this because of the disclosure of God's superabundant love expressed through the person of Jesus Christ. Like the three wise men, we have been granted an epiphany. The Christian response is endless praise, adoration, and thanksgiving—evermore and evermore. There is joy in the disclosure of such boundless love and it is shared by all of creation and all of humanity.

The chant tune that traditionally has accompanied this text expresses a sense of awe through its simplicity. Each phrase—mostly monosyllabic— gently rises and falls in a way that replicates human breath. It is in the very act of breathing that the music embodies heartfelt gratitude and reflection on the mystery revealed or disclosed.

When a singing assembly is engaged in sung prayer, many truths may disclose themselves to the group and to individuals through the hymnody sung or listened to. In addition, the singing itself may be performing or articulating a state of affairs. For example, the truth of God's mercy, or glory, or goodness may be manifested. Our own creature-hood or sinfulness in the face of God's love and power may be disclosed to us. On the other hand, an experience of unity as a state of affairs or of joy in the celebration of a special feast such as Christmas or Easter may be disclosed in a very real and tangible way. As mentioned earlier in this chapter, the singing of the "Gloria" or any other doxology may disclose God's glory by evidencing God's Trinitarian nature.

The classic hymn "The King Shall Come When Morning Dawns" is another example of how a hymn may disclose some aspect of the mystery of Christian faith. John Brownlie wrote the text in 1907. The text is frequently yoked with the tune MORNING SONG, published originally in *Wyeth's Repository of Sacred Music* (1813). Its composition is attributed to Elkanah Kelsay Dare. The text below is the revised version published in *Worship* (2011). The third and fourth stanzas in parenthesis are part of the original hymn. *Worship* (2011) omits these two stanzas as did *Worship* (1986), *RitualSong* (1996, 1998), and *One in Faith* (2016).[268]

> The King shall come when morning dawns
> And light triumphant breaks,
> When beauty gilds the eastern hills
> And life to joy awakes.
>
> Not, as of old, a little child,
> To suffer and to die,
> But crowned with glory like the sun
> That lights that morning sky.
>
> (O, brighter than the rising morn,
> When He, victorious rose,
> And left the lonesome place of death,
> Despite the rage of foes;)
>
> (O, brighter than that glorious morn,
> Shall this fair morning be,

---

268 "The King Shall Come When Morning Dawns," *Worship* (2011), #403 (minus verses in parenthesis). *Journeysongs* (2003), #319 and *Evangelical Lutheran Worship* (2007), #260, include the verses in parenthesis, but omit stanzas five and six.

When Christ, our King, in beauty comes,
And we His face shall see.)

The King shall come when morning dawns
And earth's dark night is past;
O haste the rising of that morn
Whose day shall ever last.

And let the endless bliss begin,
By weary saints foretold,
When right shall triumph over wrong,
And truth shall be extolled.

The King shall come when morning dawns
And light and beauty brings.
Hail, Christ the Lord! Thy people pray:
Come quickly, King of kings.

The closing days of the liturgical year and the days of Advent before the introduction of the "O" antiphons focus on the second coming of Christ. This eschatological focus is clear in the Lectionary readings that speak about signs and wonders at the approach of the end times. Many Advent hymns express a complex reality that includes Jesus Christ's first coming in history at his birth in Bethlehem, anticipation of his second coming at the end of time, and the Christian experience of moments of disclosure of the Lord's presence in our lives in small and sometimes quite significant ways. In the case of "The King Shall Come," the main focus is disclosing or giving some intimation of the glory, brightness, and beauty that will be experienced when Christ appears at the end of time.

The glory and beauty of the second coming are described as the experience of morning and of awakening. This dawn is triumphant and glorious! Contrasts are set up to make the extent of this morning's glory tangible. It is not, like the first coming, the humble appearance of a little child who comes to suffer and to die. Furthermore, this dawn, the text claims, will be even brighter than the resurrection morning when Christ conquered death and evil and foes. To underscore this fact, the claim is repeated in the stanza that follows. The morning of the second coming will outshine Easter morning for we shall see Christ face to face! The contrasts continue. The second coming will end dark night; daylight shall last forever. The second coming will inaugurate endless bliss; weariness shall end; right shall triumph over wrong; truth shall be extolled.

The main concrete images employed to disclose this anticipated state of affairs are dawn, light, glory, sun, morning sky, rising morn, and glorious morn. These external manifestations, however, complement and inform the inner experience of awakening joy and endless bliss. The Christian response to this future vision is joyful anticipation and ardent desire: come quickly, King of kings!

Our final example of a hymn's power to disclose truth is a contemporary hymn that may be too new to have earned the designation "classic." Shirley Erena Murray's hymn "Touch the Earth Lightly,"[269] set to the tune TENDERNESS by D. Colin Gibson, is a fine example of recent hymns on stewardship and creation. Nevertheless, it demonstrates the power of a hymn text to disclose important truths about our relationships with creation and with one another.

> Touch the earth lightly,
> Use the earth gently,
> Nourish the life of the world in our care:
> Gift of great wonder,
> Ours to surrender,
> Trust for the children tomorrow will bear.
>
> We who endanger,
> Who create hunger,
> Agents of death for all creatures that live,
> We who would foster
> Clouds of disaster
> God of our planet, forestall and forgive!

---

269 *Worship*, (2011), #808. This hymn, copyrighted in 1992, appears in 17 hymnals as of 2017, representing a variety of Christian churches. This wide reception bodes well for this hymn's potential to become a classic.

Let there be greening,
Birth from the burning,
Water that blesses, and air that is sweet,
Health in God's garden,
Hope in God's children,
Regeneration that peace will complete.

God of all living,
God of all loving,
God of the seedling, the snow, and the sun,
Teach us, deflect us,
Christ reconnect us,
Using us gently, and making us one.

The text articulates a theological understanding of humankind's relationship with creation as stewardship. It stands in contrast to a somewhat pervasive attitude that we can use and/or abuse creation as we wish without recrimination.

Stanza one exhorts us to handle God's earth with gentle care. The proper attitude or approach is characterized by words such as "lightly" and "gently." Such language contrasts with the more traditional interpretation of the first creation story in Genesis 1:28:

> God blessed them, and God said to them, "Be fruitful and multiply, and fill the earth and subdue it; and have dominion over the fish of the sea and over the birds of the air and over every living thing that moves upon the earth."

At issue is the discrepancy between our contemporary understanding of "dominion" and the meaning that was operative at the time when this primeval history was written. The ancient world understood the Creator's "dominion" as necessarily one of tending and caring for creation. From this perspective, humankind's role as standing in as a representative or steward of the Creator would require the same tending or caring attitude. This understanding of "dominion" does not involve or excuse exploitation. Rather, dominion language as it is used in Genesis is more accurately expressed by language that encourages us to nurture life and be ready to surrender the gift we have been given and that we hold in trust for future generations.

Stanza two is a confession of the sins that we, as human race, have committed against this "gift of great wonder." We have endangered living things on earth through selfish and thoughtless living. Indeed, we have fostered disasters of all sorts. For this we ask the God of the planet to stop us from wreaking any further havoc on creation and forgive us for what we have already done. The tone shifts when stanza three lays out a vision of hope. Images of God's garden and children (not just human ones) dominate the stanza. Greening, birth out of ashes, regeneration, and peace complete the idyllic description of a world where life is reverenced and creation flourishes when we embrace our role as stewards. The last stanza addresses God, the source of life and love, the only one who truly has dominion over the earth. We admit we have much to learn; we ask Christ to re-align our relationship with God, the planet, and one another. When we understand our interconnectedness and interrelatedness with each of God's creatures (when we truly "get it"), then and only then will the unity ordained by God bring peace and health to our planet. Such is the responsibility of authentic stewardship.

Murray, a New Zealand poet, begins with gentle words of encouragement. Repetition and alliteration communicate the message through the beauty of the poetry. But stanza two includes an open and stark admission of culpability. Her point is clear. The hymn text discloses the necessity of treating creation gently and lightly by using language that is gentle and music that is dance-like. The situation of a transgressed creation and of a sinful people is disclosed. We can begin to look at things in their truth and in their evidencing. Both the nature of the poetry and of the hymn tune articulate a state of affairs and invite us to allow an insight to manifest itself to us. When we are open to the disclosure of a truth or a state of affairs, the insight received may invite us to change or to transformation. This change or transformation or conversion is the topic of the last section of this chapter.

The Transformative Power of Hymn Singing

The liturgy consists of many symbols that interact with each other to express or mediate theological meaning. One of those enacted symbols is hymn singing. Because it invites participation and because it is symbolic activity that points beyond itself, hymn singing has the potential to be transformative. So, for example, by pointing beyond itself to a world where God's justice flourishes, hymn singing can challenge an assembly to live a fuller life with God in Christ and through the Spirit. By shifting our center of awareness, hymn singing, as symbolic activity, can change our values.[270] This is the case because music making, as ritual symbol, assists in transmitting the faith by forming the imagination and the affectivity of the worshiping community. This dynamic enables the worshiping community to appropriate the symbols—in this case the hymn—and "dwell in" its meaning.[271] We are invited to participate and inhabit the world of the hymn. Such activities as singing, playing, listening, or moving with the rhythms of the music can mediate a participatory knowledge, a living into the music that allows our bodies and our spirits to breathe with its rhythms and phrases in such a way that they reveal the saving presence of God and our communion with the entire assembly.[272] In this way, singing together has the potential to invite a worshiping assembly to deep conversion or transformation.

Again, to use the example above, we can say that hymn singing has the potential to transform us into "just" people or people who do justice. This is the case not only when we sing about topics one might label "justice and peace." Rather, hymn singing that provides the possibility for our transformation into more faithful followers of the Gospel of Jesus Christ has the potential to accomplish such transformation. We are speaking of the dialogic call-and-response to the Gospel—the call to discipleship. This dialogic call-and-response is ritualized in the liturgy and then lived out in daily life. And while it is important to sing songs that challenge us to live lives that promote justice and peace, our primary impulse is not to promote a particular political agenda. Rather, the Christian's agenda is to live the life of Christ who showed us how to respond to the poor and to instances of injustice. We have in Christ's life, then, the model of discipleship. This is the one whom Luke 4:18–19 records (echoing Isaiah 61:1–4) saying: "The Spirit

---

270   See Avery Dulles, *Models of Revelation* (Garden City, NY: Doubleday and Co., 1983), 136.

271   See Avery Dulles, *The Craft of Theology: From Symbol to System* (New York: The Crossroad Publishing Company, 1992), 23.

272   Nathan Mitchell, "Symbols are Actions, Not Objects," Living Worship 13 (February 1977): 1–2, and Michael Lawler, *Symbol and Sacrament: A Contemporary Sacramental Theology* (New York: Paulist Press, 1987), 23, 19.

of the Lord is upon me, because he has anointed me to bring good news to the poor. He has sent me to proclaim release to captives and recovery of sight to the blind, to let the oppressed go free, to proclaim the year of the Lord's favor." Furthermore, our concern about justice cannot be narrowly focused on the texts of our hymn repertoire. Rather, we also need to be concerned about ordering the community to worship and act justly. This is an area that challenges Christians to greater reflection and action.

Victor Zuckerkandl has investigated why people engage in singing. (Quite the opposite question Thomas Day asked many years ago!) After examining different activities and settings where people sang, Zuckerkandl concluded that people sing when they abandon themselves wholly to whatever they are doing. This abandonment is not for its own sake, that is, not simply to forget oneself. Rather, this self-abandonment is an enlargement, an enhancement of the self that results in the breaking down of barriers. In theological language, we would say that this self-abandonment is an emptying of the self in order to be open to God. Furthermore, the breaking downs of barriers allows us to be open to the other, whether God (Other) or our fellow human being (other). By drawing us into the activity of singing, we are carried out of ourselves. As a result, separation is overcome and transformed into togetherness.[273] In the case of hymn singing, that transcendent experience can allow for the possibility of an experience of the sacred or of God's presence.

This kind of dynamic is involved in the singing the Taizé chants discussed in chapter four. By means of short, simple, repetitive chants, the music draws the pilgrims in, enabling them to participate in the singing. Since Taizé attracts international visitors who speak in a great variety of languages and come from a great variety of countries, cultures, political, social, and economic settings, the Taizé music serves to break down barriers and level differences. This allows participants to experience a sense of unity and belonging.[274] In this way, the assembly's music making becomes a type of "situating" speech. This is possible because the symbolizing activity of music making invites the worshiper to participate and inhabit its world. At the pilgrimage site at Taizé, for example, the music provides the sonic environment within which

---

273 Victor Zuckerkandl, *Sound and Symbol*, vol. 2, trans. Willard R. Trask (Princeton, NJ: Princeton University Press, 1969), 23.

274 See Kubicki, *Liturgical Music as Ritual Symbol*, especially chapters 2, 3, and 4.

participants grow in awareness of their shared Christian faith and shared humanity with those with whom they are singing.

This awareness and breaking down of barriers is able to occur particularly when participants are willing and intentional in their singing or listening. Many years ago I attended the funeral of the father of a good friend. This friend and his brother were both accomplished church musicians and therefore wished to provide the best music they could for their father's funeral mass. The cathedral organist was also a friend and so they engaged him to play the funeral mass, assuming it would ensure the most wonderful organ playing for singing the funeral music. After spending several minutes delaying the funeral and attempting to figure out how to turn on the organ, they abandoned all hope of having organ music. The congregation was invited to sing a cappella (without accompaniment) except for some places where one of the sons accompanied the assembly with melody or descant on his violin. The voices carried the day. The singing was intentional and glorious in its simplicity. That *ad hoc* group of worshipers sang their hearts out in the most beautiful and inspiring ways because they paid attention and deliberately intended to participate.

The theologian Paul Tillich provides important insights regarding music as ritual symbol when he clarifies the difference between signs and symbols. According to Tillich, the movement involved in symbolizing activity introduces us into realms of awareness not normally accessible to discursive thought. In this way, ritual song as symbol puts us in touch with the power to which it points and opens up to us levels of reality that might otherwise be closed to us.[275] That is part of the reason that ritual symbols have the potential to mediate transformation. By shifting our center of awareness symbols can change our values.[276] According to Chauvet's theory of symbolizing, this dynamic is constantly in process as symbols continue to offer us new opportunities to make sense of our world and to find our identity within it. This is especially true of aesthetic or art symbols. As we are assimilated or integrated into the world of the art symbol (in this case, the hymn), we open up to the possibility of intentional self-transcendence:

---

275 Paul Tillich, *Dynamics of Faith* (New York: Harper and Row, 1957), 41–43.
276 Avery Dulles, *Models of Revelation* (Garden City, NY: Doubleday, 1983), 136.

we can become different persons if we allow ourselves to be carried away by new faith meanings and orient ourselves in new ways to our place within that faith world. According to Chauvet, by engaging with symbols and dwelling in the symbolic order, we build ourselves by building our world. This "building" of ourselves is the process of change that is inherent in the process of transformation.[277]

A few days before Bill Clinton's first inauguration, tents housing a great variety of music heard and performed in the United States were set up on the National Mall. The crowds made even simple movement from tent to a tent a real challenge. Wynton Marsalis was playing in one tent, bluegrass performers in another, and polka bands and other groups further down. The folk singers, Peter, Paul, and Mary, were just beginning their performance as I managed to find my way into their tent. I discovered as I began listening, that their songs had been part of the essential fabric of my life. I felt that in that tent they were, in fact, singing my life as I had experienced it up till that moment and now especially in that moment. For their final song, the trio invited us to sing along with them, but only if we sang the song like a prayer. Then they began singing "We Shall Overcome." The power of that song (hymn) and the great crowd of ordinary Americans like me singing it, the place in DC, the moment in time before the inauguration, and the history of the singing of that song in our country was more than I could bear. While everyone else sang full-throated, I stood there, incapable of singing, as tears welled up in my eyes. All of these songs—but especially the civil rights hymn—sang not only my life, but our life, our world, our dreams, and our very being as Americans in that moment. It was symbolizing activity that "carried me away," inviting participation, transforming and deepening my awareness, and further building my world.

ADDITIONAL EXAMPLES OF POTENTIALLY TRANSFORMATIVE HYMN TEXTS

A classic hymn that illustrates the potential for this transformative experience is "Draw Us in the Spirit's Tether." Percy Dearmer composed

---

277 Louis-Marie Chauvet, *Symbol and Sacrament: A Sacramental Reinterpretation of Christian Existence*, trans. Patrick Madigan and Madeleine E. Beaumont (Collegeville, MN: The Liturgical Press, 1995), 86, 99–109.

the text as a post-communion hymn in 1931. The tune that is now most often yoked with this text is UNION SEMINARY by Harold Friedell. Let us consider how "Draw Us in the Spirit's Tether"[278] invites us to dwell within its symbolic order.

Draw us in the Spirit's tether,
For when humbly in your name
Two or three are met together,
You are in the midst of them.
Alleluia! Alleluia!
Touch we now your garment's hem.

As disciples used to gather
In the name of Christ to sup,
Then with thanks to God the Father
Break the bread and bless the cup.
Alleluia! Alleluia!
So now bind our friendship up.

All our meals and all our living
Make as sacraments of you,
That by caring, helping, giving,
We may be disciples true.
Alleluia! Alleluia!
We will serve with faith anew.

Scripture allusions abound in Dearmer's text. Stanza one echoes the Mt 18:20 saying regarding the promise of Christ's presence where two or three are gathered. The last line of the stanza recalls the story of the woman cured of hemorrhages when she unobtrusively touches Christ's garment. The stanza is a petition that we be drawn into the space where the Spirit dwells, a space where Christ's presence is promised when two or three disciples gather in his name. Within that space, we dare touch the hem of Christ's garment. In other words, we reach out in search of Christ's healing transformation. The tether

---

278 "Draw Us in the Spirit's Tether," *Worship* (2011), #937.

and the garment's hem are two images that situate us within a space filled with the Spirit of Christ.

Stanza two recalls the experience of the early disciples and our own experience of gathering for the Lord's Supper or Eucharist. The outlines of the Eucharistic action are named: thanksgiving, breaking bread, blessing the cup. We, too, in observing Christ's mandate, are his disciples. In gathering and celebrating Eucharist, we become one (bind our friendship up) in Christ. The reality that results is not simply a social one, but an ecclesial one. We become Church; we become disciples; we become Christ. This becoming more and more Christ is the reason for our gathering. Our healing is our transformation into Christ.

The third stanza situates us beyond the ritual and moves our vision to how we live our daily life. Our experience of Eucharist is meant to transforms all that we do so that we ourselves become sacraments of the presence of Christ for the world. In this way, our ordinary meals recall our Eucharistic ones and we live to minister as Christ would do through us—caring, helping, giving to the least of our sisters and brothers. This is the transformation expressed in the hymn. Singing it often can enable us to see ourselves, our local community, and our daily life in new ways. It is the act of building ourselves and building our world by being carried away by the faith world expressed in the hymn.

Another hymn that illustrates the transformative dimension of hymn singing is "Mercy, O God"[279] by Francis Patrick O'Brien. Since this text offers much food for thought during the Lenten season, it is a good example of how singing a hymn can transform both individuals in the assembly, and the entire community. The text below includes the original six stanzas and refrain:

Refrain:
Mercy, O God, have mercy on us.
Send down your mercy to set us free.
Mercy, O God, have mercy on us.
Send down your mercy to set us free.

---

279 "Mercy, O God," *Gather* (2011), # 480. The version published in *Gather* (and quoted here) include the original six stanzas and refrain. In *RitualSong* (2016), #575, an additional set of eight verses suitable for the communion procession were published. In the interest of space, only the original six verses are analyzed here.

Gather the people, the children, the elders;
come now and gather before the Lord.
Open your hearts to compassion and mercy;
open your hearts to the Lord. *Refrain.*

Now is the hour, the day of salvation;
now is the time to return to God.
Open your lives to forgiveness and mercy;
open your lives to the Lord. *Refrain.*

Long is the journey and steep are the mountains,
come now and guide us, O gracious God.
Show us your face, give us hope for the journey;
lead us to walk in your love. *Refrain.*

Wash us anew in your life-giving water;
come quench the thirst of our yearning hearts.
Break through the silence, the fear and the longing;
embrace us with unending love. *Refrain.*

Once lost in darkness you did not forsake us,
called us your children and gave us light.
Open our eyes, come remove all our blindness.
Open our eyes to your love. *Refrain.*

Wake, O sleeper, awake from your slumber;
rise from the chains of the dark, cold tomb.
Walk in the light of compassion and mercy;
walk in the light of the Lord. *Refrain.*

The singing of the text is, in the first place, performative. The act of singing performs the plea for God's mercy. In other words, the plea is accomplished in the act of singing. However, the text also has the potential to be transformative. That is, it has the power to form the imagination and affectivity of the worshiping community as they "dwell in" its meaning. The refrain is simple and repetitive and therefore easily memorized. It gives voice to our plea for God's mercy and associates it with the experience of freedom. The refrain is not primarily an admission of sinfulness even though that is the "state of affairs." Rather, the text provides an opportunity for us to look to God as the source of merciful love and acknowledge our radical need for God's mercy. This is a rich theological theme and very appropriate for reflection during the Lenten season. The refrain's repetitive nature allows the assembly to dwell in that meaning so that it captures our imagination and seeps into our bones as we sing it over and over again.

The stanzas reflect the Scripture texts that accompany our Lenten journey. Stanza one echoes Joel's proclamation of a fast that is read on Ash Wednesday. The prophet invites the people to "gather before the Lord." Why? So that they may open their (our) hearts to the Lord's compassion and mercy. The word "open" is repeated twice in stanza one and again in stanza two. It is an invitation to a change of heart (*metanoia* or conversion). The call is not simply to repentance—although that is a part of it. The invitation is primarily to faith and trust—faith that God cares about us deeply and trust that God's mercy and compassion will truly set us free. Stanza two's insistence that "now is the hour" and "now is the time" echo Lenten scriptural themes and provide a sense of urgency. Open your hearts and open your lives to the Lord—now!

O'Brien communicates this message by using many classic images and metaphors for the spiritual life. He creatively reshapes them, thereby superimposing fresh interpretations on old meanings. This nudges us to begin to see our world in new ways. This new "seeing" also facilitates a new openness to change or transformation. Stanza three sings of the Christian life as a long journey involving steep mountains. Echoes of the transfiguration story can be heard in the plea "show us your face." Stanza four continues to employ vivid images, this time echoing the story of the Samaritan woman. Grace and mercy are expressed through the baptismal images of washing, life-giving water, and quenching thirst. God's gracious mercy embraces us and breaks through our fears and longings.

The baptismal focus is linked to the power of light to overcome darkness. O'Brien develops this in stanzas five and six where light becomes the central image. We can get lost on the journey because of the darkness (of sin) or our blindness (to God's love), but baptism calls us to be children of the light. The story of the cure of the blind man becomes our story. Once we were lost in darkness, but Christ has given us light. The final stanza borrows from a text that scholars believe is an excerpt from an ancient Christian hymn quoted in Eph 5:14: "Sleeper, awake! Rise from the dead, and Christ will shine on you." The text is replete with images of sleep, chains, tomb, and light that resonate with themes of the Easter Vigil and the Easter season. Indeed, Lent is a journey from darkness to light! When we are open to the light—that is, to God's gracious mercy—we will be set free from fear, darkness, and death. As Christians journey through life, these images and metaphors capture our imagination and allow the invitation to open ourselves to God's mercy to touch our hearts and seep into our bones. As we sing this text, we are carried away by the depiction of a world that calls us out of ourselves and out of lives of fear and darkness. Our center of awareness shifts so that we can change.

Another example of a hymn that invites participants to deep conversion or repentance is the hymn "All Who Hunger"[280] by Sylvia G. Dunstan. It serves well as either a gathering or communion processional. Dunstan creates the possibility of transformation by setting up a dynamic that is neither didactic nor hortatory, but instead invitational.

> All who hunger, gather gladly;
> Holy manna is our bread.
> Come from wilderness and wand'ring,
> Here, in truth, we will be fed.
> You that yearn for days of fullness,
> All around us is our food.
>
> *Refrain:*
> *Taste and see the grace eternal,*
> *Taste and see that God is good.*
>
> All who hunger, never strangers;
> Seeker, be a welcome guest.
> Come from restlessness and roaming.

---

280 "All Who Hunger," *Worship*, #844 with tune HOLY MANNA; *RitualSong*, #1032 with tune GRACE ETERNAL.

Here, in joy, we keep the feast.
We that once were lost and scattered
In communion's love have stood. Refrain

All who hunger, sing together;
Jesus Christ is living bread.
Come from loneliness and longing.
Here, in peace, we have been led.
Blest are those who from this table
Live their lives in gratitude. Refrain

From the very first line, this text offers an invitational embrace that includes all people. The primary verbs are "gather" gladly and "come." It explores, expresses, and celebrates the deep theological meaning of the act of gathering and of the communion rite and our participation in it. Recall that a hymn's transformative power comes from its ability to form our imagination and affectivity so that we might "dwell in" its meaning. In this case, the world we are invited to inhabit is the world where Jesus Christ invites us to approach the Eucharist so that he can satisfy our hunger.

Stanza one alludes to the story of the Israelites wandering in the desert for forty years. God satisfies their physical hunger with the gift of manna. Like the Israelites, holy manna (eucharist) is our bread and again God satisfies our hunger. However, in this instance, our hunger is spiritual—a desire for union with God and with each other. But like the Israelites, we find ourselves wandering in our own deserts or contemporary wildernesses. The stanza expresses both invitation and confident belief that we will, indeed, be fed.

The refrain is a brief, easily remembered mantra that enables the singing assembly to proclaim the marvelous grace of the moment and the generosity and goodness of God. Its earnest "taste and see" focuses on the amazing gift that is being offered. The repeated appeal to two of our senses speaks to the assembly's imagination. In this way, the singing of a hymn text can, over time, change our perceptions by capturing our imagination and helping us to see our world in a new light.

The image of table is a powerful symbol both of the Christian Eucharist and also the shared fellowship of family and friends. Shirley Erena Murray's hymn text, "A Place at the Table"[281] captures our imagination on multiple levels of meaning.

> For ev'ryone born, a place at the table,
> for ev'ryone born, clean water and bread,
> a shelter, a space, a safe place for growing,
> for ev'ryone born, a star overhead,
>
> *Refrain:*
> *And God will delight when we are creators*
> *of justice and joy, compassion and peace:*
> *yes, God will delight when we are creators*
> *of justice, justice and joy.*
>
> For woman and man, a place at the table,
> revising the roles, deciding the share,
> with wisdom and grace, dividing the power,
> for woman and man, a system that's fair. *Refrain.*
>
> For young and for old, a place at the table,
> a voice to be heard, a part in the song,
> the hands of a child in hands that are wrinkled,
> for young and for old, the right to belong. *Refrain.*
>
> For just and unjust, a place at the table,
> abuser, abused, with need to forgive,
> in anger, in hurt, a mindset of mercy,
> for just and unjust, a new way to live. *Refrain.*
>
> For ev'ryone born, a place at the table,
> to live without fear, and simply to be,
> to work, to speak out, to witness and worship,
> for ev'ryone born, the right to be free. *Refrain.*

---

281   "A Place at the Table," *Gather* (2011), #812.

Notice how the first verse manages to create a situation of equality by repeating three times in the first stanza, "for ev'ryone born."[282] There are no distinctions in terms of race, social status, or even gender. Everyone born deserves "a place at the table." This image of equality represents fundamental human dignity: the right to food and shelter, the right to belong and be accepted. Furthermore, mention of "a star overhead" introduces yet another dimension to our understanding of basic human equality. The juxtaposition of "born" and "star" conjures up in our imaginations the story of the star associated with the birth of Christ. Our dignity as human beings has deep theological foundations. We are all creatures of God, brothers and sisters of Christ, redeemed by Christ and members of Christ.

Stanza two offers a vision of gender equality, where traditional roles can be revised and shared. Wisdom, grace, and justice are lifted up as essential aspects of this project. Stanza three offers a vision of belonging, no matter what a person's age. The metaphor here becomes auditory rather than visual: all have a voice that needs to be heard; all have a part to offer in the song. Together, young and old create harmony at the table. It is when we gather for worship and for table fellowship outside worship that we truly make a place for each other. This can change the way we view our world. This is what changes or transforms our hearts. Stanza four reminds us that we are all sinners and that Christ's personal style of table fellowship welcomed sinners first of all. Forgiveness and mercy are prerequisites for justice. Yes, it is a new way to live and a new way to view our world and each other. Finally, the last stanza offers a reprise of the first line of the hymn. The fundamental human value of freedom is celebrated, especially the freedom to live without fear.

Like Jesus' parables, the refrain turns our expectations or suppositions upside down by suggesting that God delights in *our* creative efforts. We are not praying here that God will fix our broken world. Rather, we become aware that God expects us to be faithful disciples. This means carrying on Christ's mission to build a world of justice, joy, compassion, and peace. As Chauvet reminds us, we build our world as we celebrate or handle the

---

282 Perhaps the debate regarding the rights of the unborn does not have the same highly charged political ramifications in New Zealand as it does in the United States. It seems appropriate to take the phrase "for ev'ryone born" to be a comment on the equality of all people who are born rather than as a slight on those who are yet unborn.

symbols of worship. It is our mission to build a just world. The symbolizing activity of singing is integral to doing just that.

Thus, we can say that, as with all liturgical symbols, hymn singing has the potential to communicate to the worshiping assembly the challenge to live a fuller life with God in Christ. How does this happen? Don Saliers asserts that ritual music has the power of transformation by forming, over time, the imagination and affectivity (affections) of the Christian assembly. It does this by "forming and expressing those emotions which constitute the very Christian life itself.[283] Saliers is not talking about simple emotion or surface feelings, but a complex, permanent attitude or deep emotion. So, singing praise or thanksgiving, contrition or forgiveness has the ability to form the singers in those Christian attitudes. By *exhibiting* these Christian attitudes, we participate through our music making in the process of being shaped or formed in those very attitudes. In this way, specific hymn choices will either lead the assembly toward or away from the deep patterns of emotion that constitute the Christian life. Over time, for good or for ill, assemblies will be shaped by their musical choices. In this way, the emotional range of their worship music will either enhance or inhibit their ability to enter into those praisings, repentings, lamentings, hopings, longings, rejoicings, and thankings that are peculiar to the heart of Christian worship.[284]

When we speak about the potential for hymn singing to form complex Christian attitudes or emotions, we are speaking about the hymn as both text and music. Sometimes a familiar and beloved text is sung to different tunes in different communities, often because of the choices provided by the hymnal in the pew. This variety of tunes can shift emphases within the text and even encourage different responses or insights. It is all part of the richness of symbolizing activity. Nevertheless, hymn singing is not a ritual element that guarantees transformation or conversion. Instead, it provides the possibility whereby hearts and minds are touched so that they might be open to the workings of Christ's Spirit within the assembly. That is the one guarantee we do have—the promise that Christ's Spirit is present when we gather for worship.

---

283 Don Saliers, "The Integrity of Sung Prayer," *Worship* 55 (July 1981), 293.
284 Saliers, 294–295.

All of this presupposes the assembly's dynamic engagement with the process of transformation that occurs over time when individuals and communities give themselves over regularly to worship. Such dynamic engagement is encouraged or facilitated when the language and music is authentic and life-giving. Nevertheless, the ultimate purpose is not the performance of beautiful and inspiring hymns—desirable and wonderful though that is—but the transformation of the individual and the assembly into the one Body of Christ.

CHAPTER 6

WHAT'S IN A NAME?
HOW DO WE NAME GOD? HOW DO WE NAME OURSELVES?

At the beginning of each semester, I invite my undergraduate students to complete two sentence fragments. The first begins "God is . . . ." The second, "God is like . . . ." After sufficient time has been given for thoughtful scribbling and crossing out, we discuss students' reaction to doing the exercise and their responses. Sentence completions vary widely and reveal differing perspectives regarding who God is or how God is perceived. Some completed sentences use traditional images or descriptions. These include using nouns such as Father, friend, judge, love, or adjectives such as all-powerful, all-present, eternal, or all-knowing. Other responses are more creative or, sometimes, more honest. Many students point out that it seems easier to complete the phrase "God is like. . ." since it allows for comparisons that can be borrowed from human experience. Often someone describes God as mystery.

HOW DO WE NAME GOD?

Student observations open up class discussion to considering the limits of language when naming God, addressing God, or speaking about the experience of God. This is where the notion of metaphor as a way to engage in God talk becomes helpful. But as the hymn text writer, Ruth Duck, observes, "to say language about God is metaphorical is not to deny its truth claims, but to affirm a particular way of communicating truth."[285] We use metaphors in order to come to fresh insights about God who is truly mystery. Metaphor uses the "God is like. . ." approach to God talk since, if God is truly mystery, our grasp of God or our ability to speak about God can only be tentative at best.[286] The word "mystery" suggests that our knowledge is not only incomplete, but also ambiguous. Indeed, one of the challenges of religious speech is becoming comfortable with ambiguity and imprecision. This can be especially daunting for the person inclined to seeking mathematical or scientific precision. Yet, referencing God only as "mystery" can be unsatisfying, or at least less compelling, especially in worship and particularly in hymn singing. As human persons, we desire relationship with God on a more personal level. Certainly Scripture and Tradition provide a wealth of metaphors and descriptions for naming or addressing God, some personal and others inanimate. Many of these have been an integral part of our hymns and our prayers for centuries. How we name God is important since language shapes our understanding and our ability to enter into a personal relationship with the Divine.

The hymn text writer Brian Wren rightly observes:

> Naming God is important, since to name God untruthfully is to
> delude ourselves and worship an idol. Naming God truthfully
> is especially important if language shapes and angles thinking
> and behavior, since untruthful God-language will then hinder
> our encounter with God and our knowledge of God.[287]

We cherish and reverence the language for naming and addressing God that Scripture and Tradition have handed down to us. Tapping into these two sources provides us with confidence that we can name God truthfully. It is important to remember, however, that the language of written texts may long outlive the world or culture from which they originally emerged. As a result,

---

285 Ruth Duck, *Gender and the Name of God: The Trinitarian Baptismal Formula* (Cleveland, OH: Pilgrim Press, 1991), 22.
286 Recall that when this text speaks of metaphor, it employs a definition that goes beyond the grammatical distinctions between simile and metaphor. As several thinkers referenced in chapter three assert, metaphor appeals in new ways to the imagination and is particularly appropriate when speaking about such religious notions as transcendence and mystery. See chapter three.
287 Brian Wren, *What Language Shall I Borrow? God-Talk in Worship: A Male Response to Feminist Theology* (New York: Crossroad Publishing, 1989), 61.

language that meant one thing for its original audience may come to mean something radically different to subsequent generations. This is particularly true when dealing with texts read in translation. The process of translating always represents an adaptation of a texts' original social world to the social world implied in the language of the translation.[288] So, for example, English has no precise equivalent for the ancient Hebrew ab (abba) or Greek pater. As L. William Countryman explains:

> We translate them [ab, pater] "father," and with reason, since the ancient and modern terms do overlap. All three terms designate the "biological male parent." Yet, in a world where the male head of household no longer simply *embodies* the whole family for public purposes, a world where women and adult children have legal and political rights, a world where we are expected to make our own choices regarding occupation, marriage, and even religion, our ordinary word for "biological male parent" cannot possibly convey the power or social significance of the ancient *ab* or *pater*—or his role as public personification of the household and source of identity for wife, children, and servants or slaves. Thus translation is never more than an approximation—even when dealing with something as seemingly fundamental as names of God or the gender of pronouns applied to God.[289]

Indeed, every translation is an interpretation. In order to compensate for this liability, whether when translating from one language to another and/or from one culture to another, we need to proceed with caution and an open mind. Furthermore, we want to examine the breadth of our resources in order to discover the rich and varied field of descriptive language used to speak or address God in the Scriptures and in the tradition.

The Canadian-born professor Janet Martin Soskice specializes in religious language and naming God at the University of Cambridge. Her work explores

---

288 L. William Countryman, "Biblical Origins of Inclusive Language," in *How Shall We Pray? Expanding Our Language about God*, Liturgical Studies 2, Ruth A. Meyers, ed. (New York: The Church Hymnal Corporation, 1994), 17.
289 Countryman, 17–18.

the many metaphorical names for God in the biblical literature, including such familiar images as rock, shepherd, lamb, fortress, door, and way. However, she notes that privileged among all of these are the anthropomorphic[290] titles for God. She reasons that if the biblical writers hoped to do justice to describing a God whose acts they wished to chronicle, then using anthropomorphism would best accomplish this goal. In the biblical texts, we meet a God who cajoles, chastises, soothes, alarms, and loves. In our experience, Soskice reasons, it is human beings who do such things. For this reason, early Christian writers realized that a plenitude of divine titles serves to reveal the way in which God, while remaining one and holy mystery, is also, in diverse ways, very much "God *with us*."[291] As the Judeo-Christian tradition has chronicled the experience of God's presence in human history, so it has described this God as being "in relationship" with us.

Recall (from chapter three) that the act of using language is symbolizing activity. Because it is symbolizing activity, language enables us to build or negotiate relationships with God, each other, and ourselves. Language is the basis of our relationships. Language is therefore fundamental to Christian belief since the Trinity expresses God-self in relationship and the structure of worship is dialogic or relational. As Mark Searle wrote, "the role of liturgical language is not simply to convey supernatural 'facts' but to engage us in relationship."[292]

Soskice lists three registers of anthropomorphic titles: offices of governance (Lord, King, Judge); offices of service (Shepherd, Watchman, Servant, Teacher); and offices of love (Father, Brother, Son, Spouse, Lover). The last of these categories is the most intimate because all of these titles are kinship titles.[293] In other words, the terms of the third category refer to persons in relationship. For Soskice, the notion of kinship is key to understanding our human inclination to speak of God in anthropomorphic terms. Soskice explains that kinship imagery has a distinct advantage because it is all about birth, growth, and change.[294] From their first appearance in

---

290 Anthropomorphism is the practice of attributing human characteristics to gods, objects, animals, etc. This word is sometimes incorrectly used interchangeably with personification which is a person or thing thought of as representing some quality, thing or idea; embodiment, type, or perfect example.
291 Janet Martin Soskice, *The Kindness of God: Metaphor, Gender, and Religious Language* (Oxford: Oxford University Press, 2007), 1.
292 Mark Searle, "Liturgy as Metaphor," *Worship* 55:1(1981), 100.
293 Soskice, *Kindness of God*, 1.
294 Soskice, *Kindness of God*, 6.

the Hebrew Scriptures, Soskice observes, divine kinship titles are names of promise, holding before us the vision of a love that is both now and not yet. The family of God is both now and yet to come, and what we will be—either individually or collectively—is not yet apparent. Metaphors of kinship open up for us an eschatological[295] anthropology wherein our constant becoming is our way of being children of God.[296]

Soskice's observation highlights two important aspects of kinship. The first is that human beings experience change when they are in relationship. The second is that change, as a function of being in relationship, is integral to the Christian life. Two metaphors are used to express this fundamental way of being. The first is that we are always on the way to becoming more the Body of Christ. The second is that we are children of God and thus in relationship with both God and one another. This "condition" of being the body of Christ and children of God is not static. We are constantly on our way toward becoming more of what we are called to be. So while we acknowledge that God is mystery or pure spirit, we realize that it is much easier, as human persons, to be in a relationship with a God whom we imagine in anthropomorphic, that is human, terms. The fact of the Incarnation appears to suggest that God thought so, too.

These titles of kinship for God, however, are necessarily embedded in a complex web of relationships that today—under the scrutiny of theological anthropology, psychology, and social developments—no longer fit so easily into clear or neat categories. In patriarchal cultures, the default for God has always been the male gender. Hence, our traditional metaphors for God were king, lord, prince, shepherd, and father. On the other hand, contemporary cultures, especially in the West, have made significant progress in affirming the equality of all human persons. Part of the impetus for this work is often referred to as "feminism." Barbara Reid, borrowing from Joan Chittister, defines feminism as "a commitment to the humanity, dignity, and equality of all persons to such a degree that one is willing to work for changes in structures and in relationship patterns so that these occur to the equal good of all."[297]

---

295 See chapter three for a fuller treatment of eschatology.
296 Soskice, *Kindness of God*, 6.
297 Reid, 124. See also Joan Chittister, "Yesterday's Dangerous Vision: Christian Feminism in the Catholic Church," *Sojourners* 16:7(July 1987), 18.

This definition captures the best of the impulses of feminism, a term that includes many different subsets and ways of thinking. And, like all movements that promote the common good, there has often been more success in articulating the theory than in carrying it out. This feminist way of thinking has contributed to raising questions regarding equating God with the male gender and the subsequent consequences of this mindset and practice for the flourishing of women. Furthermore, new issues and understanding continue to emerge today. For example, we are beginning to realize that in the area of human sexuality, it is not always possible to say definitively that someone is either male or female. The reality of transgender designations for human persons has provided yet another challenge for language that typically operates in either/or categories or labels.

Nevertheless, while we may describe God in anthropomorphic terms, we also need to keep in mind that the Triune God is gracious and personal mystery. In addition, this God is pure spirit. Does this mean that God is genderless since God does not possess a human body? The five senses cannot grasp mystery. Certainly the triune God (we are not speaking here of the historical Jesus who was indeed a man!) cannot be grasped by our five exterior senses of seeing, hearing, tasting, touching, or smelling.

We know from experience that it is difficult, if not nearly impossible to conceive of a personal being without gender. So how can we successfully employ anthropomorphic metaphors for God and still remember that God is holy mystery, pure spirit? There is another approach to this quandary and it is part of our Christian tradition. In the *Odes of Solomon*, probably a second century CE collection of poems, there is a wealth of bodily and gendered metaphors for the persons of the Trinity, but they are layered in paradoxical and conflicting sequences. This collection of 42 hymns, perhaps our earliest non-biblical literature from the Syrian Orient, are sometimes hauntingly poignant, sometimes elusive and obscure in their meanings.[298] Ode 19, perhaps the most famous of the collection, reads as follows:

> A cup of milk was offered to me
> And I drank it with the sweetness of the Lord's kindness.

---

[298] Susan Ashbrook Harvey, "Feminine Imagery for the Divine: The Holy Spirit, the Odes of Solomon, and Early Syriac Tradition," *St. Vladimir's Theological Quarterly* 37:2–3 (1993), 122.

The Son is the cup,

And He who was milked is the Father,

And she who milked Him is the Holy Spirit.

Because His breasts were full,

And it was not necessary for His milk to be poured out
without cause.

The Holy Spirit opened her womb,

and mixed the milk of the two breasts of the Father.

And She gave the mixture to the world without their knowing,

And those who received it are in the perfection of the right hand.

The womb of the Virgin caught it,

and She received conception and gave birth.

And the Virgin became a mother with many mercies.

And she labored and bore a son and there was no pain for her.

Because it was not without cause.

And she did not need a midwife

Because He [God] delivered her.

Like a man she gave birth by will.

And she bore with manifestation

And she acquired with much power.

And she loved with redemption,

And she guarded with kindness

And she manifested with greatness.

Hallelujah.[299]

Susan Ashbrook Harvey's analysis of this poem highlights the complex dynamic that is at work here when she explains that "gender imagery becomes a force beyond the scope of the Spirit's role. . . God the Father is imaged in wholly feminine terms: nursing from his breasts, and midwife at Mary's birthgiving."[300] The images recall familiar Old Testament metaphors: God as midwife (Ps 22:9–10), God as comforting mother (Is 49:15 and 66:13) and God in the throes of divine labor pangs (Is 42:14b).[299]

---

299   Harvey, 125–126. Soskice discusses Harvey's analysis of the Odes of Solomon in *The Kindness of God*, 114–115.
300   Harvey, 126.
301   Harvey, 126.

About this Ode, Harvey observes that:

> gender is played with for all participants in the salvation drama, both human and divine. Roles are reversed, fused, inverted: no one is simply who they seem to be. More accurately, everyone is more than they seem to be—Mary is more than a woman in what she does; the Father and the Spirit are more than one gender can convey in the effort to glimpse their works. Gender is thus shown to be important, even crucial to identity—but *not one specific gender* (emphasis added). Here gender imagery leads us to see that categories of identity are far wider than what has been culturally defined as masculine and feminine.[302]

In layering gendered images, the poem creates paradox. The experience of grace ("the sweetness of the Lord's kindness") is likened to a cup of milk. The Syriac word for cup, *casa'*, often refers to the ritual cup of the Eucharist in later writings. Here, the Son is appropriately called the cup. The Spirit is God's agent, she who milked him in order to bestow God's grace on the world.[303]

Soskice does not find anthropomorphism surprising in a religious tradition whose God is a God of calling and address. In human experience, it is people who speak and a "speaking God" will necessarily be spoken of in personal terms.[304] Therefore, gender is considered important, even crucial to identity, for both Harvey and Soskice. Their conclusion is that God does not lack gender, but exceeds gender.[305] This ancient collection of poems demonstrates how all three persons of the Trinity can be expressed in the imagery of both the human feminine and human masculine. This interplay of gendered imagery both supports symbols of desire, fecundity, and parental love while de-stabilizing any possible over-literalistic reading.

In addition to offering the second-century example of the *Odes of Solomon*, Soskice also appeals to the work of the medieval mystic Julian of Norwich (c.1342–c.1416). For her time, Julian was unusual in her embrace

---

302 Harvey, 126–127.
303 Harvey, 126.
304 Soskice, *Kindness of God*, 78.
305 Harvey, 127 and Soskice, *Kindness of God*, 115.

of bodiliness and temporality. While much attention has been given to Julian's dramatic portrayal of Christ as mother, less attention has been given to how Julian's *Revelation of Divine Love* (*Shewings*)[306] is actually an example of Trinitarian theology. Furthermore, to be fully appreciated, her theology must be understood as configured by her notion of kinship.[307]

Throughout this work, Julian portrays all three persons of the Trinity as mother. We know historically that Jesus was male. Yet, if he represents the perfection of our humanity, Julian reasons, he must be the perfection of both male and female humanity. The passage that expresses these ideas is found in chapter 59 of *Showings*. Julian writes:

> As verely as God is oure Fader, as verely is God oure Moder. And that shewde he in all, and namely, in theyse swete words there he seyth, I it am. That is to sey, I it am, the myght and the goodness of faderhode. I it am, the wysdom and the kyndnes of moderhode. I it am, the lyght and the grace that is all blessyd love. I it am, the Trynyte. I it am, the unyte. I it am, the hye sovereyn goodnesse of all manner thyng. I it am that makyth the to long. I it am, the endless fulfyllying of all true desyers.[308]

In proceeding this way, Julian follows the route of excess rather than displacement. She complements the gendered scriptural terms of divine Fatherhood and Sonship with maternal and functional imagery, describing God as Maker, Keeper, Lover. Yet, just as God is both Mother and Father, so too is Christ Maker, Lover, and Keeper.[309]

In her book, *Julian's Gospel: Illuminating the Life and Revelations of Julian of Norwich*, Veronica Mary Rolf devotes an entire chapter to exploring

---

306   Sometimes the title, *Revelation of Divine Love*, is simply called *Shewings*. Often the medieval spelling is observed. Writers on Julian of Norwich seem to alternate between the two spellings, shewings and showing.

307   Soskice, *Kindness of God*, 115, 126. Contemporary editions include Julian of Norwich, *The Showings of Julian of Norwich*, ed. Denise N. Baker, Norton Critical Edition (New York: W.W. Norton, 2005). Also ed. Edmund Colledge and James Walsh, *Classics of Western Spirituality*, (Mahwah, NJ: Paulist Press, 1978).

308   Julian of Norwich, *Showings*, Authoritative Text, Contexts, Criticism, ed. by Denise N. Baker. A Norton Critical Edition (New York: W.W. Norton, 2005), 92. "As truly as God is our Father, so truly is God our Mother, and he revealed that in everything, and especially in these sweet words, where he says, I am he, the power and goodness of fatherhood; I am he, the wisdom and the lovingness of motherhood; I am he, the light and grace which is all blessed love. I am he the Trinity. I am he, the unity. I am he, the high sovereign goodness of all manner of things. I am he that makes desire. I am he, the endless fulfilling of all true desires." See also Soskice, *Kindness of God*, 116.

309   Soskice, *Kindness of God*, 116.

Julian's understanding of the motherhood of God. Julian's thinking is part of a long-standing tradition that preceded even her writings. The Greek word for wisdom is *sophia*, a feminine word. The Hebrew word for Divine Wisdom in the Hebrew Scriptures is *Hochma*, also a feminine noun. Furthermore, both the Book of Proverbs and the Book of Wisdom attribute the qualities of *Sophia* to God.[310] There are also non-scriptural examples in the tradition of speaking of God as mother. In the eleventh century, St. Anselm speaks of Christ as mother in his "Prayer to St. Paul."

> And you, Jesus, are you not also a mother?
> Are you not the mother who, like a hen,
> Gathers her chickens under her wings?
> Truly, Lord, you are a mother;
> For both they who are in labour
> And they who are brought forth
> Are accepted by you.
> You have died more than they that they may labour to bear.
> It is by your death that they have been born,
> For if you had not been in labour,
> You could not have borne death;
> And if you had not died, you would not have brought forth.[311]

The scriptural references found in Anselm's prayer (Luke 13:34, Matthew 23:37, and John 16:21) make clear the connection between this creative work and tradition. It shows that this example is not an anomaly, but rather a metaphorical thread that weaves in and out of the Church's thinking from the Gospels and into the Medieval period.

The writings of such twelfth-century Cistercian monks such as Bernard of Clairvaux, William of Thierry, and Aelred of Rievaulx continue Anselm's approach. These medieval writers used maternal analogies to suggest Christ's compassion and spiritual nurturing as well as the intimate bond between God and the human soul. The scholastic writers of the twelfth and

---

310   Veronica Mary Rolf, *Julian's Gospel: Illuminating the Life and Revelations of Julian of Norwich*, (Maryknoll, NY: Orbis Books, 2013), 512.
311   Rolf, 513. See also St. Anselm, *Prayer to St. Paul*, from *The Prayers and Meditations of St. Anselm, with the Proslogion*, translated by Benedicta Ward, SLG (New York: Penguin, 1973), 153–156.

thirteenth centuries, including Peter Lombard, Abelard, St. Albert the Great, St. Thomas Aquinas and St. Bonaventure, employed maternal imagery to described the Creator, the Wisdom of Christ, and the Holy Spirit. In addition, the thirteenth-century document *Ancrene Riwle*, written for anchoresses following a solitary life of prayer, portrayed Jesus Christ as a kindly mother. Visionary nuns of Helfta, including Mechthild of Hackeborn, Mechthild of Magdeburg, and St. Gertrude the Great, described divine motherhood as expressive of both authority and merciful love. Julian's contemporaries, Brigit of Sweden and Catherine of Siena, also employed tender and protective maternal images for God. Therefore, by the time of Julian (14th–15th c.), there already existed a long and varied tradition of monks, scholastics, nuns, and laywomen who referred to Wisdom, God, and Christ in maternal terms. All of these understood such speech to be metaphorical.[312]

However, for Julian, something different is going on here. She does not interpret speaking of the motherhood of God to be metaphorical speech. Neither does she think of it as apt simile. Rather, Julian considers the Motherhood of the Son of God as perfectly equal to the Fatherhood. For her, it was a matter of divine revelation.[313] For Julian the question is why should we desire to flee our physical nature if God has chosen to become our kind? It is this "kindness" of God that renders all kinship metaphors so appropriate when speaking of God, according to Soskice.[314] Julian does not limit her descriptions to any one kinship metaphor:

> Our great Father, almighty God, who is being, knows us and loved us before time began. Out of this knowledge, in his most wonderful deep love, by the prescient eternal counsel of all the blessed Trinity, he wanted the second person to become our Mother, our brother and our savior. From this it follows that as truly as God is our Father, so truly is God our Mother (§59)."[315]

---

312 Rolf, 513–514.
313 Rolf, 515.
314 Soskice, *Kindness of God*, 150. Indeed, this seems to be the inspiration for the title of Soskice's book, *The Kindness of God*.
315 Soskice, *Kindness of God*, 150.

We can glean an important insight from the interplay of the words "kin" and "kindness" in these writings. Scripture speaks of Jesus Christ taking on human flesh to become "one of us" or God "with us." So the word "kindness" might also be interpreted as God being "of our kind," one of us. Being God, that "kindness" would be beyond fullness, and in this particular instance, exceeding gender.

This brief survey of instances of the existence of feminine metaphors for God uncovers a long tradition of this practice in classic Christian texts. The data suggests that contemporary interest in exploring these ideas is not a new perspective, recently contrived by inspired or disgruntled feminists. Rather, it is a legacy of rich poetry and song that can inspire contemporary writers and composers and has already done so in many instances. When it comes to speaking of God, a multiplicity of metaphors enriches our understanding. Indeed, no one metaphor can capture the mystery and the wonder that is God. In speaking of the Christian effort to name God, Sallie McFague asserts that "many metaphors and models are necessary, that a piling up of images is essential, both to avoid idolatry and to attempt to express the richness and variety of the divine-human relationship."[316]

This same type of behavior is similar to that observed when someone attempts to describe falling in love. Whether the object of one's affection is man or woman, the attempt to describe this wonderful person always falls short of capturing the wonder of the beloved. Using metaphors, descriptions and superlatives, the person "piles up" images in order to create a fuller understanding for those who have not had the good fortune of knowing the beloved. This understanding can likewise be applied to worship. In regard to the way in which we name God, the overarching concern is not only about "inclusive" language, but also about "expansive" language.[317] What is necessary is to employ multiple metaphors to speak of the inexhaustible mystery of God.[318] In fact, much of the richness we find in the language about God used in the Bible is founded on and grows out of not so much

---

316   Sallie McFague, *Metaphorical Theology: Models of God in Religious Language* (Philadelphia: Fortress Press, 1982), 20. In this work, McFague argues that the Protestant tradition is metaphorical while the Catholic tradition is symbolical or analogical. I would argue, as a Catholic, that it is both/and.

317   Refer to chapter three for a more detailed discussion of the expansive dimension of metaphor.

318   Ruth Meyers, "Principles for Liturgical Language," in *How Shall We Pray? Expanding Our Language about God*, ed. Ruth Meyers (New York: The Church Hymnal Corporation, 1994), 93.

names or titles, but rather descriptive language about God. This language is allusive and metaphorical since, at least on this side of the grave, our experience of God is indirect and interior. Such experiences do not give rise to direct, straightforward, or precise ways of speaking, but rather inspire more pointing or gesturing than anything else. God resists our futile attempts to be pinned down.[319]

Thus mystery leaves us with more questions than answers. Nevertheless, Christians believe that the historical Jesus was truly God and truly human. The mystery of the Incarnation (what we celebrate at Christmas) highlights Christian faith in the mystery of God (pure Spirit) taking on human flesh (the male, Jewish, first-century body of Jesus Christ). The Triune God of Christian faith is pure spirit. Jesus Christ is God incarnate. Or, to put it another way, Jesus Christ is the pure spirit of God taking on a human body.

From what we know about the first-century social and cultural life into which Jesus was born, we can make some tentative, but informed, assumptions. First of all, it would have been nearly impossible for him to successfully proclaim the message of God's love and mercy as a woman. No one would have listened. A woman's word had no value in a court of law or in the religious life of Israel. Because of the social and cultural milieu into which he was born, Jesus necessarily took on human flesh as a man. Yet even in this ancient environment, Jesus was always pushing boundaries and challenging expectations. For example, the fact that the Risen Christ chose Mary Magdalene to announce the news of his resurrection to the disciples is truly amazing. At that time and in that culture, a woman's word had no credibility or weight in any official capacity. To entrust such an important and world-changing piece of news to a woman was quite risky.

So while God became incarnate as a man, that God—as Jesus the Christ—challenged many of the social conventions of his day regarding public interaction of men with women. As the Scripture scholar Barbara Reid points out, Christian feminists find a liberating message for women in the way Jesus interacted with women and his vision for them as human beings. Many of those healed were women. Jesus touched and was touched by women, including those considered unclean by Jewish law. Women were friends of

---

319 Countryman, 18.

Jesus and among his most ardent and faithful disciples. Jesus engaged in theological discussions with women (e.g., the Samaritan woman at the well) and taught them. According to the Gospel accounts of Matthew and John (already referred to above), the risen Christ first appeared to women.[320]

We are heirs of a Christian tradition that has used male metaphors for God almost exclusively. This widespread practice has reinforced the misconception that God is male. This is the case even when God's nature as pure spirit is enthusiastically affirmed. Common and widely used metaphors include those listed earlier by Soskice: king, lord, shepherd, prince, and especially, father. Barbara Reid points out that while there are some fifteen references to God as father in the Hebrew Scriptures (Old Testament), "father" is the most frequent designation for God in the New Testament.[321] Another scripture scholar, Robert Hamerton-Kelly, finds that while God is designated "father" in the Old Testament, God is never invoked as "father" in prayer.[322] There is an indirect reference to God as father in the phrase "the God of the fathers." This is the earliest evidence of an association between the idea of God and the idea of father, a notion rooted in the family life of ancient Israel.[323] This usage appears in the early stories in the Book of Exodus, where God is not described as "father," but rather as the God of *our* fathers. As Paul Ricoeur points out, God's relationship with the Hebrews is not so much one of kinship as it is one of covenant. The primary name of God in Exodus is spoken from the burning bush: "I Am Who I Am."[324]

So how should we interpret the significance of the title "Father" for God in the Sacred Scriptures? Gail Ramshaw suggests that the context of the usage is what is informative. As she points out, in nearly every instance in the Hebrew Scriptures, the title "Father" is available only to especially chosen

---

320 Barbara Reid, "Liturgy, Scripture and the Challenge of Feminism," in *Living No Longer for Ourselves: Liturgy and Justice in the Nineties*, ed. by Kathleen Hughes and Mark R. Francis (Collegeville, MN: Liturgical Press, 1991), 130–131.

321 Reid, 125. Examples for the OT include Dt 32:6; Is 63:16; Jer 3:4. NT examples include Mk 14:36; Mt 11:25; Lk 23:34; Jn 17:1.

322 Robert Hamerton-Kelly, "God the Father in the Bible and in the Experience of Jesus: The State of the Question," ed. by Johannes-Baptist Metz, Edward Schillebeeckx, Marcus Lefébure, in *God as Father?* (New York, Seabury Press, 1981), 96–98.

323 Hamerton-Kelly, 96.

324 Soskice, *Kindness of God*, 75–76. See also Paul Ricoeur, "Fatherhood: From Phantasm to Symbol," in *The Conflict of Interpretations: Essays in Hermeneutics*, ed. Don Ihde, trans. Robert Sweeney (Evanston, IL: Northwestern University Press, 1974), 485–486.

and loved ones. That is, the filial relationship is by adoption. Speaking of Solomon, the builder of the temple, God promises David that "I will be his father, and he shall be my son" (2Sa 7:14; 1Ch 17:13; 22:10; 28:6). Here, as also in Psalm 89:26, David's dynasty is called to a unique relationship with God. Because the king is chosen to be the son of God, God is Father. But the idea that God is the father of all humanity is rare because God is seen as creator of the universe. The context of most occurrences of God as Father suggests that God's fatherhood is a gracious gift since it makes the people of the covenant, especially the king, children of God.[325]

This Hebrew understanding of God as loving father of his adopted people extends into intertestamental times and is also found in the New Testament where the old covenant notion of anointed king as adopted son of God is epitomized in Jesus' title Messiah.[326] Joachim Jeremias argues that Jesus' use of the Aramaic Abba in prayer (Mk 14:36) was unique in Palestinian Judaism. As such it was a distinctive claim on the part of Jesus to be the one chosen by God.[327] Ramshaw notes that "In the words introducing the Lord's Prayer, 'audemus dicere,' 'we are bold to say,' classical liturgy demonstrates a similar awareness of the privileged state of the baptized in addressing God as Father."[328]

The fact that Jesus prayed to God as his father became increasingly important in Christian consciousness. However, the use of that term is often, particularly for Paul, grammatically connected with the name Lord Jesus Christ. For example, Paul uses the expression "the God and Father of our Lord Jesus Christ" (e.g., Ro 15:6, 2Co 1:3). Extending this relationship, through the Spirit received in baptism, Christians are also able to say "God our Father and the Lord Jesus Christ" (e.g., Ro 1:7; 1Co 1:3).[329]

However, the "two dominant biblical strains, the typological—the elect of Israel, especially the king, as God's children—and the theological—Jesus' intimate address to God as "my Father"—are joined by a third, increasingly philosophical usage, the Trinitarian naming of God as Father to denote the

---

325   Gail Ramshaw Schmidt, "Lutheran Liturgical Prayer and God as Mother," *Worship* 52(1978): 525–526.
326   Ramshaw Schmidt, 526.
327   Joachim Jeremias, *The Prayers of Jesus*, (Naperville, IL: Allenson, 1967), 29, 97, 111.
328   Ramshaw, 526.
329   Ramshaw, 526–527.

origin of the Son."[330] This concept, rooted in those passages that describe the coming of the Son of man from the Father (e.g., Mk 8:38; Mt 16:27; Lk 10:22), comes to prominence in John's Gospel, where God's name Father signifies the divine origin of Jesus Christ, the Logos (e.g., Jn 1:8; 1:14; 16:28).[331] In these passages, "the relationship of the Father to the Son is neither adoptive and salvific nor intimate and forgiving, but essential and identity-producing . . . In affirming the preexistent Christ of John's Gospel, the Church stressed Christ's identity with God as the Father's Logos, rather than Jesus' intimacy with God in prayer."[332]

We can confidently assert that the four Gospel accounts record "father" as the primary (but not only) way that Jesus refers to God. Nevertheless, the repertoire of images for God in the Scriptures is much more varied, including many that are feminine. God is shown as giving birth and mothering in several instances. In the Book of Deuteronomy, God speaks through Moses, reminding the Israelites that it was God who gave them birth (Dt 32:18). Isaiah likens God's anguish over Israel to a woman in labor (Is 42:14) and compares God's tenderness to that of a woman for the child of her womb (Is 49:15).[333] God is also spoken of using non-human metaphors. Instances comparing God to a rock occur in several places, including Deuteronomy 32:15 and also in the psalms (e.g., Ps 42). God is described as a consuming fire (Dt 4:24), a lion (Hos 5:14) and compared to a mother eagle (Dt 32:11–12 and Ps 91:4).[334]

What does reflection on this data suggest? Perhaps our designation of God as strictly male ought to be more tentative. This does not mean that the God that we thought was male is really female. Rather, as our earlier discussion of the *Odes of Solomon* and the *Revelations of Divine Love* of Julian of Norwich suggests, God is neither a single gender nor genderless, but rather beyond gender. For this reason, our use of metaphors needs to be even more expansive and abundant rather than narrow and limited.

The Gospel according to Luke is particularly noteworthy in regard to its juxtaposing feminine and masculine images for God. So, for example,

330 Ramshaw, 527.
331 Ramshaw, 527.
332 Ramshaw, 527.
333 Reid, 125–126.
334 Reid, 126.

the parable of the Good Shepherd in search of the lost sheep (Lk 15: 1–7) is followed by the parable of the woman searching for the lost coin (Lk 15:8–10).[335] We may know many great works of art that portray the Good Shepherd. Perhaps art works portraying the woman in search of the lost coin do not come as readily to mind. They do, however, exist. Nevertheless, art—visual and musical and poetic—shapes the imagination and carries the tradition in concrete and subtle ways. That is why promoting the creation of hymns and other works of art that explore the expansiveness of the mystery of God is so important. Such work can enliven and expand our imaginations so that we might more fully benefit from the abundant and varied ways of exploring the mystery of God.

Concern for varied metaphors or images for God may elicit negative or disinterested responses. Some may counter that a word or phrase choice is "merely metaphor" or "only words." However, such disclaimers remain unconvincing when the usage referred to persists, is widespread, or may have unintended consequences. Those consequences can include imagining God as exclusively male—a mindset that can encourage or even unwittingly support the subordination of women. Persistent and widespread usage usually expresses what the speakers really think and matches how they behave. By extension, we could conclude that the way we speak of mystery—and in particular, the gracious and personal mystery we call God—can shape or misshape our understanding of God.[336] Furthermore, while we understand God to be pure spirit, we also believe that God is personal. The way gender functions in the English language makes it difficult—if not impossible—to imagine a personal God without gender.

Depicting Christ as the Good Shepherd has been a popular subject for artists for centuries. Plockhorst's painting presents a familiar depiction of Christ as the good shepherd attending to the one lost sheep. It is a visual depiction of Luke 15:1–7. Similarly, musical settings of Psalm 23 abound in numerous languages and musical styles.

---

335 Reid, 126.
336 Ruth A. Meyers, "Introduction: A Theological Consultation on Language and Liturgy," in *How Shall We Pray? Expanding Our Language about God*, Liturgical Studies 2 (New York: The Church Hymnal Corporation, 1994), 70.

Figure 1. "The Lord Is My Good Shepherd" by Bernhard Plockhorst (1825–1907).

Figure 2. "The Lost Drachma" (1886–1895) by James Tissot (1836–1902).

"The Lost Drachma" by James Tissot (figure 2) is owned by the Brooklyn Museum although at the time of this writing, it was not on display. This painting visually tells the parable recorded in Luke 15:8–10. The main point, however, is that both pictures (Blockhorst's and Tissot's) are meant to be a window into what God is like. Jesus told the parable about the good shepherd (Lk 13:3–7; Mt 18:12–14) and the woman in search of a lost coin (Lk 13:8–10) to provide his hearers with insights into the depth of God's solicitude and care for each person.

Barbara Reid captures the significance of the variety of biblical images for God when she says:

> All of these images are attempts by the biblical writers to describe what God is like yet no image adequately expresses who God is. God is like a loving father, a birthing and nursing mother, a midwife, a steady rock, a mother eagle who hovers over her brood, a woman who searches for the lost. But God is *not* any of these. All of our language about God ultimately falls short of the reality of God's being. God is more than our words can express.[337]

Yet, the point often missed is that while using a rich and varied repertoire of metaphors for God helps us to imagine more of what the mystery of God might be, God is *not* any of these things. They are metaphorical, not literal descriptions. The issue, as Gail Ramshaw and others[338] have pointed out, is that by overusing one metaphor or category of metaphor (such as God as male), we forget that we are speaking metaphorically and interpret what is being said literally. When I shared with my students my completed sentence, "God is like the ocean," they all understood that I was not trying to say that God is wet or salty. But when religion operates within mystery and ambiguity, reading metaphors literally can quickly deteriorate into fundamentalism. The end result is not a metaphor that has many layers of meaning, but "dead" metaphors that no longer trigger new insights nor speak in fresh ways to our imagination.

---

337 Reid, 127.
338 Some of the discussion of metaphor was introduced in chapter three. Other writers, among many others, on this topic include Sallie McFague and Brian Wren.

Figure 3. "The Last Supper" (1495–1498) by Leonardo Da Vinci (1452–1519)

Perhaps another visual example may clarify the point about the power of art to shape our imagination. Leonardo da Vinci's "The Last Supper" (figure 3) has become the standard for imagining Christ's gathering with his disciples the night before he died. Da Vinci's intention was to capture the moment in John 13:21 when Jesus declares that one of his disciples is going to betray him. That moment of shock and disbelief is what Da Vinci intended to paint. His depiction, despite its beauty and fame, is not a historical depiction of the Last Supper. The painting shows daylight coming through the windows. The meal would have begun after sunset. The disciples are all on one side of the table and the room itself looks more like a Renaissance structure than a first-century dining room.

Figure 4. "The Last Supper" by Bohdan Piasecki[339]

339 This painting was commissioned by B.A.S.I.C. (Brothers and Sisters in Christ) in 1998 to depict an actual Passover Seder. A Passover Seder would always have men, women, and children present together. Some scripture scholars today question whether the Last Supper was the Passover meal itself, or a meal around the time of Passover. © We Are Church Ireland (www.wearechurchireland.ie).

While many have mimicked Da Vinci's famous rendering, others, such as the Polish artist Bohdan Piasecki (b. 1941), offer us another interpretation and therefore another way of imagining. In figure 4, women and children are depicted in this gathering of the last meal Christ celebrated with his disciples. Some may contend that women and men ate separately, but the Gospels are full of examples of Jesus breaking with social and religious norms when it came to meals and his relationships with women. The Gospels also make clear that women were disciples throughout Christ's ministry. Why would he exclude them from this key event?

Sometimes our suppositions regarding Christ and his revelation of who God is have not always reflected the fullness of the Gospel narrative. Sometimes separate accounts are conflated and sometimes certain stories are favored—that is, highlighted—over others. When this happens, we tend to limit the mystery of God to small and manageable pieces. We settle into our familiar comfort zones that don't challenge us to look beyond our limited experience to the fullness of the Gospel message.

CONTEMPORARY HYMN TEXT WRITING ABOUT THE MYSTERY OF GOD

Contemporary hymn text writers, influenced by their own social and cultural environment, bring new sensitivity and insights into the use of metaphors for exploring and expressing the mystery of God. In our time, the biblical scholarship of the twentieth century continues to have a significant impact on the work of twenty-first century theologians and hymn text writers. Furthermore, the reforms of the Second Vatican Council have provided a new context for understanding the role of music and hymn singing in worship.

The activities of composing and singing hymn texts enable Christians to praise, petition, and thank the Triune God who is gracious mystery and who became incarnate in the person of Jesus Christ. To do this, faith communities address God under many titles and speak about their experience of God in their individual lives and in the life of the church. Since this singing is, indeed, symbolizing activity, the very act of hymn singing enables us to negotiate our relationship with God, with ourselves and with each other. Such activity has the potential ultimately to strengthen and to deepen all of these relationships.

In order to tap into that potential, however, the symbols and metaphors that are celebrated in the liturgy need to be authentic, polyvalent (comprised of many layers of meaning), and living. Otherwise, there is the danger that those celebrating will forget that the language of worship is metaphorical. This can drain the life out of metaphor and lead to literalist interpretations that eliminate the ambiguity and the richness of the liturgy's symbolic activity.

Hymns and hymnals are theological artifacts that both express the faith of the church and also shape that faith. Such claims require that we acknowledge that words do matter. That is, the words and phrases and sentences that are crafted by hymn text writers carry our faith and help to determine how we understand that faith. In addition, these hymn texts express our understanding of God, of our faith communities, and of ourselves as individuals and as the Body of Christ. All language possesses this power to shape and to express our understanding of reality. Religious language is all the more powerful because it deals with mystery on many levels.

The British composer, Bernadette Farrell, wrote the music and text for the hymn "God, beyond All Names."[340] It is a wonderful example of a hymn that explores and celebrates the mystery of God in the contemporary context. Here is the text in full:

> God, beyond our dreams, you have stirred in us a mem'ry;
> You have placed your pow'rful spirit in the hearts of humankind.
>
> *Refrain:*
> *All around us we have known you, all creation lives to hold you.*
> *In our living and our dying we are bringing you to birth.*
>
> God, beyond all names, you have made us in your image;
> We are like you, we reflect you; we are woman we are man.
> *Refrain*
>
> God, beyond all words, all creation tells your story;
> You have shaken with our laughter, you have trembled with
>   our tears. *Refrain*

---

340   "God, beyond All Names," *Journeysongs* (2003), #634.

God, beyond all time, you are laboring within us;
We are moving, we are changing in your spirit ever new. *Refrain*

God of tender care, you have cradled us in goodness,
You have mothered us in wholeness, you have loved us into birth.
Refrain

Although the title of the hymn is "God beyond All Names," Farrell begins with a description of God who is beyond "dreams" and "memory." Both nouns are intangible and suggest aspects of ambiguity and lack of control. The word "beyond" is repeated at the beginning of each of the first four stanzas. Yet while God is "beyond," God is also within our hearts. Thus from the very first stanza, Farrell sets up a lively tension between God's transcendence (being beyond us) and God's immanence (being present within us). In addition, this first stanza introduces the inclusive word "humankind," rather than the more traditional "mankind."

The two-line refrain serves as a type of mantra, reminding us—again— that this God who is beyond us is yet present in all of creation. Signs of God's presence and loving activity surround us. Furthermore, this presence is "in relationship." Amazing as it sounds, our living and dying are part of the way that God's presence comes to birth in our world.

Stanza two resonates with much that this chapter has been considering regarding God and gender. God is beyond the names or the images we might assign Divine Mystery. However, as the Book of Genesis declares, God made us human beings in God's image. As woman and man in relationship with each other and with God, we reflect the fullness that is God. Together, this expansiveness serves to unfold Divine Mystery.

Stanza three reminds us that who God is in God-self cannot be confined to the words we might use to express our understanding. Nor is the description of God confined to what humankind might articulate. Instead of focusing on humankind, as did the previous two stanzas, the first two phrases makes the point that all of creation speaks God's mystery. Not just one part of creation (humankind), but all of creation tells God's story. Nevertheless, the second part of the stanza expresses God's immanence in a touchingly human fashion. The concrete description of God shaking with our laughter and trembling with our tears captures an intimacy God shares with us that is truly beyond our dreams and imagination.

The fourth stanza focuses on time, movement, and change. Farrell's use of the verb "laboring" is significant for its ability to suggest both feminine and masculine aspects of work. The word can mean both the specific female work of giving birth and the general idea of physical labor. Even more amazing, we discover that the effort of laboring to bring new life to birth is mutual. As God labors within us to bring about our transformation, so we—as the refrain repeatedly acknowledges—are bringing God to birth by our efforts to live a life rooted in God. In either case, God partners with us in our daily work or labor (whether exercised by woman or man). Furthermore, God's labor within us is beyond time because it is part of the eternal now of God into which God's spirit gently draws us. And while for us, transformation can only happen over time, for God movement and change are beyond time.

The fifth and final stanza employs anthropomorphism to depict God's tender care cradling us like a mother. God's watchfulness is poised toward our flourishing or wholeness. As God loved us into birth, so God continues to love us into the fullness of life. This last stanza is the first time that Farrell's metaphor for God seems to be focused more exclusively on the female role of mothering. Nevertheless, contemporary parenting practices often involve the father in caring, nurturing, and cradling a child more than ever before.

The entire text presents an understanding of God's immanence and transcendence as involved in the life and flourishing of humankind and all of creation. God is depicted as intimately involved in a loving relationship with all creation, including us. Creation is depicted as responding to that love with praise and wonder. Furthermore, the music—almost chant-like in its texture—supports the awe and wonder of the poetry. It does this by communicating a sense of mystery through its melodic movement, its minor key, and the open intervals of the harmonies.

The Trinitarian Formulation Today

The classic Trinitarian formulation, articulated at the Council of Nicea in 325, reaffirmed the three persons of the Trinity—Father, Son, and Spirit—

as co-equal and co-eternal. This expression of the oneness of God in three persons emerged from a patriarchal culture—ecclesial, political, cultural, and familial. Today, alternate ways of expressing that formula have become the subject of much study, discussion, and some experimentation. Classic Christian hymns often conclude with a doxology in praise of the one God in three persons. The text expresses praise to Father, Son, and Holy Spirit. Thomas Ken wrote one of the most well-known formulations in 1674:

> Praise God, from whom all blessings flow;
> praise Him, all creatures here below;
> praise Him above, ye heavenly host;
> praise Father, Son, and Holy Ghost.

According to Brian Wren, Ken's purpose was "to give believers a formative worship language, theologically accurate and clearly understood."[341] Today, however, there is disagreement about the text's accuracy, adequacy, and clarity. The text is classic but questionable for many since its compactness obscures rather than reveals the nature of God as relatedness rather than monarchical apartness.[342]

Because of the theological issues regarding God language, many have begun to question the theological appropriateness of the classic, glorious, but male-centered doxology. One of those efforts included an adaptation of Thomas Ken's text. World Library published this revision of Thomas Ken's doxology in its 2003 edition of *People's Mass Book*.[343]

> Praise God, from whom all blessings flow;
> Sing praise, all creatures here below;
> Joined with the praise of heav'nly host;
> Praise Father, Son, and Holy Ghost.

This text preserves the "Father, Son and Holy Ghost" language, but removes two instances of the masculine pronouns "him." It has the effect of softening the strong masculine emphasis without disturbing—in the words of Brian

---

341 Wren, *Praying Twice*, 238.]
342 Gail Ramshaw, *God beyond Gender: Feminist Christian God Language* (Minneapolis: Augsburg Press, 1995), 84–85.
343 *People's Mass Book*, Franklin Park, IL: World Library Publications, 2003, #483

Wren—the singer's memory bank.[344] On the other hand, many Christians sing this doxology with gusto from memory. Churches that have been singing this hymn since the late seventeenth century would probably resist the changes in lines two and three. Catholics' history of singing of this hymn is much shorter (post Vatican II) than other Christian groups. The changes in lines two and three might be considered acceptable. However, changing the final line likely would not be well received and World Library understood that. Nevertheless, the editors of *People's Mass Book* took a risk with this text and continue to be forward looking in their editing. This early revision of the doxology appears again in the *One in Faith* (2016) hymnal. Outside the assemblies that use WLP, however, the original version is still heartily being sung.

Because the words of the Trinitarian doxology "interlock with each other in a unique linguistic and theological system," Wren believes that major alterations in the Trinitarian doxology may prove unfeasible.[345] However, an American Camaldolese monk, Cyprian Consiglio, has made a modest attempt to create some new poetic expressions by delving thoughtfully into the theological and scriptural tradition in a publication entitled *Lord, Open My Lips*.[346] This collection, which comprises printed music and compact disc, includes settings of Morning and Evening Prayer (the Liturgy of the Hours). Consiglio composed the chants for the psalms and canticles. Since the Church's tradition has been to conclude the psalms and New Testament canticles with a Trinitarian doxology (Glory to the Father, and to the Son, and to the Holy Spirit . . .) Consiglio takes the opportunity to offer some alternative doxologies. The new texts vary in how closely they follow the traditional formula. So, for example, the doxology for the Liturgy of the Hours for Christmas Day includes all of the traditional "Father, Son, Spirit" language, but reworks the turn of phrase significantly:

> Great is the Father's glory
> Revealed in his Son, Jesus Christ,
> Who was born a child for us:
> The Spirit of the Lord has done this.

---

344 Wren, *Praying Twice*, 306.
345 Wren, *Praying Twice*, 241.
346 Cyprian Consiglio, *Lord, Open My Lips* (Portland, OR: Oregon Catholic Press, 2003).

In this doxology, all three traditional names for the persons of the Trinity are mentioned—Father, Son, and Spirit. However, the text highlights additional aspects of the persons of the Trinity. This aids in deepening an understanding both of their relationship with each other and with us. The doxology for the Lenten season, however, does not include traditional titles:

> Glory to you, Jesus Christ,
> Who, with the sign of the cross,
> Have revealed in the Holy Spirit
> The salvation that comes from our God.

Here the titles "Father" and "Son" are omitted. The role of Jesus Christ is central to the text as it was composed for the Lenten season. Once again, the interrelationship of the three Persons and humankind is clearly expressed.

In some cases, editors, composers, or other well-intentioned persons, have attempted to avoid the traditional titles by addressing God as Creator, Redeemer, and Sanctifier. The danger here is that it suggests that each person of the Trinity has a separate task not shared by the others and that they act independently. The Trinitarian God is One. That means that Father, Son and Spirit were all present at the creation of the world, all save us and sanctify us. This theological point has challenged rewriting efforts. Furthermore, we are baptized into the Christian church with the traditional "Father, Son, and Spirit." Hence, while it is advantageous to expand and supplement poetic expressions of Trinitarian praise so that we form our imaginations in true teaching (ortho-doxy), it is likewise important to continue to sing traditional formulations.

How Do We Name Ourselves?

The reverse side of the question regarding how we name God is how we name ourselves, specifically how we name ourselves in hymn texts that are a significant component of worship. Once again, sacred Scripture, Tradition, and cultural usage must figure into our effort to answer this question. Our goal is to determine whether our language practice (male centered) continues to support worship in a way that provides the possibility for an epiphany or disclosure of God's love active in our lives today.

The book of Genesis provides two separate accounts of creation, the first in chapter one and the second in chapter two. They are distinctly different. In the first story, man and woman were created simultaneously and were declared created in the image of God (Ge 1:27). In the second account (Ge 2:18–24), man is created first and woman is created as the culmination of God's creative efforts. Some have interpreted the second version to indicate the superiority of man and the subservience of woman as "helpmate." However, a look at the original language offers an alternate way of interpreting these events.[347]

The two stories recorded in Genesis are stories of primeval events, not historical events. Both are a product of the efforts of ancient scribes to explain the world as they saw it. Both accounts present creation as a deliberate plan of God (Ge 1:26 and Ge 2:18). However, the second account need not be interpreted as a depiction of woman's creation as an afterthought. Rather, God sees a deficiency. Man needs a companion like himself and no other element of creation will satisfy that need.[348] Two additional points challenge preconceptions of women's secondary status. The first is the detail that woman is taken from man's rib and the second is the fact that woman's role is described as "helpmate."

Barbara Reid offers an important insight on translating the word "rib":

> The idea of "rib" for the creation of woman may reflect a word play in Sumerian. In that language, *ti* means both "rib" and "to make live." If the author of Genesis 2:21 wanted to make that association, then derivation of woman from man was not what the story intended to convey. Furthermore, the Hebrew word for rib, *sela'*, everywhere else in the Old Testament means "side." So in Genesis 2:21, the woman is taken from the man's side, a notion that speaks more of equality than subordination.[349]

Reid's closer look at of the use of "helpmate" in Genesis 2:18 is also enlightening:

---

347 Reid, 127.
348 Reid, 127–128.
349 Reid, 128.

The Hebrew word 'ezer, usually translated "helpmate," occurs over twenty times in the Old Testament. In the majority of those instances, it refers to the strength or salvation that comes from God. For example, the psalmist prays, "The Lord answer you in time of distress; the name of the God of Jacob defend you! May he send you help ['ezer] from the sanctuary, from Zion may he sustain you" (Ps 20:2–3). The notion of "power" or "strength" stands behind the word 'ezer. And the next word in Genesis 2:18, kenegdo, means "corresponding to him." So in Genesis 2:18, God's intention in creating the woman is to make for the man "a power like his own" or a "strength corresponding to his." This suggests that God's design for human existence is that relations between male and female be marked by mutual strength, partnership, support.[350]

These first two chapters of Genesis offer an idyllic description of the beginnings of creation. Chapter three, however, offers another story that attempts to explain sin and suffering in human existence. While the traditional interpretation is that Eve was the weaker of the two and led Adam into sin, a closer look at the story may reveal some interesting and new perspectives.

In the dialogue with the serpent, Eve is the spokesperson. Adam remains silent even though it is clear that he is present. In her conversation with the serpent, Eve is intelligent, informed and perceptive in the way she participates in a theological discussion. Furthermore, she acts independently, not asking Adam what he thinks. Adam is silent and passive. When Eve offers him the fruit, he acquiesces without argument. Both Eve and Adam are responsible for sin.[351]

When God confronts Adam, his response is to blame the woman (and indirectly God!) for his sin. Eve, on the other hand, admits her sin, but blames the serpent rather than God or Adam.[352] Reid points out that both man and woman are responsible for introducing sin into the word. Both admit their guilt before God. But what is even more significant and worthy

---

350 Reid, 128.
351 Reid, 129.
352 It is interesting to note that in Romans 5, Paul only mentions Adam when speaking of the sin of our first parents. In verses 12–21, sin is identified as the result of "one man." Eve is not mentioned at all.

of our attention are the consequences of sin that are described in Genesis 3:14–19. Reid sums up these stanzas by saying:

> The harmony of God's creation is now disrupted. The distinctions in creation now result in opposition. What had been made for delight now ends in pain and alienation. The divine, human, animal, and plant worlds are all adversely affected. None of this is God's original intent; it is the result of human choice, for which both man and woman are responsible. Man's rule over woman (v. 16) is part of the disorder and is already in place by the end of the story. The woman has disappeared from the scene. God speaks of the man having become "like one of us," and God sends him forth from the garden (vv. 22–24).[353]

Perhaps the most pertinent phrase in the quote above (for our concern regarding inclusive language) is the claim that man's rule over woman is part of the disorder that resulted from sin. Before sin there was harmony between the sexes. After sin man exerts power over woman. The mutuality of the sexes disintegrates.

We all know the historical manifestations of this breakdown of mutuality. Western civilization has been built on patriarchal foundations. And while we affirm that the Bible was written under the inspiration of the Holy Spirit, we still need to acknowledge that the human instruments of the Holy Spirit were primarily men who wrote for men and about men.[354]

In the English language, the use of male nouns and pronouns has traditionally been interpreted to include women. However, social and cultural movements have heightened awareness of the need to promote the dignity and equality of all human beings—both men and women. As a result, there have been significant efforts to address some of the gender issues in English usage. This is not a trivial pursuit. It does matter whether one uses "man," "woman," or "human being." As Reid points out, "the English-speaking world is recognizing that woman is not included in the word 'man' and that

353 Reid, 130.
354 Reid, 125.

'brothers' does not mean 'brother and sisters.'"[355] This is the situation, despite the fact that the Roman Catholic Church published the 2001 instruction on translation entitled *Liturgiam Authenticam* with no helpful provisions for dealing meaningfully with these gender issues.

The secular and political spheres have also been attentive to changes in usage whereby the masculine includes the feminine. This practice has an interesting history. Sexist language—the presumption that the norm for humanity is male—was used for over 150 years in English legislative texts. This "masculine rule"—that *he* subsumed *she*—first appeared in British legislation in 1827. The introduction of this policy ended almost 300 years of using female terms to represent women in legislative texts that originated in the Elizabethan period.[356] In 1971, the *Oxford English Dictionary* declared the generic usage of "man" obsolete, as have many publishing and educational guidelines. Yet this usage persists in many of our religious and secular institutions.[357]

How has this practice survived into the twenty-first century? On the one hand, the continued use of "man" for man and woman may be a thoughtless holdover from the past that nevertheless generates confusion and inaccuracy.[358] On the other hand, "it may represent a commitment to maintaining the kinds of unequal power relationships between men and women in our culture that are both represented and constituted by this kind of pseudo-generic terminology."[359] Whatever the reason, language generates imagery and imagery is more powerful, more lasting, and more formative and integrative than ideas or concepts.[360]

EDITING CLASSIC TEXTS

As noted earlier, hymns and hymnals are both theological artifacts and cultural artifacts. Studying them carefully reveals a particular community's understanding of God and of themselves. It also reveals aspects of the

---

355 Reid, 134.
356 Christopher Williams, "The End of the 'Masculine Rule'? Gender-Neutral Legislative Drafting in the United Kingdom and Ireland," in *Statute Law Review* 29:3(2008), 139–140.
357 Christie Cozad Neuger, "Image and Imagination: Inclusive Language Matters, in *Engaging the Bible in a Gendered World: An Introduction to Feminist Biblical Interpretation in Honor of Katharine Doob Sakenfeld*, eds. Linda Day and Carolyn Pressler (Louisville, KY: Westminster John Knox Press, 2006), 155. See also Letty M. Russell, "Inclusive Language and Power," *Religious Education* (Fall 1985), 584.
358 Neuger, 155.
359 Neuger, 155.
360 Neuger, 155.

community's faith and those elements that are or were most important to daily living. Furthermore, that faith is expressed by means of cultural elements such as language, (usage, idioms, imagery, symbols, metaphors), music (vocal, instrumental), movement (dance), and visual art (paintings, architecture, sculpture, furnishings). Since the life of Christian communities, like all of life, is organic, it involves change over time. The history of church music attests to this reality.

The Hebrew Scriptures record the ongoing transformation of Israel's understanding of God and of its relationship with God. Originally a polytheistic nation like its neighbors, Israel only gradually came to embrace monotheistic faith—a faith in one God, the God of Israel. The same can be said of the early Christian community. The New Testament records how early Christians, as they gathered for worship, gradually came to fuller understanding of Christ and of themselves as a distinct faith community. For example, it was only over time that they gradually understood that the Christ they gathered to remember was both human and divine. The Church continues to respond to Christ's invitation to become ever more the Body of Christ—the presence of Christ in the world for the salvation of all humankind. This is the Church that sings its worship and opens itself to transformation and conversion day by day, week by week, and year by year. All this is done so that it may continue to evolve as the presence of Christ in the world.

This transformation and conversion is necessarily reflected in the changes and edits that are made—even to classic texts. As Brian Wren argues in his book, *Praying Twice: The Music and Words of Congregational Song*, it is not the case that editing texts is a modern phenomenon:

> However, much we value our past, our present interest in congregational song is not antiquarian, but immediate. We sing to God from today, in lyrics which—whether ancient or recent—express today's faith. When a lyric from the past gets too archaic to be understood, or too out of sync with today's hope, faith, and issues to speak for us, it will eventually cease to be sung, or amended to keep it singable.[361]

---

361 Wren, *Praying Twice*, 298.

Indeed, the task of supporting and encouraging the editing of hymns and creating new hymns is the responsibility of each generation of Christians.

History provides evidence of the truth of this claim. During one of the most prolific periods of hymn writing, the eighteenth century, there was a great deal of editing of texts. Indeed, the very project of taking a psalm from the Book of Psalms and creating metrical hymns (metrical psalmody) was an exercise in editing classic texts. Beginning with the Reformation in the sixteenth century and continuing to the present day, hymn text writers have crafted revised texts so that their worshiping assemblies were singing hymns that related to their own faith experience. Isaac Watts, the Father of English Hymnody, made allowances for the editing of texts and John Wesley devoted much time and energy to the task of editing hymn texts.

Perhaps one of the most interesting examples is the extended (over several years) editing of the Christmas carol, "Hark! The Herald Angels Sing." Charles Wesley's original version was published in 1739 in *Hymns and Sacred Poems* and entitled "Hymn for Christmas Day." The hymn text originally consisted of four line stanzas without a refrain. The first line read: "Hark how all the welkin rings!" George Whitefield made changes to the text in 1753 that included changing the first line to the familiar text we sing today. Martin Madan added the word "Bethlehem" in 1760. Additional changes appeared in Tate and Brady's *New Versions of the Psalms of David* in 1782, and John Kempthorne added the word "Emmanuel" in 1810. In the twentieth century, the *United Methodist Hymnal* of 1989 made several changes by eliminating the exclusive expressions "man," "men," and "sons" and replacing them with "we," "us" and "flesh."[362] Many hymnals, including those published for Roman Catholic congregations, have also adopted this approach. World Library's most recent publications read "pleased on earth with us to dwell," OCP and GIA Publications read "pleased as man with us to dwell."

Here are the texts of Charles Wesley's original version and the version sung by many congregations today:

---

362 Wren, 299–306. These pages offer a more in depth analysis of the editing of "Hark! The Herald Angels Sing."

Hymn for Christmas Day (1739)[363]

Hark how all the welkin rings!
"Glory to the King of kings,
Peace on earth and mercy mild,
God and sinners reconciled."

Joyful, all ye nations, rise,
Join the triumph of the skies;
Universal nature say:
"Christ the Lord is born today."

Christ by highest heaven adored,
Christ the everlasting Lord,
Late in time behold him come,
Offspring of a Virgin's womb.

Veiled in flesh the Godhead see!
Hail the incarnate Deity!
Pleased as man with men to appear,
Jesus, our Immanuel here!

Hail the heavenly Prince of Peace!
Hail the Sun of Righteousness!
Light and Life to all he brings,
Risen with healing in his wings.

Mild he lays his glory by,
Born that man no more may die,
Born to raise the sons of earth,
Born to give them Second birth.

Come, Desire of Nations, come.
Fix in us thy humble home;
Rise, the woman's conquering seed,
Bruise in us the serpent's head.

---

363   Version published in Wren, *Praying Twice*, 301–302.

Now display thy saving power,
Ruined nature now restore,
Now in mystic union join
Thine to ours, and ours to thine.

Adam's likeness, Lord efface;
Stamp thy image in its place;
Second Adam from above,
Reinstate us in thy love.

Let us Thee, though lost, regain,
Thee the life, the heavenly Man;
O! to all thyself impart,
Formed in each believing heart.

Or here:

Hark! The Herald Angels Sing (2011)[364]

Hark! The herald angels sing,
"Glory to the newborn King!
Peace on earth and mercy mild,
God and sinners reconciled!"
Joyful, all you nations, rise;
Join the triumph of the skies'
With the angelic host proclaim,
"Christ is born in Bethlehem!"
Hark! The herald angels sing,
"Glory to the newborn King!"

Christ, by highest heav'n adored,
Christ the everlasting Lord!
Late in time behold him come,
Offspring of the Virgin's womb.
Veiled in flesh the Godhead see;

Hail the incarnate Deity,

Pleased as man with us to dwell,

Jesus, our Emmanuel.

Hark! The herald angels sing,

"Glory to the newborn King!"

Hail the heav'n born Prince of Peace!

Hail the Sun of Righteousness!

Light and life to all he brings,

Ris'n with healing in his wings.

Mild he lays his glory by,

Born that we no more may die,

Born to raise each child of earth,

Born to give us second birth.

Hark! The herald angels sing,

"Glory to the newborn King!"

The early revisions of Charles Wesley's text, "Hark how all the welkins ring," added details that contributed to the story-telling aspect of the text. More recent changes focus on the inclusivity of the "people" language (how we name ourselves). These latest changes demonstrate attentiveness to cultural and social change and a heightened awareness of the dignity and equality of all persons. For a Church that seeks to promote a discipleship of equals, such efforts can provide the possibility for conversion and transformation.

The Transcendence and Immanence of God

A theological perspective focuses on worship as the primary context for discussing religious language. This is specifically the case when its celebration provides a sense of awe, wonder, and mystery that reminds us of the inevitable distance between our words and the divine reality. Without that sense of mystery, we may mistakenly identify God with our words. That is, God becomes father, mother, lover, friend. Nevertheless, without a sense of the nearness of God, the metaphors can go awry in the direction of idolatry, irrelevancy, or both.[365]

---

365 McFague, *Metaphorical Theology*, 2.

In attempting to answer these questions—how do we name God and how do we name ourselves—we discover that, like a well-crafted fugue, themes of God's transcendence and immanence weave in and out of the fabric of our faith, our experience of God, and the way we express an understanding of this reality through language and song.

CODA

Each of us knows intuitively when we experience a liturgy where the various ritual elements, including the hymn singing, come together to create a grace-filled moment. Such an experience can leave us with a profound sense of joy, peace, or gratitude. Sometimes it is simply awe and humility. When this happens, we abandon ourselves to the grace of the moment. We catch a glimpse of divine mystery disclosed to us in a personal way. The Spirit takes hold of us and we don't resist. Alas, that does not happen every time we do Eucharist or some other liturgy. Such is the human condition. Nevertheless, we prepare, rehearse, and study, knowing that the Spirit works through our time, our culture, our efforts, our gifts, and our limitations.

My hope is that this book will assist liturgical ministers so that the assembly's song may be enabled and that its theology may be more deeply grasped. The approach includes studying hymn singing as a particular assembly performs it. It also involves examining hymn texts within the context of music, the space or architecture, the ritual, and the historical moment. The purpose of such an examination is to discover theological meaning as it is expressed in the hymn and as it is generated in the act of singing in a specific time and place. Congregational hymn singing needs to be explored, not simply as words interlined with notes on a page, but as dynamic action, because it is one of the symbolizing activities of the ritual we call liturgy. The concrete images, metaphorical language, and other literary devices disclose theological meaning and draw the assembly into the world of the hymn. In this way the song of the singing assembly can potentially generate theological meaning, express and shape belief, constitute an assembly as Church, and transform that assembly as individuals and as community into the One Body of Christ. Furthermore, if done well, the assembly's song enables participants to go forth into the world with Christ's message of Good News. That is what disciples do.

Since celebrating liturgy is participating in symbolizing activity, all of the symbolic elements enable participants to negotiate both identity and relationships. Hymn singing, therefore, is part of the process—let loose in the liturgy—that transforms individuals and the community into disciples. This is what Chauvet means when he explains that symbols enable us to build our world.[366] This is one of the ways that we constitute ourselves as church.

Yes, there is theological meaning in the hymn texts and in the assembly's very act of singing. Because of this, that very act of singing is integral to the liturgical celebration, to the formation of the assembly as individuals and as community, and to the possibility of sending forth the assembly as the presence of Christ in the world to announce the Good News and to help build a just world. Since these goals are not optional for the Church, neither should be our ongoing effort to enhance and enliven the song of each liturgical assembly. This can be achieved by appropriating the best resources at our disposal in order to promote excellence in hymns, their performance, the preparation of the assembly, and musical and liturgical leadership.

The last stanza of "When in Our Music God Is Glorified" sums it up well:

> Let ev'ry instrument be tuned for praise!
> Let all rejoice who have a voice to raise!
> And may God give us faith to sing always: ALLELUIA!

---

366 Chauvet, *Symbol and Sacrament*, 84–85, 112.

BIBLIOGRAPHY

HYMNALS and MUSIC

African American Heritage Hymnal. Chicago: GIA Publications, 2001.

Consiglio, Cyprian. *Lord, Open My Lips.* Portland: Oregon Catholic Press, 2003.

Evangelical Lutheran Worship, Evangelical Lutheran Church in America. Minneapolis: Augsburg Fortress Press, 2006.

Gather, 3rd edition. Chicago: GIA Publications, 2011.

Gather Comprehensive, 2nd edition. Chicago, IL: GIA Publications, 2004.

The Hymnal of the Protestant Episcopal Church in the United States of America. New York: The Church Pension Fund, 1940.

Hymns Ancient and Modern: Historical Edition, W. H. Frere, ed. London: William Clowes and Sons Limited, 1909.

Journeysongs, 3rd edition. Portland: Oregon Catholic Press, 2012

Journeysongs, 2nd edition. Portland: Oregon Catholic Press, 2003.

One in Faith. Franklin Park, IL: World Library Publications, 2016.

Our Parish Prays and Sings: Dialogue Mass, Hymns, Chants. Collegeville, MN: Liturgical Press, 1959.

People's Mass Book. Cincinnati, OH: World Library of Sacred Music, 1964.

People's Mass Book. Franklin Park, IL: World Library Publications, 2003.

RitualSong, 2nd edition. Chicago: GIA Publications, 2016.

RitualSong. Chicago: GIA Publications. 1996, 1998.

Worship, 4th edition. Chicago: GIA Publications, 2011.

Worship, 3rd edition. Chicago: GIA Publications, 1986.

Worship II. Chicago: GIA Publications, 1975.

DOCUMENTS

Bishops' Committee on the Liturgy. *Music in Catholic Worship*. Washington, DC: USCCB Publications Office, 1972, 1982.

Committee on Divine Worship. *Sing to the Lord: Music in Divine Worship*. Washington, DC: United States Conference of Catholic Bishops, 2008.

Catechism of the Catholic Church, 2nd edition. Washington: DC: Libreria Editrice Vaticana—USCCB, 2000.

Flannery, Austin, gen. ed. "Constitution on the Sacred Liturgy." *Vatican Council II: Constitutions, Decrees, Declarations; A Completely Revised Translation in Inclusive Language*, 117–161. Northport, NY: Costello Publishing Company, 1996.

Flannery, Austin, gen. ed. "Decree on Ecumenism." *Vatican Council II: Constitutions, Decrees, Declarations; A Completely Revised Translation in Inclusive Language*, 499–523. Northport, NY: Costello Publishing Company, 1996.

Flannery, Austin, gen. ed. "Dogmatic Constitution on the Church." *Vatican Council II: Constitutions, Decrees, Declarations; A Completely Revised Translation in Inclusive Language*, 1–95. Northport, NY: Costello Publishing Company, 1996.

General Instruction on the Roman Missal. Washington, DC: United States Conference of Catholic Bishops, 2002.

The Holy Bible: New International Version. Grand Rapids, MI: Zondervan Publishing, 2011.

The New Oxford Annotated Bible: New Revised Standard Version with the Apocrypha. Michael D. Coogan, ed. New York: Oxford University Press, 2001.

Roman Missal, Translation according to the Third Typical Edition. Collegeville, MN: Liturgical Press, 2011.

SECONDARY SOURCES

Aune, Michael. "Liturgy and Theology: Rethinking the Relationship." *Worship* 81 (January 2007): 46–68.

Austin, John Langshaw. *How to Do Things with Words*. Cambridge, MA: Harvard University Press, 1962.

Bellinger Jr., W. H. Psalms: *A Guide to Studying the Psalter*, 2nd edition. Grand Rapids, MI: Baker Academic, 2012.

———. "The Psalms as a Place to Begin for Old Testament Theology, 28–39." In *Psalms and Practice: Worship, Virtue and Authority*, ed. Stephen Breck Reid. Collegeville, MN: Liturgical Press, 2001.

Black, Max. *Models and Metaphors: Studies in Language and Philosophy*. Ithaca, NY: Cornell University Press, 1962.

Boccardi, Donald. *The History of American Catholic Hymnals Since Vatican II*. Chicago: GIA Publications, 2001.

Bradshaw, Paul. "Difficulties in Doing Liturgical Theology." *Pacifica* 11 (June 1998): 181–194.

Brink, Emily R. and Bert Polman, ed. *Psalter Hymnal Handbook*. Grand Rapids, MI: CRC Publications, 1998.

Brown, Raymond E. *The Birth of the Messiah: a Commentary on the Infancy Narratives in the Gospels of Matthew and Luke*. New updated version. New York: Doubleday, 1993.

Brown, William. *Seeing the Psalms: a Theology of Metaphor*. Louisville, KY: Westminster John Knox Press, 2002.

Brueggemann, Walter. *The Message of the Psalms: a Theological Commentary*. Minneapolis, MN: Augsburg Press, 1984.

———. "The Psalms and the Life of Faith: A Suggested Typology of Function," 1–25. In *Soundings in the Theology of Psalms: Perspectives and Methods in Contemporary Scholarship*, ed. Rolf A. Jacobson. Minneapolis, MN: Fortress Press, 2011.

Burghardt, Walter J. "Just Word and Just Worship: Biblical Justice and Christian Liturgy." *Worship* 73 (September 1999): 386–398.

Burns, Rita J. *Has the Lord Indeed Spoken Only through Moses? A Study of the Biblical Portrait of Miriam*. SBL Dissertation Series 84. Atlanta: Scholars Press, 1987.

Caird, George Bradford. *The Language and Imagery of the Bible*. London: Westminster Press, 1980.

Chauvet, Louis-Marie. *Symbol and Sacrament: A Sacramental Reinterpretation of Christian Existence*. Translated by Patrick Madigan and Madeleine Beaumont. Collegeville, MN: Liturgical Press, 1995.

Chittister, Joan. "Yesterday's Dangerous Vision: Christian Feminism in the Catholic Church." *Sojourners* 16 (July 1987): 18–21.

Cone, James. "Black Spirituals: A Theological Interpretation," 41–51. In *Music and the Experience of God*, ed. Mary Collins, et al. Edinburgh: T&T Clark, Ltd., 1989.

Congar, Yves M.J. "L'Ecclesia ou communauté chrétienne, sujet integral de l'action liturgique." *La Liturgie après Vatican II*, ed. J. P. Jossua and Y. Congar. Paris: Cerf, 1967.

Congregational Union of England and Wales. *Congregational Praise*. London: Independent Press for the Congregational Union of England and Wales, 1951.

Coogan, Michael D. *The Old Testament: A Historical and Literary Introduction to the Hebrew Scriptures*, 2nd edition. New York: Oxford University Press, 2011.

Countryman, L. William. "Biblical Origins of Inclusive Language," 16–27. In *How Shall We Pray? Expanding Our Language about God*, Liturgical Studies 2, ed. Ruth A. Meyers. New York: The Church Hymnal Corporation, 1994.

Culler, Jonathan D. *The Literary in Theory*. Cultural Memory in the Present series, ed. Mieke Bal and Hent de Vries. Stanford, CA: Stanford University Press, 2007.

———. *Literary Theory: A Very Short Introduction*, 2nd edition. New York: Oxford University Press, 2011.

De Clerck, Paul. "'Lex orandi, lex credendi': The Original Sense and Historical Avatars of an Equivocal Adage." *Studia Liturgica* 24 (1994): 178–200.

de Lubac, Henri. *Corpus Mysticum: The Eucharist and the Church in the Middle Ages*. Translated by Gemma Simmonds. South Bend, IN: University of Notre Dame Press, 2007.

Denzinger, H. and A. Schönmetzer, ed. *Enchiridion Symbolorum. Definitionum et Declarationum de Rebus Fidei et Morum*. Freiburg im Bresigau: Herder and Herder, 1965.

Dillon, Richard J. *The Hymns of Saint Luke: Lyricism and Narrative Strategy in Luke 1–2*. The Catholic Biblical Quarterly Monograph Series 50. Washington, DC: The Catholic Biblical Association of America, 2013.

Duck, Ruth C. *Gender and the Name of God: The Trinitarian Baptismal Formula*. Cleveland, OH: Pilgrim Press, 1991.

———. and Patricia Wilson-Kastner. "Trinitarian Language in Hymns," 81–97. In *Praising God: The Trinity in Christian Worship*. Louisville, KY: Westminster John Knox Press, 1999.

Dulles, Avery. *The Craft of Theology: From Symbol to System*. New York: The Crossroad Publishing Company, 1992.

———. *Models of Revelation*. Garden City, NY: Doubleday and Co., 1983.

———. *Models of the Church*, expanded edition. New York: Doubleday and Co., 2002.

Fackre, Gabriel. "Christian Teaching and Inclusive Language Hymnody." *The Hymn* 50:2 (April 1999): 26–32.

Field-Bibb, Jacqueline. "'By any other name': The Issue of Inclusive Language." *Modern Churchman* 31(1989): 5–9.

Fitzmyer, Joseph A. *The Gospel According to Luke (I–IX)*. The Anchor Bible series, vol. 28, gen. ed. William Foxwell Albright and David Noel Freedman. Garden City, New York: Doubleday & Co., 1981.

Ford, John T. "Paschal Mystery," "Psalmody." *Glossary of Theological Terms*. Winona, MN: St. Mary's Press, 2006.

Gadamer, Hans-Georg. *Truth and Method*, second, revised edition. Translated by Joel Weinsheimer and Donald G. Marshall. New York: Continuum, 1993.

Gilligan, Michael J. "Psalm." *Worship Music: A Concise Dictionary*, ed. Edward Foley. Collegeville, MN: Liturgical Press, 2000.

Goodman, Nelson, *Languages of Art: an Approach to a Theory of Symbols*. Indianapolis: Bobbs-Merrill, 1968.

Gottwald, N. K. *Interpreter's Dictionary of the Bible*. Nashville, TN: Abingdon Press, 1962.

Grendel, Gracia. "Inclusive Language in Hymns: A Reappraisal." *Currents in Theology and Mission* 60 (June 1989): 187–193.

Griffiss, James E. Naming the Mystery: *How Our Words Shape Prayer and Belief*. Cambridge, MA: Cowley Publications, 1990.

Hamerton-Kelly, Robert. "God the Father in the Bible and in the Experience of Jesus: The State of the Question," In *God as Father?* ed. Johannes –Baptist Metz, Edward Schillebeecks, Marcus Lefébure, 95–102. Concilium series no. 143. New York: Seabury Press, 1981.

Harvey, Susan Ashbrook. "Feminine Imagery for the Divine: The Holy Spirit, the Odes of Solomon, and Early Syriac Tradition." *St. Vladimir's Theological Quarterly* 37 (1993): 111–139.

Hotz, Kendra G. and Matthew T. Mathews, *Shaping the Christian Life: Worship and the Religious Affections*. Louisville, KY: Westminster John Knox Press, 2006.

Hughes, Graham. *Worship as Meaning: A Liturgical Theology for Late Modernity*. Cambridge: Cambridge University Press, 2003.

Huh, Paul Junggap. "John Calvin and the Presbyterian Psalter. *Liturgy* 27 (2012): 16–22.

Jacobson, Rolf A. "'The Faithfulness of the Lord Endures Forever': The Theological Witness of the Psalter," 111–137. In *Soundings in the Theology of Psalms: Perspectives and Methods in Contemporary Scholarship*, ed. Rolf A. Jacobson. Minneapolis, MN: Fortress Press, 2011.

Jeremias, Joachim. *The Prayers of Jesus*. Naperville, IL: Alec R. Allenson, Inc., 1967.

Johnson, Elizabeth A. *She Who Is: The Mystery of God in Feminist Theological Discourse*. New York: Crossroad Press, 1992.

Johnson, Maxwell E. *Praying and Believing in Early Christianity: The Interplay between Christian Worship and Doctrine*. Collegeville, MN: Liturgical Press, 2013.

Julian of Norwich, ed. Edmund Colledge and James Walsh. *Classics of Western Spirituality*. Mahwah, NJ: Paulist Press, 1978.

———. *The Showings of Julian of Norwich*, ed. Denise N. Baker, Norton Critical Edition. New York: W.W. Norton & Company, 2005.

Kaplan, Cora, "Language and Gender," 57–69. In *The Feminist Critique of Language: A Reader*, ed. Deborah Cameron. New York: Routledge, 1990.

Kavanagh, Aidan. "Beyond Words and Concerts to the Survival of Mrs. Murphy." Pastoral Music 1:4 (April–May 1977), 17-20.

———. "Response: "Primary Theology and Liturgical Act: Response." *Worship* 57 (July 1983): 321–324.

Kelleher, Margaret Mary. "Liturgical Theology: A Task and a Method." *Worship* 62 (January 1988): 2–25.

———. "Liturgy: An Ecclesial Act of Meaning." *Worship* 59 (November 1985): 482–497.

———. *Liturgy as an Ecclesial Act of Meaning: Foundations and Methodological Consequences for a Liturgical Spirituality*, PhD diss., Washington, DC: The Catholic University of America, 1983.

Kraus, Hans-Joachim. *Theology of the Psalms*. Translated by Keith Crim. Minneapolis, MN: Augsburg Publishing House, 1986, 1992.

Kramer, Lawrence. *Music as Cultural Practice*, 1800–1900. Berkeley: University of California Press, 1990.

Kubicki, Judith Marie. *Liturgical Music as Ritual Symbol: A Case Study of Jacques Berthier's Taizé Music*. Leuven: Peeters, 1999.

———. *The Presence of Christ in the Gathered Assembly*. New York: Continuum, 2006.

———. "Hymn Text Master Class." *GIA Quarterly* 26:3 (2015), 20–21; 25:3 (2014), 18–19; 24:2 (2013), 18–19; 23:1 (2011), 16–17.

Kugel, James L. *The Idea of Biblical Poetry: Parallelism and Its History*. New Haven: Yale University Press, 1981.

LaCugna, Catherine Mowry. *God for Us*. San Francisco: HarperCollins, 1991.

Ladriére, Jean. "The Performativity of Liturgical Language." In *Liturgical Experience of Faith*, ed. H. Schmidt and David N. Power, 50–62. Concilium series no. 82. New York: Herder and Herder, 1973.

Lane, Dermot A. "Eschatology." In *The New Dictionary of Theology*, ed. Joseph A. Komonchak, Mary Collins, and Dermot A. Lane, 329–342. Collegeville, MN: Liturgical Press, 1991.

Langer, Susanne K. *Philosophy in a New Key: A Study in the Symbolism of Reason, Rite and Art*, 3rd edition. Cambridge, MA: Harvard University Press, 1967.

Lawler, Michael. *Symbol and Sacrament: A Contemporary Sacramental Theology*. New York: Paulist Press, 1987.

Leaver, Robin A. and James H. Litton, ed. *Duty and Delight: Routley Remembered*. Norwich: Canterbury Press, 1985.

———. "Hymn." *Worship Music: A Concise Dictionary*, ed. Edward Foley. Collegeville, MN: Liturgical Press, 2000.

Leonard, John K. "Psalmody." *Worship Music: A Concise Dictionary*, ed. Edward Foley. Collegeville, MN: Liturgical Press, 2000.

Lovelace, Austin. *Anatomy of Hymnody*. New York: Abingdon Press, 1965.

Loxley, James. *Performativity*. New York: Routledge, 2007.

Marshall, Madeleine Forell and Janet Todd. *English Congregational Hymns in the Eighteenth Century*. Lexington: The University Press of Kentucky, 1982.

Marshall, Paul V. "Reconsidering 'Liturgical Theology': Is there a *Lex Orandi* for All Christians?" *Studia Liturgica* 25 (1995): 129–150.

Mays, James Luther. *The Lord Reigns: A Theological Handbook to the Psalms*. Louisville, KY: Westminster John Knox Press, 1994.

McBrien, Richard P. *Catholicism: Study Edition*. New York: HarperCollins, 1981. *Catholicism: Completely Revised and Updated Study Edition*, 1994.

McCant, Jerry W. "Inclusive Language and the Gospel." *Religious Education* 94 (Spring 1999): 172–188.

McFague, Sallie. *Metaphorical Theology: Models of God in Religious Language*. Philadelphia: Fortress Press, 1982.

Metz, Johannes-Baptiste, Edward Schillebeeckx, and Marcus Lefébure, ed. *God as Father?* Concilium series no. 143. New York: Seabury Press, 1981.

Meyers, Ruth A. ed. *How Shall We Pray? Expanding Our Language about God.* Liturgical Studies 2. New York: The Church Hymnal Liturgical Commission, 1994.

———. "Introduction: A Theological Consultation on Language and Liturgy," vii–xiii. In *How Shall We Pray? Expanding Our Language about God*, Liturgical Studies 2, ed. Ruth A. Meyers. New York: The Church Hymnal Corporation, 1994.

———. "Principles of Liturgical Language," 85–96. In *How Shall We Pray? Expanding Our Language about God*, ed. Ruth A. Meyers. New York: The Church Hymnal Corporation, 1994.

Mitchell, Nathan. "Symbols Are Actions, Not Objects." *Living Worship* 13 (February 1977): 1–2.

Moati, Raoul. *Derrida/Searle: Deconstruction and Ordinary Language.* Translated by Timothy Attanucci and Maureen Chun. New York: Columbia University Press, 2014.

Nasuti, Harry P. *Defining the Sacred Songs: Genre, Tradition and the Post-Critical Interpretation of the Psalms.* Journal for the Study of the Old Testament Supplement Series 218. Sheffield, England: Sheffield Academic Press, 1999.

———. "God at Work in the Word: A Theology of Divine-Human Encounter in the Psalms," 27–48. In *Psalms and Practice: Worship, Virtue, and Authority.* Stephen Breck Reid, ed. Collegeville, MN: The Liturgical Press, 2001.

———. "The Sacramental Function of the Psalms in Contemporary Scholarship and Liturgical Practice,"78–89. In *Psalms and Practice: Worship, Virtue, and Authority*, ed. Stephen Breck Reid. Collegeville, MN: The Liturgical Press, 2001.

Neuger, Christie Cozad. "Image and Imagination: Why Inclusive Language Matters," 153–165. *Engaging the Bible in a Gendered World: an Introduction to Feminist Biblical Interpretation in Honor of Katharine Doob Sakenfeld*, ed. Linda Day and Carolyn Pressler. Louisville, KY: Westminster John Knox Press, 2006.

Noth, Martin. "The Re-Presentation of the Old Testament in Proclamation." In *Essays on Old Testament Hermeneutics*, ed. Claus Westermann, 76–88. Richmond, VA: John Knox Press, 1963.

The Oxford Dictionary of the Christian Church, 3rd revised edition, ed. F. L. Cross and E. A. Livingstone. Oxford University Press, 2005. www.oxfordreference.com/view/10.1093/acref/9780199659623.001.0001/acref-9780199659623

Polanyi, Michael and Harry Prosch. *Meaning*. Chicago: University of Chicago Press, 1975.

Power, David N. "Doxology: The Praise of God in Worship, Doctrine and Life." *Worship* 55 (Jan. 1981): 61–69.

The Prayers and Meditations of St. Anselm, with the Proslogion. Translated by Benedicta Ward, SLG. New York: Penguin, 1973.

Quinn, Frank C. "Psalter." *Music: A Concise Dictionary*, ed. Edward Foley. Collegeville, MN: Liturgical Press, 2000.

Ramsey, Boniface, ed. *The Works of Saint Augustine: A Translation for the 21st Century. Exposition of the Psalms, 121–150*. Translation and notes by Maria Boulding. Hyde Park, NY: New City Press, 2004.

Ramshaw, Gail. *God beyond Gender: Feminist Christian God Language*. Minneapolis, MN: Augsburg Press, 1995.

———. *Reviving Sacred Speech: the Meaning of Liturgical Language*, Akron, OH: OSL Publications, 2000.

Ramshaw Schmidt, Gail. "Lutheran Liturgical Prayer and God as Mother." *Worship* 52 (November 1978): 517–542.

Reid, Barbara. "Liturgy, Scripture, and the Challenge of Feminism," 124–137. In *Living No Longer for Ourselves: Liturgy and Justice in the Nineties*, ed. Kathleen Hughes and Mark R. Francis. Collegeville, MN: Liturgical Press, 1991.

Ricoeur, Paul. "Fatherhood: From Phantasm to Symbol," 468–497. Translated by Robert Sweeney, edited by Don Ihde. In *The Conflict of Interpretations: Essays in Hermeneutics*. Evanston, IL: Northwestern University Press, 1974.

———. *The Rule of Metaphor: Multi-disciplinary Studies of the Creation of Meaning in Language*. Translated by Robert Czerny with Kathleen

McLaughlin and John Costello. Toronto: University of Toronto Press, 1975, 1979.

Rienstra, Debra, and Ron Rienstra. *Worship Words: Discipling Language for Faithful Ministry*. Grand Rapids, MI: Baker Academic, 2009.

Robert, Brother. "Taizé Music . . . A History." Pastoral Music 11 (February–March 1987): 19–22.

Rolf, Veronica Mary. *Julian's Gospel: Illuminating the Life and Revelations of Julian of Norwich*. Maryknoll, New York: Orbis Books, 2013.

Routley, Erik. *Church Hymns Observed: When in Our Music God Is Glorified*. Princeton: Prestige Publications, 1982.

———. *Church Music and the Christian Faith*. Carol Stream, IL: Agape, 1978.

———. *Church Music and Theology*. Philadelphia: Fortress Press, 1959.

———. *An English-Speaking Hymnal Guide*. Collegeville, MN: Liturgical Press, 1979.

———. *The Music of Christian Hymns*. Chicago: GIA Publications, 1981.

———. *A Panorama of Christian Hymnody*. Collegeville, MN: Liturgical Press, 1979.

Saliers, Don E. "The Integrity of Sung Prayer." *Worship* 55 (July 1981): 290–303.

———. "The Nature of Worship: Community Lived in Praise of God," 35–45. In *Duty and Delight: Routley Remembered*, ed. Robin A. Leaver, James H. Litton and Carlton R. Young. Norwich: Canterbury Press, 1985.

Schillebeeckx, Edward. "The Crisis in the Language of Faith as a Hermeneutical Problem." Translated by David Smith, 31–45. In *The Crisis of Religious Language*, ed. Johann Baptist Metz and Jean-Pierre Jossua. Concilium series no. 85. New York: Herder and Herder, 1973.

Schmemann, Alexander. "Liturgical Theology, Theology of Liturgy, and Liturgical Reform." *St. Vladimir's Theological Quarterly* (1969): 217–224.

———. "Liturgy and Theology." *The Greek Orthodox Theological Review* 17(1972): 86–100.

Searle, John R. "Austin on Locutionary and Illocutionary Acts." In *Essays on J. L. Austin*, ed. Isaiah Berlin, et al., 141–159. London: Oxford University Press, 1973.

Searle, Mark. "Liturgy as Metaphor." *Worship* 55 (March 1981): 98–120.

Shea, John. "The Second Naiveté: Approach to a Pastoral Problem." In *The Persistence of Religion*, ed. Andrew Greeley and Gregory Baum, 106–116. Concilium series no. 81. New York: Herder and Herder, 1973.

Sokolowski, Robert. *Introduction to Phenomenology*. Cambridge: Cambridge University Press, 2000.

Soskice, Janet Martin. *The Kindness of God: Metaphor, Gender, and Religious Language*. New York: Oxford University Press, 2007.

———. *Metaphor and Religious Language*. New York: Oxford University Press, 1985, 2002.

Tannehill, Robert C. "The Magnificat as Poem." *Journal of Biblical Literature* 93 (1974): 263–275.

Tavard, George H. *The Church, Community of Salvation: An Ecumenical Ecclesiology*. New Theological Studies I, gen. ed. Peter C. Phan. Collegeville, MN: Liturgical Press, 1992.

Tillich, Paul. *Dynamics of Faith*. New York: Harper and Row Publishers, 1957.

Tracy, David. *The Analogical Imagination: Christian Theology and the Culture of Pluralism*. New York: Crossroad Publishing Co., 1981.

Trask, Robert Lawrence. *Language and Linguistics: The Key Concepts*, second edition, ed. Peter Stockwell. New York: Routledge, 2007.

Tuchman, Shera Aranoff and Sandra E. Rapoport. *Moses' Women*. Jersey City, NJ: KTAV Publishing House, Inc., 2008.

Turbayne, Colin M. *The Myth of Metaphor*. New Haven: Yale University Press, 1962.

Turner, Victor, "Process, System, and Symbol: A New Anthropological Synthesis." In *On the Edge of the Bush: Anthropology as Experience*, ed. Edith L. B. Turner, 151–173. Tucson: The University of Arizona Press, 1985.

Wainwright, Geoffrey. "In Praise of God." *Worship* 53 (1979): 496–511.

Warnock, Geoffrey James. "Some Types of Performative Utterance." In *Essays on J. L. Austin*, ed. Isaiah Berlin, et al., 69–89. London: Oxford University Press, 1973.

Westermeyer, Paul. *Te Deum: The Church and Music*. Minneapolis, MN: Fortress Press, 1998.

Wheelwright, Philip. *The Burning Fountain: A Study in the Language of Symbolism*. Bloomington: Indiana University Press, 1954.

———. *Metaphor and Reality*. Bloomington: Indiana University Press, 1962.

Williams, Christopher. "The End of the 'Masculine Rule'? Gender-Neutral Legislative Drafting in the United Kingdom and Ireland." Statute Law Review 29:3 (2008): 139–153.

Williams-Tinajero, Lace Marie. *The Reshaped Mind: Searle, the Biblical Writers, and Christ's Blood*. Boston: Brill, 2011.

Wilkey, Jay W. "Prolegomena to a Theology of Music." *Review and Expositor* 69 (Fall 1972): 507–517.

Winter, Miriam Therese. *Why Sing? Toward a Theology of Catholic Church Music* Washington, DC: The Pastoral Press, 1984.

Wren, Brian. *Praying Twice: The Music and Words of Congregational Song*. Louisville, KY: Westminster John Knox Press, 2000.

———. *What Language Shall I Borrow? God-Talk in Worship: A Male Response to Feminist Theology*. New York: Crossroad Publishing Company, 1989.

Zuckerkandl, Victor. *Sound and Symbol*, vol. 2. Translated by Willard R. Trask. Princeton, NJ: Princeton University Press, 1969.

INDICES

MAIN INDEX

"Praise God, from whom all blessings flow" 192

"Prayer to St. Paul" (Anselm) 176

"religious" classic 132

"right attitudes" 61

"Sing a New Church" 120, 121, 122

"Sing to the Lord: Music in Divine Worship" 122

"situating" speech 154

"steno-language" 67

"systematic" theology 13

"tensive language" 67

"The Church's One Foundation" 109, 122

"The King of Love My Shepherd Is"

"The King Shall Come When Morning Dawns" 148

"The Old Rugged Cross" 80, 81

"The Strife Is O'er" 138, 139

"Touch the Earth Lightly" 150

"Urbs beata Jerusalem" 103

"ut legem credendi lex statuat supplicandi" 9, 10, 27

"We Shall Overcome" 156

"We Three Kings" 19

"Were You There" 82

"When I Behold the Wondrous Cross" 81

"When I Survey the Wondrous Cross" 74

"When the Lord in Glory Comes" 72

1 Samuel 2:1–10 53

abandonment 154

Abelard 177

abundant (use of metaphor) 182

act of singing 56, 122

active participation (Polanyi) 56, 59

active participation 97, 126, 128

addressing God 168

Advent 71, 137, 149

Aelred of Rievaulx 176

affectivity 165

Alford, Henry 69, 72

all reality is mediated (Chauvet) 58

allusion(s) 56, 80

Altar Hymnal (1884) 115

ambiguity/-ies 65, 67, 75, 168, 186

ambiguous 66, 68

Ancrene Riwle 177

Anthropomorphism 170, 191

ANTIOCH 46

apophatic theology 72

Aristotle 64

Ash Wednesday 90

assembly 97

assembly as *subject* 97

assembly's song xxiii

Aune, Michael 11

AURELIA 102, 111

Aurelius Prudentius 145

Austin, J. L. 135, 136

Avery Cardinal Dulles 101, 113, 122

Baker, Harry W. 38, 42, 43

Baker, Henry W.: Ps 23 "The King of Love My Shepherd Is" 42

baptism 129

baptismal focus 160

baptismal responsibility 128

Bar form 24

Barth, Karl 32

Barton, William 83

battle 77

BEACH SPRING 24, 27

Belief(s) 5, 6, 8, 15

Bennard, George 80

Bernard of Clairvaux 176

Berthier, Jacques 124, 125, 126, 137

Bible 133

biblical 29

biblical language 30, 51

birth of the Messiah 45

Black spiritual(s) 80, 82

bodiliness 68

Biblical Citations

Hymn Titles/First Lines

HYMN TUNES

ABOUT THE AUTHOR

Judith Marie Kubicki, PhD, is a Felician Franciscan Sister from Buffalo, New York. She has a BA in Music from Daemen College in Williamsville, NY, an MA in English from Canisius College in Buffalo, NY, and a Master of Liturgical Music and a PhD in Liturgical Studies both from The Catholic University of America in Washington, DC.

Sr. Judith has published two previous books: *Liturgical Music as Ritual Symbol: A Case Study of Jacques Berthier's Taizé Music* by Peeters in 1999 and *The Presence of Christ in the Gathered Assembly* published by Continuum in 2006. She has also written a pamphlet, How to Pray the Liturgy of the Hours, published by Pauline Books and Media. Her articles and reviews have appeared in *Worship, Theological Studies, Studia Liturgica, New Theology Review, The Living Light, Pastoral Music, Rite, Pastoral Liturgy, GIA Quarterly, Aim,* and *INTAMS review*. She served on the editorial board of the revised *New Catholic Encyclopedia*, for which she also contributed several articles. She also contributed an article on Taizé in *The Grove Dictionary of American Music, 2nd ed.*

Before her current position as Associate Professor in the Department of Theology at Fordham University in New York City, Dr. Kubicki was the Director of Music and later the Academic Dean at Christ the King Seminary, a Graduate School of Theology in East Aurora, New York. She is a former Chair of the Board of Directors of the National Association of Pastoral Musicians and is a past President of the North American Academy of Liturgy.

Sr. Kubicki has given presentations on liturgical topics in the United States, Canada, Great Britain, Germany, Italy, Switzerland, and Australia.